T0212115

Lecture Notes in Computer Science 11823

More information about this series at http://www.springer.com/series/7408

Dirk Beyer · Chantal Keller (Eds.)

Tests and Proofs

13th International Conference, TAP 2019
Held as Part of the Third World Congress on Formal Methods 2019
Porto, Portugal, October 9–11, 2019
Proceedings

 Springer

Editors
Dirk Beyer (iD)
Ludwig-Maximilians-Universität München
Munich, Germany

Chantal Keller
University of Paris-Sud
Orsay, France

ISSN 0302-9743 ISSN 1611-3349 (electronic)
Lecture Notes in Computer Science
ISBN 978-3-030-31156-8 ISBN 978-3-030-31157-5 (eBook)
https://doi.org/10.1007/978-3-030-31157-5

LNCS Sublibrary: SL2 – Programming and Software Engineering

This Springer imprint is published by the registered company Springer Nature Switzerland AG
The registered company address is: Gewerbestrasse 11, 6330 Cham, Switzerland

Preface

Welcome to TAP 2019, the 13th edition of the International Conference on Tests and Proofs. TAP 2019 is part of the Third World Congress on Formal Methods (FM Week 2019). The conference is held in the Alfândega Porto Congress Centre in Porto, Portugal, during October 9–11, 2019.

Conference Description. The TAP conference promotes research in verification and formal methods that targets the interplay of proofs and testing: the advancement of techniques of each kind and their combination, with the ultimate goal of improving software and system dependability.

Research in verification has recently seen a steady convergence of heterogeneous techniques and a synergy between the traditionally distinct areas of testing (and dynamic analysis) and of proving (and static analysis). Formal techniques for counter-example generation based on, for example, symbolic execution, SAT/SMT-solving, or model checking, furnish evidence for the potential of a combination of tests and proofs. The combination of predicate abstraction with testing-like techniques based on exhaustive enumeration opens the perspective for novel techniques of proving correctness. On the practical side, testing offers cost-effective debugging techniques of specifications or crucial parts of program proofs (such as invariants). Last but not least, testing is indispensable when it comes to the validation of the underlying assumptions of complex system models involving hardware or system environments. Over the years, there has been a growing acceptance in research communities that testing and proving are complementary rather than mutually exclusive techniques.

TAP's scope encompasses many aspects of verification technology, including foundational work, tool development, and empirical research. Its topics of interest center around the connection between proofs (and other static techniques) and testing (and other dynamic techniques).

Focus on Replicability of Research Results. We consider that reproducibility of results is of the utmost importance for the TAP community. Therefore, we encouraged all authors of accepted papers to submit an artifact for evaluation. For the first time, TAP 2019 included an optional artifact evaluation (AE) process for accepted papers. An artifact is any additional material (software, data sets, machine-checkable proofs, etc.) that substantiates the claims made in a paper and ideally makes them fully replicable. The evaluation and archival of artifacts improves replicability and traceability for the benefit of future research and the broader TAP community.

Paper Selection. This year, 19 papers were submitted to TAP. After a rigorous review process, with each paper reviewed by at least three Program Committee (PC) members, followed by an online discussion, 10 papers were accepted by the PC for publication in these proceedings and presentation at the conference.

Invited Talks. The conference program and the proceedings also include a keynote by Heike Wehrheim from Paderborn University, Germany, on "Extracting Unverified Program Parts from Software Verification Runs" and an invited tutorial by

Ana Cavalcanti from University of York, UK, on "RoboStar Technology - Testing in Robotics Using Process Algebra."

Artifact-Evaluation Process. For the first time, TAP 2019 used an AE process. The goals of AE are (1) to have more substantial evidence for the claims in the papers, (2) simplify the replication of results in the paper, and (3) reward authors who create artifacts, i.e., any additional material like software, tools, data sets, test suites, and machine-checkable proofs that substantiates the claims made in the paper.

To valorize their papers, authors of accepted papers could submit an artifact for evaluation to the TAP 2019 artifact-evaluation committee (AEC). Artifacts had to be provided as .zip files including all necessary software for AE and a README file that explains the artifact and guides the user through the replication of the results. AE had to be possible in the TAP 2019 virtual machine, which runs a Ubuntu 19.04 with Linux 5.0.0.

Each artifact was evaluated by four members of the AEC. The AE proceeded in two phases. In the first phase, the reviewers checked if the artifacts were functional, e.g., no corrupted or missing files exist and the evaluation does not crash on simple examples. All submitted artifacts passed the first phase without any problems and we skipped the author clarification phase in which authors could respond to problems in the test-phase evaluation. In the second phase, the assessment phase, the reviewers tried to reproduce any experiments or activities, and evaluated the artifact with respect to the following five questions:

1. Is the artifact consistent with the paper and the claims made by the paper?
2. Are the results of the paper reproducible using the artifact?
3. Is the artifact complete, i.e., how many of the results of the paper are replicable?
4. Is the artifact well-documented?
5. Is the artifact easy to use?

All submitted artifacts also passed this second phase. Corresponding papers were granted the TAP evaluation badge and two additional pages to describe the artifact. Unfortunately, for only one of the ten accepted papers an artifact was submitted. However, this artifact was of very good quality.

Acknowledgments. We would like to thank, first of all, the authors who submitted their papers to TAP 2019. The PC and the AEC, who did a great job of reviewing, contributed informed and detailed reports, and took part in the discussions during the virtual PC meeting. Special thanks go to the general chair of the FM Week 2019, José Nuno Oliveira, and his overall organization team, for taking care of the local organization. We also thank Alfred Hofmann and his publication team at Springer for their support.

August 2019

Dirk Beyer
Chantal Keller
PC Chairs

Daniel Dietsch
Marie-Christine Jakobs
AEC Chairs

Organization

Program Committee

Dirk Beyer (PC Chair)	LMU Munich, Germany
Chantal Keller (PC Chair)	LRI, Université Paris-Sud, France
Bernhard Beckert	KIT, Germany
Marcel Böhme	Monash University, Australia
Achim D. Brucker	University of Exeter, UK
Catherine Dubois	ENSIIE-Samovar, France
Reiner Hähnle	TU Darmstadt, Germany
Klaus Havelund	Jet Propulsion Laboratory, USA
Marieke Huisman	University of Twente, The Netherlands
Marie-Christine Jakobs	TU Darmstadt, Germany
Nikolai Kosmatov	CEA List, France
Laura Kovacs	Vienna University of Technology, Austria
Peter Lammich	TU Munich, Germany
Caroline Lemieux	University of California, Berkeley, USA
Martin Nowack	Imperial College London, UK
Corina S. Păsăreanu	CMU/NASA Ames Research Center, USA
François Pessaux	ENSTA ParisTech, France
Alexander K. Petrenko	ISP RAS, Russia
Michael Tautschnig	Queen Mary University of London, UK
Burkhart Wolff	LRI, Université Paris-Sud, France

Artifact Evaluation Committee (AEC)

Daniel Dietsch (AEC Chair)	University of Freiburg, Germany
Marie-Christine Jakobs (AEC Chair)	TU Darmstadt, Germany
Martin Bromberger	MPI, Germany
Maryam Dabaghchian	University of Utah, USA
Simon Dierl	TU Dortmund, Germany
Rayna Dimitrova	University of Leicester, UK
Mathias Fleury	MPI, Germany
Marcel Hark	RWTH Aachen, Germany
Martin Jonáš	Masaryk University, Czech Republic
Sven Linker	University of Liverpool, UK
Felipe R. Monteiro	Federal University of Amazonas, Brazil
Marco Muñiz	Aalborg University, Denmark
Gabriel Radanne	University of Freiburg, Germany
Cedric Richter	Paderborn University, Germany
Asieh Salehi Fathabadi	University of Southampton, UK

| Christian Schilling | IST Austria, Austria |
| Martin Tappler | TU Graz, Austria |

Steering Committee

Bernhardt K. Aichernig	TU Graz, Austria
Jasmin Blanchette	Vrije Universiteit Amsterdam, The Netherlands
Achim D. Brucker	University of Sheffield, UK
Catherine Dubois	ENSIIE, France
Martin Gogolla	University of Bremen, Germany
Nikolai Kosmatov	CEA, France
Burkhart Wolff	LRI, France

Additional Reviewers

Richard Bubel
Michael Forster
Eduard Kamburjan
Matthieu Lemerre
Yakoub Nemouchi
Thuan Pham
Alexander Weigl
Nicky Williams
Nina Yevtushenko

Contents

Invited Contributions

When Are Software Verification Results Valid for Approximate Hardware?

Tobias Isenberg[1], Marie-Christine Jakobs[2], Felix Pauck[1],
and Heike Wehrheim[1(✉)]

[1] Paderborn University, Paderborn, Germany
wehrheim@upb.de
[2] TU Darmstadt, Darmstadt, Germany

Abstract. Approximate computing (AC) is an emerging paradigm for energy-efficient computation. The basic idea of AC is to sacrifice high precision for low energy by allowing hardware to carry out only "approximately correct" calculations. This provides a major challenge for software quality assurance: Programs successfully verified to be correct might be erroneous on approximate hardware.

In this paper, we present a novel approach for determining under what conditions a software verification result is valid for approximate hardware. To this end, we compute the allowed *tolerances* for AC hardware from successful verification runs. More precisely, we derive a set of constraints which – when met by the AC hardware – guarantee that the verification result carries over to AC. Our approach is based on the framework of *abstract interpretation*. Furthermore, we show (1) how to practically extract tolerances from verification runs employing predicate abstraction, and (2) how to check such constraints on hardware designs. We have implemented all techniques, and exemplify them on example C programs and a number of recently proposed *approximate adders*.

1 Introduction

Approximate computing (AC) [17,27,30] is a new computing paradigm which aims at reducing energy consumption at the cost of computation *precision*. A number of application domains can tolerate AC because they are inherently resilient to imprecision (e.g., machine learning, big data analytics, image processing, speech recognition). Computation precision can be reduced by either directly manipulating program executions on the algorithmic level (e.g. by loop perforation [12]) or by employing approximate hardware for program execution [33].

For software verification, the use of approximate hardware challenges soundness, and raises the question of whether the achieved verification result will really be valid when the program is being executed. So far, correctness in the

This work was partially supported by the German Research Foundation (DFG) within the Collaborative Research Centre "On-The-Fly Computing" (SFB 901).

D. Beyer and C. Keller (Eds.): TAP 2019, LNCS 11823, pp. 3–20, 2019.
https://doi.org/10.1007/978-3-030-31157-5_1

```
int arr[1000];                          int u:=input();
                                        int sum:=1;
for(int j:=0;j<990;) {
    j:=j+10;                            if (u>0)
    if (!(j>=0 && j<1000))                  sum:=1+u;
        ERR: ;                          if (sum==0)
    arr[j]:=0;                              ERR: ;
}
```

Fig. 1. Programs `Array` (left) and `AddOne` (right)

context of approximate computing has either studied *quantitative reliability*, i.e., the probability that outputs of functions have correct values [13,29] (employed for the language Rely), or differences between approximate and precise executions [18,19] (applying differential program verification). Alternatively, some approaches plainly use types and type checking to separate the program into precise and approximate parts (language EnerJ) [33]. All of these techniques take a hardware-centric approach: take the (non-)guarantees of the hardware, and develop new analysis methods working under such weak guarantees. The opposite direction, namely use standard program analysis procedures and have the verification impose constraints on the allowed approximation, has not been studied so far. This is despite the fact that such an approach directly allows re-use of existing verification technology for program verification.

In this paper, we propose a new strategy for making software verification reliable for approximate computing. Within the broad spectrum of AC techniques, we focus on *deterministic* approximate designs, i.e., approximate hardware designs with deterministic truth tables. We start with a verification run proving general safety properties or termination of a program. Our approach derives from this verification run requirements (called *tolerance constraints*) on the hardware executing the program. A tolerance constraint acts like a pre/postcondition pair, and describes the expected output of a hardware design when supplied with specified inputs. The derived tolerance constraints capture the assumptions the verification run has made on the executing hardware. Thus, they are specific to the program and property under consideration. Typically, tolerance constraints are much less restrictive than the precise truth table of a hardware operation.

We develop a general theory for tolerance constraint extraction based on abstract interpretation. To see our technique in practice, we instantiate this framework with predicate abstraction [4,16]. In this case, tolerance constraints are pairs (p,q) of predicates on inputs and expected outputs of a hardware operation. As a first example, take a look at the left program in Fig. 1. The left program writes to an array within a for-loop. The property to be checked (encoded as an error state ERR) is an array-index-inside-bounds check. Using x and y as inputs and z as output (i.e., $z = x + y$), the tolerance constraint on addition $(+)$ derived from a verification run showing correctness is

$$(x \geq 0 \wedge x \leq 989 \wedge y = 10 \Rightarrow z \geq 0 \wedge z \leq 999)$$

It states that the hardware adder should guarantee that adding 10 to a value in between 0 and 989 never brings us outside the range $[0, 999]$, and thus the program never crashes with an index-out-of-bounds exception.

Using the analysis tool CPACHECKER [10] for verification runs, we implemented the extraction of tolerance constraints from abstract reachability graphs constructed during verification. The constraints will be in SMT-Lib format [5]. To complete the picture, we have also implemented a procedure for *tolerance checking* on hardware designs. This technique constructs a specific checker circuit out of a given hardware design (in Verilog) and tolerance constraint. We have evaluated our overall approach on example C programs using as AC hardware different approximate adders from the literature. Our evaluation shows that in particular termination is a fragile property for AC: programs involving standard iterations over arrays which can easily be shown to terminate on precise hardware might not terminate anymore on AC.

A short version of this work has appeared in [23].

2   Background

We start by formally defining the syntax and semantics of programs, and by introducing the framework of abstract interpretation [15].

Programs. For our formal framework, we assume programs to only use integer variables[1], $Ops = \{+, -, *, \backslash\}$ to be the set of binary operators on integers, $\mathbb{Z}$ to be the integer constants and $Cmp = \{<, \leq, >, \geq, =\}$ the set of comparison operators on integers. Programs use variables out of a set Var, and have two sorts of statements from a set Stm: (1) conditionals **assume b** (b boolean condition over Var and $\mathbb{Z}$ formed using Ops and Cmp) and (2) assignments **v:=expr**, $v \in Var$, *expr* expression over Var and $\mathbb{Z}$ formed with Ops. Formally, programs are given by control-flow automata.

Definition 1. *A* control-flow automaton *(CFA)* $P = (L, \ell_0, E, Err)$ *consists of a finite set of* locations L, *an* initial location $\ell_0 \in L$, *a set of* edges $E \subseteq L \times Stm \times L$, *and a set of* error locations $Err \subseteq L$.

Note that we mark the error locations in programs with the label **ERR** (or similar). A concrete state of a program is a mapping $s : Var \to \mathbb{Z}$, and Σ is the set of all states. For a state s, we define a *state update* wrt. $u \in Var$ and $c \in \mathbb{Z}$ to be $s[u := c](u) = c$, $s[u := c](v) = s(v)$ for $u \neq v$. For a state s and a boolean condition b, we write $s \models b$ to state that b is true in s. A configuration of a program is a pair (s, ℓ), $s \in \Sigma, \ell \in L$.

The semantics of program statements is given by the following (partial) *next transformers* $next_{stm} : \Sigma \to \Sigma$ with

$$next_{stm}(s) = s' \text{ with } \begin{cases} s' = s & \text{if } stm \equiv \textbf{assume b} \land s \not\models b \\ s' = s[v := s(expr)] & \text{if } stm \equiv \textbf{v:=expr} \end{cases}$$

---

[1] For the practical evaluation we, however, allow arbitrary C programs.

We lift $next_{stm}$ to sets of states by $next_{stm}(S) = \{next_{stm}(s) \mid s \in S\}$. Note that this lifted function is total. The next transformers together with the control-flow determine the transition system of a program.

Definition 2. *The* concrete transition system $T(P) = (Q, q_0, \rightarrow)$ *of a CFA* $P = (L, \ell_0, E, Err)$ *consists of*

- *a set of configurations* $Q = \Sigma \times L$,
- *an initial configuration* $q_0 = (s_0, \ell_0)$ *where* $s_0(v) = 0$ *for all* $v \in Var$,
- *a transition relation* $\rightarrow \subseteq Q \times Stm \times Q$ *with* $(s, \ell) \xrightarrow{stm} (s', \ell')$ *if* $next_{stm}(s) = s'$ *and* $(\ell, stm, \ell') \in E$.

An error location is *reachable* in $T(P)$ if there is a path from (s_0, ℓ_0) to a configuration $(*, \ell)$ with $\ell \in Err$. If no error location is reachable, we say that the transition system is *free of errors*.

Abstract interpretation. For verifying that a program is free of errors, we use the framework of abstract interpretation (AI) [15]. Thus, we assume that the verification run from which we derive tolerance constraints is carried out by an analysis tool employing abstract interpretation as basic verification technology.

Instead of concrete states, instances of AI frameworks employ abstract domains *Abs* and execute abstract versions of the next transformers on it. Abstract domains are equipped with an ordering $\sqsubseteq_{Abs}$, and $(Abs, \sqsubseteq_{Abs})$ has to form a complete lattice (as does $(2^{\Sigma}, \subseteq)$). To relate abstract and concrete domain, two monotonic functions are used: an abstraction function $\alpha : 2^{\Sigma} \rightarrow Abs$ and a concretisation function $\gamma : Abs \rightarrow 2^{\Sigma}$. The pair (α, γ) has to form a *Galois connection*, i.e. the following has to hold: $\forall S \in 2^{\Sigma} : S \subseteq \gamma(\alpha(S))$ and $\forall abs \in Abs : \alpha(\gamma(abs)) \sqsubseteq_{Abs} abs$. We require the least element of the lattice $(Abs, \sqsubseteq_{Abs})$ (which we denote by $a_{\perp}$) to be mapped onto the least element of $(2^{\Sigma}, \subseteq)$ which is the empty set $\emptyset$.

On the abstract domain, the AI instance defines a total abstract next transformer $next_{stm}^{\#} : Abs \rightarrow Abs$. To be useful for verification, the abstract transformer has to faithfully reflect the behavior of the concrete transformer.

Definition 3. *An abstract next transformer* $next_{stm}^{\#} : Abs \rightarrow Abs$ *is a* safe approximation *of the concrete next transformer if the following holds:*

$$\forall abs \in Abs, \forall stm \in Stm : \alpha(next_{stm}(\gamma(abs)) \sqsubseteq_{Abs} next_{stm}^{\#}(abs)$$

Using the abstract next transformer, we can construct an abstract transition system of a program.

Definition 4. *The* abstract transition system $T^{\#}(P) = (Q, q_0, \rightarrow)$ *of a CFA* $P = (L, \ell_0, E, Err)$ *with respect to an abstract domain Abs and functions* $next_{stm}^{\#}$ *consists of*

- *a set of configurations* $Q = Abs \times L$,

- an initial configuration $q_0 = (a_0, \ell_0)$ where $a_0 = \alpha(\{s_0\})$ with $s_0(v) = 0$ for all $v \in Var$,
- a transition relation $\rightarrow \subseteq Q \times Stm \times Q$ with $(a, \ell) \xrightarrow{stm} (a', \ell')$ if $next^{\#}_{stm}(a) = a'$ and $(\ell, stm, \ell') \in E$.

An abstract configuration (a, ℓ) is *reachable* in $T^{\#}(P)$ if there is a path from $q_0 = (a_0, \ell_0)$ to a configuration (a, ℓ). We denote the set of reachable configurations in $T^{\#}(P)$ by $Reach(T^{\#}(P))$ or simply $Reach^{\#}$. An error location is reachable in $T^{\#}(P)$ if there is a path from (a_0, ℓ_0) to a configuration (a, ℓ) with $\ell \in Err$, $a \neq a_\perp$. Note that we allow paths to configurations $(a_\perp, \ell)$, $\ell \in Err$, in the abstract transition system, since $a_\perp$ represents the empty set of concrete states, and, thus, does not stand for a concretely reachable error.

The abstract transition system can be used for checking properties of the concrete program whenever the abstract transformers are safe approximations. This is a standard result of abstract interpretation.

Theorem 1. *Let P be a CFA, T its concrete and $T^{\#}$ its abstract transition system according to some abstract domain and safe abstract next transformer. Then the following holds: If $T^{\#}$ is free of errors, so is T.*

3 Transformer Constraints

The framework of abstract interpretation is used to verify that a program is free of errors. To this end, the abstract transition system is built and inspected for reachable error locations. However, the construction of the abstract transition system and, thus, the soundness of verification relies on the fact that the abstract transformer safely approximates the concrete transformer. In particular, this means that we verify properties of a program execution using the concrete transformers for next state computation. This assumption is not true anymore when we run our programs on approximate hardware.

For a setting with approximate hardware, we have *approximate next transformers* $next^{AC}_{stm}$ for (some or all) of our statements instead of the precise transformers $next_{stm}$. The key question is now the following: Under which conditions on these approximate transformers will our verification result carry over to the AC setting? To this end, we need to find out what "properties" of a statement the verification run has actually used. This can be seen in the abstract transition system by looking at the transitions labeled with a specific statement, and extracting the abstract states before and after this statement. A *tolerance constraint* for a statement includes all such pairs of abstract states, specifying a number of pre- and postconditions for the statement.

Definition 5. *Let $T^{\#} = (Q, q_0, \rightarrow)$ be an abstract transition system of a CFA P and $stm \in Stm$ a statement.*

The tolerance constraint *for stm in $T^{\#}$ is the family of pairs of abstract states $((a^i_1, a^i_2))_{i \in I}$ such that for every $i \in I$ there exists locations ℓ^i_1, ℓ^i_2 with $((a^i_1, \ell^i_1) \xrightarrow{stm} (a^i_2, \ell^i_2))$ and $a^i_2 \neq a_\perp$.*

While the concrete transformers fulfill all these constraints thanks to safe approximation, the approximate transformers might not adhere to the constraints.

Definition 6. *A next transformer* $next_{stm}^{AC} : \Sigma \to \Sigma$ *fulfills a tolerance constraint* $((a_1^i, a_2^i))_{i \in I}$ *if the following property holds for all* $i \in I, s \in \Sigma$:

$$s \in \gamma(a_1^i) \Rightarrow next_{stm}^{AC}(s) \in \gamma(a_2^i).$$

When programs are run on approximate hardware, the execution will use some approximate and some precise next transformers depending on the actual hardware. For instance, the execution might employ an approximate adder, and, thus, all statements using addition will be approximate. We let $T^{AC}(P)$ be the transition system of program P constructed by using $next_{stm}^{AC}$ for the approximate statements and standard concrete transformers for the rest. This lets us now formulate our main theorem about the validity of verification results on approximate hardware.

Theorem 2. *Let P be a CFA and $next_{stm}^{AC}$ be a next transformer for stm fulfilling the tolerance constraint on stm derived from an abstract transition system* $T^{\#}(P)$ *wrt. some abstract domain Abs and safe abstract next transformers. Then, we get:*

$$\text{If } T^{\#}(P) \text{ is free of errors, so is } T^{AC}(P).$$

Proof: Let $((a_1^i, a_2^i))_{i \in I}$ be the tolerance constraint for *stm* in $T^{\#}(P)$. Assume the contrary, i.e., there exists a path to an error location in $T^{AC}(P)$: $(s_0, \ell_0) \xrightarrow{stm_0} (s_1, \ell_1) \xrightarrow{stm_1} \ldots \xrightarrow{stm_{n-1}} (s_n, \ell_n)$ such that $\ell_n \in Err$. We show by induction that there exists a path $(a_0, \ell_0) \xrightarrow{stm_0} (a_1, \ell_1) \xrightarrow{stm_1} \ldots \xrightarrow{stm_{n-1}} (a_n, \ell_n)$ in the abstract transition system $T^{\#}(P)$ such that $s_j \in \gamma(a_j)$.

Induction base. $s_0 \in \gamma(a_0)$ since $a_0 = \alpha(\{s_0\})$ and $\{s_0\} \subseteq \gamma(\alpha(\{s_0\}))$ by Galois connection properties.

Induction step. Let $s_j \in \gamma(a_j)$, $next_{stm_j}(s_j) = s_{j+1}$ and $(\ell_j, stm_j, \ell_{j+1}) \in E$. Let $S_j = \gamma(a_j)$ (hence $s_j \in S_j$). Now, we need to consider two cases:

Case (1): $stm_j \neq stm$: Then, the next transformer applied to reach the next configuration is the standard transformer. Thus, let $next_{stm_j}(\gamma(a_j)) = S_{j+1}$. By safe approximation of $next^{\#}$, we get $\alpha(S_{j+1}) \sqsubseteq_{Abs} next_{stm_j}^{\#}(a_j) = a_{j+1}$. By monotonicity of γ: $\gamma(\alpha(S_{j+1})) \subseteq \gamma(a_{j+1})$. By Galois connection: $S_{j+1} \subseteq \gamma(\alpha(S_{j+1}))$. Hence, by transitivity $s_{j+1} \in \gamma(a_{j+1})$.

Case (2): $stm_j = stm$: Let $next_{stm}^{\#}(a_j) = a_{j+1}$. By definition of tolerance constraint extraction, the pair (a_j, a_{j+1}) has to be in the family of tolerance constraints, i.e., $\exists i \in I : (a_j, a_{j+1}) = (a_1^i, a_2^i)$. Since $next_{stm}^{AC}$ fulfills the constraint, $next_{stm_j}^{AC}(s_j) \in \gamma(a_{j+1})$.   □

4   Preserving Termination

So far, we have been interested in the preservation of already proven safety properties on approximate hardware and these have been stated by marking states as error states. Another important issue is the preservation of program *termination*: whenever we have managed to show that a program terminates on precise hardware, we would also like to get constraints that guarantee termination on AC hardware. In order to extend our approach to termination, we make use of an approach for encoding termination proofs as safety properties [14].

We start with explaining standard termination proofs. Non-termination arises when we have loops in programs and the loop condition never gets false in a program execution. In control-flow automata, a *loop* is a sequence of locations $\ell_0, \ldots, \ell_n$ such that there are statements stm_i, $i = 0..n - 1$, with $\ell_i \xrightarrow{stm_i} \ell_{i+1}$ and $\ell_0 = \ell_n$. In this, a location $\ell = \ell_i$ is said to be on the loop. Every well-structured loop has a condition and a loop body: the *start* of a loop body is a location ℓ such that there are locations ℓ', ℓ'' and a boolean condition b s.t. $\ell' \xrightarrow{assume\ b} \ell$ and $\ell' \xrightarrow{assume\ !b} \ell''$ are in the CFA and ℓ' is on a loop, but either ℓ'' is not on a loop, or is on a different loop. Basically, we just consider CFAs of programs constructed with while or for constructs, not with gotos or recursion. However, the latter is also possible when the verification technique used for proving termination covers such programs.

Definition 7. *A non-terminating run of a CFA $P = (L, \ell_0, E, Err)$ is an infinite sequence of configurations and statements $(s_0, \ell_0) \xrightarrow{stm_1} (s_1, \ell_1) \xrightarrow{stm_2} \ldots$ in the transition system $T(P)$. If P has no non-terminating runs, then P terminates.*

Proposition 1. *In every non-terminating run, at least one loop start ℓ occurs infinitely often.*

We assume some standard technique to be employed for proving termination. Such techniques typically consist of (a) the synthesis of a termination argument, and (b) the check of validity of this termination argument. Termination arguments are either given as monolithic ranking functions or as disjunctively well-founded transition invariants [32]. Here, we will describe the technique for monolithic ranking functions:

1. For every loop starting in ℓ, define a *ranking function* f_ℓ on the program variables, i.e., $f_\ell : \Sigma \rightarrow W$, where $(W, >)$ is a well-founded order with least element $\perp_W$.
2. Show f_ℓ to decrease with every loop execution, i.e., if $(s, \ell) \xrightarrow{stm_1} (s_1, \ell_1) \xrightarrow{stm_2} \ldots \xrightarrow{stm_n} (s', \ell)$ is a path in $T(P)$, show $f_\ell(s) > f_\ell(s')$.
3. Show f_ℓ to be greater than the least element of W at loop start, i.e., for all starts of loop bodies ℓ and $(s, \ell) \in Q_{T(P)}$ (states of transition system), show $f_\ell(s) > \perp_W$.

If properties (2) and (3) hold, we say that the ranking function is *valid*. Note that we are not interested in computing ranking functions here; we just want to make use of existing verification techniques. The following proposition states a standard result for ranking functions (see e.g. [3, 28]).

```
sum=0;                          sum=0;
i=0;                            i=0;
while (i<N) {                    while (i<N) {
                                    if (!(N-i > 0))
                                        ERR: ;
                                    old_i=i;
    sum=sum+i;                      sum=sum+i;
    i=i+1;                          i=i+1;
                                    if (!(N-old_i > N-i))
                                        ERR: ;

}                               }
```

Fig. 2. Program Sum (on the left) and its instrumented version (on the right).

Proposition 2. *Let P be a program. If every loop ℓ of P has a valid ranking function, then P terminates.*

As an example consider the program Sum on the left of Fig. 2. It computes the sum of all numbers from 0 up to some constant N. It terminates since variable i is constantly increased. As ranking function we can take $N - i$ using the well-founded ordering $(\mathbb{N}, >)$ with bottom element $\perp_\mathbb{N} = 0$.

In order to encode the above technique in terms of assertions (or error states as we have done so far), we instrument a program P along the lines used in the tool TERMINATOR [14] thereby getting a program $\widehat{P}$ as follows. Let $Var = \{x_1, \ldots, x_n\}$ be the set of variables occurring in the program. At starts of loop bodies ℓ we insert

```
if (!(f_l(x1, ..., xn) > bot_W)
    ERR:
old_x1 := x1;
...
old_xn := xn;
```

and at loop ends we insert

```
if (!(f_l(old_x1, ..., old_xn) > f_l(x1, ..., xn))
    ERR:
```

when given a ranking function f_ℓ and a well-founded ordering $(W, >)$ with bottom element bot_W. Checking for the reachability of error states now amounts to checking validity of the encoded ranking function (a standard result from termination analysis).

Proposition 3. *If $\widehat{P}$ is free of errors, then P terminates.*

Hence, we can use standard safety proving for termination as well (once we have a ranking function), and thereby derive tolerance constraints. On the right of Fig. 2 we see the instrumented version of program Sum. Here, we have already applied an optimization: we only make a copy of variable i since the ranking function only refers to i and N, and N does not change anyway.

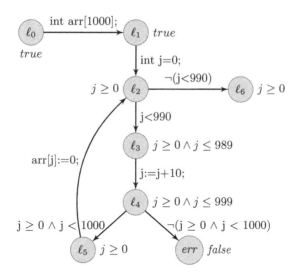

Fig. 3. Abstract transition system of program `Array`. For the sake of presentation, we only show the condition b of all assume statements `assume b`.

5 Constraint Extraction for Predicate Analysis

Section 3 has formally defined the extraction of tolerance constraints from abstract transition systems and has proven its soundness. Now, we will take a closer look at constraint extraction in practice. To this end, we choose an instance of the abstract interpretation framework, namely predicate abstraction [4,16]. Furthermore, instead of deriving constraints for statements, we derive constraints for *operators* since in practice we do not have specific hardware for whole statements but just for the operations used in expressions within a statement.

We start with defining predicate abstraction. For this, we fix a set of predicates $\mathcal{P}$ over *Var*, *Cmp*, $\mathbb{Z}$ and *Ops*. In practice, these predicates will be incrementally computed by a counter-example-guided abstraction refinement approach [20], which we just assume to exist (and which is provided by the tool that we employ for our experiments). We define $\neg\mathcal{P} := \{\neg p \mid p \in \mathcal{P}\}$ and let the abstract domain *Abs* be conjunctions of predicates or their negations (also directly written as set of literals, hence $\emptyset$ is true, $\mathcal{P} \cup \neg\mathcal{P}$ is false):

$$(\{\bigwedge_{q \in Q} q \mid Q \subseteq \mathcal{P} \cup \neg\mathcal{P}\}, \Rightarrow)$$

(where $\Rightarrow$ is logical implication). The Galois connection is given by $\alpha(S) := \{q \in \mathcal{P} \cup \neg\mathcal{P} \mid \forall s \in S : s \models q\}$ and $\gamma(Q) := \{s \in \Sigma \mid \forall q \in Q : s \models q\}$. We write $s \models Q$ iff $s \models q$ for all $q \in Q$. For the definition of the abstract next transformers see for instance [4]. Note that tolerance constraints in this domain take the form $(Q_1, Q_2), Q_j \subseteq \mathcal{P} \cup \neg\mathcal{P}, j \in \{1, 2\}$.

This abstract domain can be used to show that program `Array` of Fig. 1 is free of errors. Figure 3 shows the abstract transition system of program `Array` using the predicate set $\mathcal{P} = \{j \geq 0, j \leq 989, j \leq 999\}$. The predicates holding in an abstract configuration (a, ℓ), i.e., the abstract state a, are written next to the purple locations. We see that the location labeled err occurs in the graph, but the abstract state in this configuration is $a_\perp = false$, and, thus this error is not reachable.

For the extraction of tolerance constraints for operators $op \in Op$, we assume our statements to take the form of *three-address code* (3AC) [1]. In three-address code form, all operators op occur in programs only in statements $v := a\,op\,b$, where a and b are variables or constants. Every program can be brought in such a form (e.g., intermediate representations generated during compilation take this form). We use this 3AC form because we need to isolate operators and only have statements with one (possibly approximate) operator. Note that program `Array` is in 3AC form as is `Sum`.

The tolerance constraints, i.e., pre- and postcondition predicates, derived from abstract transition systems are specified over the *program variables*. As an example, take the operator $+$. In the program `Array` this operator occurs in the statement `j:=j+10`. The tolerance constraint for this statement derived from the abstract transition system in Fig. 3 is $(j \geq 0 \wedge j \leq 989, j \geq 0 \wedge j \leq 999)$. This constraint refers to the program variable j. If the approximate adder used for $+$ has inputs x and y and output z, this constraint first of all needs to be brought into a form using variables x, y, and z. This is achieved by using the following replacement operator.

Definition 8. *Let $Q \in \mathcal{P} \cup \neg\mathcal{P}, p \in Q, v_1, v_2 \in Var$. The predicate $p[v_2 \rhd v_1]$ is obtained from p by replacing all occurrences of v_2 by v_1. We lift this to sets by letting $Q[v_2 \rhd v_1] := \{q[v_2 \rhd v_1] \mid q \in Q\}$. For constants $c \in \mathbb{Z}$, we define $Q[c \rhd v_1] := Q \cup \{v_1 = c\}$.*

Proposition 4. *For all $q \in \mathcal{P} \cup \neg\mathcal{P}$ such that $x \notin vars(q)$:*

$$s[x := s(u)] \models q[u \rhd x] \quad \Leftrightarrow \quad s \models q$$

For constraint $(Q_1, Q_2) = (j \geq 0 \wedge j \leq 989, j \geq 0 \wedge j \leq 999)$, statement `j:=j+10` and adder with inputs x and y, output z, the replacement we need to make is $(Q_1[j \rhd x, 10 \rhd y], Q_2[j \rhd z]) = (x \geq 0 \wedge x \leq 989 \wedge y = 10, z \geq 0 \wedge z \leq 999)$. This is the constraint which ultimately needs to be checked on the AC hardware.

As another example, consider the program `Sum` used for exemplifying termination proofs. The abstract transition system for the instrumented version of `Sum` is given in Fig. 4. Note once more that locations labeled *false* are unreachable. Again, we take a look at the (potentially) approximately implemented operator $+$. It occurs on the statements leading from location ℓ_5 to ℓ_6 and ℓ_6 to ℓ_7. For the first statement, the constraint can be discarded as the predicates occurring on the locations do not mention variable `sum` which is changed by the statement. Thus this constraint is always fulfilled. The second statement is

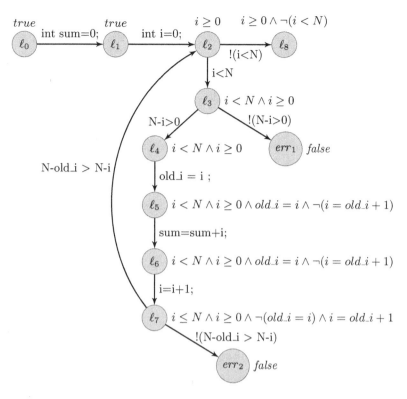

Fig. 4. Abstract transition system of program Sum. For the sake of presentation, we only show the condition b of all assume statements assume b.

more interesting: Using again inputs x and y and output z for addition (i.e., the general form of addition is $z := x + y$), the constraint for transition ℓ_6 to ℓ_7 is

$$\big(x < N \wedge x \geq 0 \wedge old\_i = x \wedge \neg(x = old\_i + 1) \wedge y = 1,$$
$$z \leq N \wedge z \geq 0 \wedge \neg(old\_i = z) \wedge z = old\_i + 1\big)$$

In the following, we assume all binary operators to have signature $(x : \mathbb{Z}, y : \mathbb{Z}) \to (z : \mathbb{Z})$, $x, y,$ and z to not occur as variables in the program nor in the predicates, and use $(\widehat{Q}_1, \widehat{Q}_2)$ to refer to the constraints obtained after the replacement.

Definition 9. *An approximate operator* $op^{AC} : \mathbb{Z} \times \mathbb{Z} \to \mathbb{Z}$ *adheres to a tolerance constraint* $(\widehat{Q}_1, \widehat{Q}_2)$ *(i.e., over* x, y *and* z*) if*

$$\forall s \in \Sigma : s \models \widehat{Q}_1 \Rightarrow s[z := op^{AC}(s(x), s(y))] \models \widehat{Q}_2$$

Adherence to constraints by operators implies adherence to constraints by statements using these operators.

Lemma 1. *Let (Q_1, Q_2) be a tolerance constraint extracted from $T^{\#}$ for stm $\equiv$ $u := v\, op\, w$. If op^{AC} adheres to $(Q_1[v \triangleright x, w \triangleright y], Q_2[u \triangleright z])$, then $next_{stm}^{AC} :\equiv u :=$ $v\, op^{AC}\, w$ adheres to (Q_1, Q_2).*

Proof: We need to show that $next_{stm}^{AC}$ adheres to (Q_1, Q_2). We first of all take the definition of it and rewrite it a little.

$$s \in \gamma(Q_1) \Rightarrow next_{stm}^{AC}(s) \in \gamma(Q_2)$$
$$\Leftrightarrow \quad \{ \text{ definition of } next_{stm}^{AC} \quad \}$$
$$s \in \gamma(Q_1) \Rightarrow s[u := op^{AC}(s(v), s(w))] \in \gamma(Q_2)$$
$$\Leftrightarrow \quad \{ \text{ definition of } \gamma \quad \}$$
$$s \models Q_1 \Rightarrow s[u := op^{AC}(s(v), s(w))] \models Q_2$$

The last implication is now shown as follows:

$$s \models Q_1 \Rightarrow s[x := s(v), y := s(w)] \models Q_1[v \triangleright x, w \triangleright y]$$
$$\Rightarrow s[x := s(v), y := s(w), z := op^{AC}(s(v), s(w))] \models Q_2[u \triangleright z]$$
$$\Rightarrow s[x := s(v), y := s(w), u := op^{AC}(s(v), s(w))] \models Q_2$$
$$\Rightarrow s[u := op^{AC}(s(v), s(w))] \models Q_2$$

$\square$

This finally gives us our main soundness result for predicate analysis which is an immediate corollary of Lemma 1 and Theorem 2.

Corollary 1. *Let $T^{\#}$ be an abstract transition system constructed using safe approximations and let all approximate operators op^{AC} adhere to the constraints derived from $T^{\#}$. Then: If $T^{\#}$ is free of errors, so is T^{AC}.*

Implementation. As proof of concept we implemented our proposed constraint extraction within the software analysis tool CPACHECKER [10], a tool for C program analysis which is configurable to abstract interpretation based analyses. Mainly, we added a constraint extraction algorithm plus some additional helper classes. Our constraint extraction algorithm builds on top of CPACHECKER's predicate analysis, which uses the technique of adjustable block encoding [9], a technique which allows the user to specify at which locations an abstraction should be computed. For our extraction, we need to make sure that we have an abstract state immediately before and after each statement that uses the operation of interest op^2. To identify these abstraction points and later the tolerance constraints, we first need to identify the statements using the operation op. Afterwards, we run CPACHECKER's standard predicate analysis, which provides us with an abstract reachability graph (ARG), a structure similar to the

---

[2] The operation of interest is made configurable in CPACHECKER.

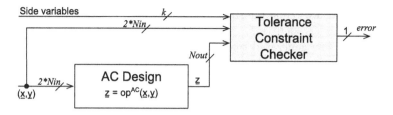

Fig. 5. Adherence Checker combining AC design with Tolerance Constraint Checker

abstract transition system. In the ARG, the predicates are given in SMT-Lib format [5] since CPACHECKER is using state-of-art SMT solvers for predicate analysis. From the ARG, we extract the tolerance constraints and write one SMT file per constraint (Q_1, Q_2), which is in the input format required by our next tool building the hardware checker. The SMT file mainly contains the description of (Q_1, Q_2) pairs plus additional information about the signature of the statement for which the constraint was extracted. The signature is needed by the next tool to construct $(\widehat{Q_1}, \widehat{Q_2})$.

To run the tolerance constraint extraction within CPACHECKER, one can use the configuration file `predicateAnalysis-ToleranceConstraints Extraction- PLUS.properties` that we used in our evaluation to extract tolerance constraints for additions.

6   Constraint Checking

The final, also automatic step of our technique checks the extracted constraints on actual hardware designs of approximate operations. For simplicity of representation, we restrict the following explanations to the case of a single constraint[3]. The input to the checking phase thus consists of a constraint (Q_1, Q_2), an approximate operator op^{AC} and the corresponding program statement $u := v\, op\, w$. The checking of the constraint on a given hardware design with inputs x, y and output z (in our case specified in Verilog) proceeds in three steps:

Mapping. The mapped tolerance constraint $(\widehat{Q}_1, \widehat{Q}_2) = (Q_1[v \triangleright x, w \triangleright y], Q_2[u \triangleright z])$ is constructed. As a result, the tolerance constraint $(\widehat{Q}_1, \widehat{Q}_2)$ uses the variables x, y, and z when referring to the inputs and output of op^{AC}. Additional variables of the program that are unequal to u, v, and w and are, thus, not used in the hardware design, may still occur in the constraint. We denote these variables as *side variables*.

Transformation. The mapped constraint is transformed into Verilog code resulting in a *checker circuit*. The checker circuit is created as Verilog code in two steps. First, the logical formulae of the tolerance constraints are compiled to Verilog code (see [31]). Thereby, side variables are treated like normal

---

[3] A generalization to a family of constraints is straightforward.

inputs. Second, we define the single output of the checker called *error* by setting $error := \neg(\widehat{Q}_1 \Rightarrow \widehat{Q}_2)$.

Combination. The generated tolerance constraint checker is afterwards combined with the hardware design of op^{AC} into an *adherence checker*. For our examples, the AC hardware designs are also given in Verilog. The combination is done using a top module that contains and wires the design of op^{AC} and the tolerance checker as sub-modules. Wiring is done as shown in Fig. 5.

The resulting adherence checker circuit is then checked for safety, i.e., that for no combinations of values on the primary inputs the error flag is raised. This check can be done using standard hardware verification techniques that apply unsatisfiability checking. An example for program `Array` can be found in our technical report [22].

7 Experiments

In our experiments, we used the software analysis tool CPACHECKER to extract the tolerance constraints from a verification run. We employed the tools *Yosys* [37] and *ABC* [6] for synthesis and generation of a CNF formula that encodes the value of the error flag in dependence on all the inputs. Using PicoSAT [11], we checked the unsatisfiability of the formula, denoting that the error flag is never raised, i.e., the tolerance constraints are met by the implementation.

In the following, we give the results of our experiments. In our experiments, we studied tolerance constraints for addition (because this is one of the few operations for which approximate hardware is currently publicly available). We extracted tolerance constraints from the verification of a number of handcrafted programs (including our three examples) and some programs from the subcategory `ControlFlow` and `ProductLines` of the SV-COMP[4] [8]. We chose our programs as to get tolerance constraints for a variety of verification problems. The handcrafted programs `AddOne`, `EvenSum`, `SpecificAdd` and `MonotonicAdd` are constructed as to examine the addition of positive numbers. Programs `Sum`, `Quotient`, and `Mirror_Matrix` use the previously described technique to encode termination proofs with assertions. The programs from SV-COMP (the last ten programs in Table 1) check protocol properties, e.g. correct locking behavior.

We checked the tolerance constraints on a standard, non-approximate ripple carry adder (RCA) and a set of approximate adders provided by the Karlsruhe library of [35] (called ACA-I [36], ACA-II (ACA_II_N16_Q4) [26], ETAII [39], GDA [38] and GeAr, see https://ces.itec.kit.edu/lpAClib.php). Table 1 shows our results. For each program, we show the number of additions ($\#+$), the number of program statements ($\#stm$), the number of constraints extracted ($\#tc$) and whether an adder meets the tolerance constraints ✓ or does not ✗.

---

[4] Some additions first had to be brought into three-address code form and in some programs we replaced some constant assignments by proper addition.

Table 1. Results of experiments

		Program	#+	#stm	#tc	RCA	ACA-I	ACA-II	ETAII	GDA	GeAr
Sample Programs	Addition Properties	AddOne	1	22	1	✓	×	×	×	×	×
		Array	1	15	1	✓	✓	✓	✓	✓	✓
		Attach/Detach	1	26	1	✓	✓	✓	✓	✓	✓
		EvenSum	2	24	4	✓	×	×	×	×	×
		MonotonicAdd	1	20	1	✓	×	×	×	×	×
		SpecificAdd	1	13	1	✓	✓	×	✓	✓	✓
	Termi- nation	Mirror_Matrix	2	42	2	✓	×	×	×	×	×
		Quotient	2	35	2	✓	×	×	×	×	×
		Sum	2	26	2	✓	×	×	×	×	×
SV-COMP	Protocol Properties	locks_5	5	114	31	✓	✓	✓	✓	✓	✓
		locks_8	8	171	255	✓	✓	✓	✓	✓	✓
		cdaudio	13	1888	23	✓	✓	✓	✓	✓	✓
		diskperf	19	981	12	✓	✓	✓	✓	✓	✓
		floppy4	31	1370	34	✓	✓	✓	✓	✓	✓
		kbfiltr2	11	759	15	✓	✓	✓	✓	✓	✓
		minepump_s5_p64	2	741	3	✓	✓	✓	✓	✓	✓
		minepump_s5_simulator	2	811	3	✓	✓	✓	✓	✓	✓
		clnt_4	13	575	18	✓	✓	✓	✓	✓	✓
		srvr_8	19	668	14	✓	✓	✓	✓	✓	✓

Our first observation is that except for program `SpecificAdd`, which we created to show that the behaviour between the approximate adders differs, either all approximate adders meet the extracted tolerance constraint or none of them does. This is because all approximate adders use the same principle: reduction of the carry chain. In their addition, they use a set of subadders and the carry bit of the previous subadder is either dropped or imprecisely predicted. The effect of this reduction only shows off for specific numbers and these specific numbers differ among the approximate adders.

Interestingly, the approximate adders meet the extracted tolerance constraints for all of the SV-COMP programs. Note, however, that none of these required a proof of termination. On the one hand, not all additions in the programs have an effect on the correctness of the program (and, thus, verification imposes no constraints on them). On the other hand, the additions considered during verification that had an effect increase a variable value in the range $[0, 9]$ by one, which can be computed precisely by the first subadder of all approximate adders.

For our own programs, one can see that all sorts of cases occur: all approximate adders satisfy the extracted constraints (as is the case for program `Array`), some do and some do not (on program `SpecificAdd`), and all do not. An instance of the latter case is our example program `AddOne` from the right of Fig. 1. The variable u, which is increased by one, can be any positive integer (it is an input). The derived constraint for operator $+$ is $((1 \leq u)[u \triangleright x, 1 \triangleright y], (sum \neq 0)[sum \triangleright z]) = (1 \leq x \wedge y = 1, z \neq 0)$. For our verification of the property, we require that the increase of that variable does not result in value zero, which can be the case if the carry propagation is imprecise. Thus, here the approximate designs fail to satisfy the constraint. Hence, an execution of the program on approximate hardware with these adders could reach the error state.

The imprecise carry propagation is also the reason why the approximate adders cannot guarantee termination of programs `Mirror_Matrix`, `Quotient`, and `Sum`. For termination, all three programs rely on an addition that is strongly monotonic up to a certain threshold (maximal int value). However, due to the imprecise carry propagation an addition of two positive integers may result in value zero. We conjecture that this is a general problem for termination on approximate hardware: all programs that contain iterations over arrays are potentially threatened to not terminate on AC.

8   Conclusion

In this paper, we have proposed a new way of making software verification robust against approximate hardware. Its basic principle is the derivation of constraints on AC hardware from verification runs. We have shown our technique to be sound, i.e., shown that the verification result carries over to a setting with AC hardware when the hardware satisfies the derived constraints. First experimental results have shown that the verification result often but not always carries over. In particular, the experiments indicate that termination might be most critical. More experiments are, however, necessary when further AC implementations of operations become available.

Discussion. As future work, we intend to investigate how a compaction of the extracted tolerance constraints can be achieved. At the moment, we extract one constraint for every occurrence of an operation (and either check all separately or join these into one). An alternative would be to model the approximate operation as a function call. This would allow us to apply verification techniques (like [34]) which compute function summaries [21]. The function summary for the approximate operation – in principle a description of a pre-/postcondition pair – would then give us a single constraint on the AC hardware. Another option is to use verification techniques like maximal specification synthesis [2], which compute the weakest specification for the approximate operation under which the program is still safe. Yet another idea is to use techniques described in [7] or [24,25] to first of all weaken the abstract reachability graph (in such a way that it still shows correctness of the program), and extract constraints from this weaker abstract reachability graph.

An adaption of software verification to AC could also be achieved by modeling the approximate operations by undefined function symbols plus specifying certain properties (the properties of the adders) for these function symbols. A complete specification of an adder's properties would, however, possibly be almost as complex as its truth table and thus prohibitly large.

References

1. Aho, A.V., Sethi, R., Ullman, J.D.: Compilers: Principles, Techniques, and Tools. Addison-Wesley, Boston (1986)
2. Albarghouthi, A., Dillig, I., Gurfinkel, A.: Maximal specification synthesis. In: Proceedings of the POPL, pp. 789–801. ACM (2016)
3. Apt, K.R., de Boer, F.S., Olderog, E.R.: Verification of Sequential and Concurrent Programs. Springer, London (2009). https://doi.org/10.1007/978-1-84882-745-5
4. Ball, T., Podelski, A., Rajamani, S.K.: Boolean and cartesian abstraction for model checking C programs. STTT **5**(1), 49–58 (2003)
5. Barrett, C., Fontaine, P., Tinelli, C.: The SMT-LIB Standard: Version 2.5. Technical report, Department of Computer Science, The University of Iowa (2015). http://www.SMT-LIB.org
6. ABC, Berkeley: A system for sequential synthesis and verification (2005)
7. Besson, F., Jensen, T.P., Turpin, T.: Small witnesses for abstract interpretation-based proofs. In: De Nicola, R. (ed.) ESOP 2007. LNCS, vol. 4421, pp. 268–283. Springer, Heidelberg (2007). https://doi.org/10.1007/978-3-540-71316-6_19
8. Beyer, D.: Software verification and verifiable witnesses. In: Baier, C., Tinelli, C. (eds.) TACAS 2015. LNCS, vol. 9035, pp. 401–416. Springer, Heidelberg (2015). https://doi.org/10.1007/978-3-662-46681-0_31
9. Beyer, D., Keremoglu, M.E., Wendler, P.: Predicate abstraction with adjustable-block encoding. In: Proceedings of the FMCAD, pp. 189–198. IEEE (2010)
10. Beyer, D., Keremoglu, M.E.: CPACHECKER: a tool for configurable software verification. In: Gopalakrishnan, G., Qadeer, S. (eds.) CAV 2011. LNCS, vol. 6806, pp. 184–190. Springer, Heidelberg (2011). https://doi.org/10.1007/978-3-642-22110-1_16
11. Biere, A.: Picosat (2013). http://fmv.jku.at/picosat
12. Carbin, M., Kim, D., Misailovic, S., Rinard, M.C.: Verified integrity properties for safe approximate program transformations. In: Proceedings of the PEPM, pp. 63–66. ACM (2013)
13. Carbin, M., Misailovic, S., Rinard, M.C.: Verifying quantitative reliability for programs that execute on unreliable hardware. In: Proceedings of the OOPSLA, pp. 33–52. ACM (2013)
14. Cook, B., Podelski, A., Rybalchenko, A.: Termination proofs for systems code. In: Proceedings of the PLDI, pp. 415–426. ACM (2006)
15. Cousot, P., Cousot, R.: Abstract interpretation: a unified lattice model for static analysis of programs by construction or approximation of fixpoints. In: Proceedings of the POPL. ACM (1977)
16. Graf, S., Saidi, H.: Construction of abstract state graphs with PVS. In: Grumberg, O. (ed.) CAV 1997. LNCS, vol. 1254, pp. 72–83. Springer, Heidelberg (1997). https://doi.org/10.1007/3-540-63166-6_10
17. Han, J., Orshansky, M.: Approximate computing: an emerging paradigm for energy-efficient design. In: Proceedings of the ETS, pp. 1–6. IEEE Computer Society (2013)
18. He, S., Lahiri, S.K., Rakamarić, Z.: Verifying relative safety, accuracy, and termination for program approximations. In: Rayadurgam, S., Tkachuk, O. (eds.) NFM 2016. LNCS, vol. 9690, pp. 237–254. Springer, Cham (2016). https://doi.org/10.1007/978-3-319-40648-0_19
19. He, S., Lahiri, S.K., Rakamaric, Z.: Verifying relative safety, accuracy, and termination for program approximations. JAR **60**(1), 23–42 (2018)

20. Henzinger, T.A., Jhala, R., Majumdar, R., McMillan, K.L.: Abstractions from proofs. In: Proceedings of the POPL, pp. 232–244. ACM (2004)
21. Hoare, C.A.R.: Procedures and parameters: an axiomatic approach. In: Engeler, E. (ed.) Symposium on Semantics of Algorithmic Languages. LNM, vol. 188, pp. 102–116. Springer, Heidelberg (1971). https://doi.org/10.1007/BFb0059696
22. Isenberg, T., Jakobs, M.C., Pauck, F., Wehrheim, H.: Deriving Approximation Tolerance Constraints from Verification Runs. CoRR abs/1604.08784 (2016). http://arxiv.org/abs/1604.08784
23. Isenberg, T., Jakobs, M., Pauck, F., Wehrheim, H.: Validity of software verification results on approximate hardware. ESL 10(1), 22–25 (2018)
24. Jakobs, M.-C.: Speed up configurable certificate validation by certificate reduction and partitioning. In: Calinescu, R., Rumpe, B. (eds.) SEFM 2015. LNCS, vol. 9276, pp. 159–174. Springer, Cham (2015). https://doi.org/10.1007/978-3-319-22969-0_12
25. Jakobs, M.-C., Wehrheim, H.: Compact proof witnesses. In: Barrett, C., Davies, M., Kahsai, T. (eds.) NFM 2017. LNCS, vol. 10227, pp. 389–403. Springer, Cham (2017). https://doi.org/10.1007/978-3-319-57288-8_28
26. Kahng, A.B., Kang, S.: Accuracy-configurable adder for approximate arithmetic designs. In: Proceedings of the DAC, pp. 820–825. ACM (2012)
27. Kugler, L.: Is "good enough" computing good enough? Commun. ACM 58(5), 12–14 (2015)
28. Manna, Z., Pnueli, A.: Temporal verification of reactive systems: progress (1996)
29. Misailovic, S., Carbin, M., Achour, S., Qi, Z., Rinard, M.C.: Chisel: reliability- and accuracy-aware optimization of approximate computational kernels. In: Proceedings of the OOPSLA, pp. 309–328. ACM (2014)
30. Mittal, S.: A survey of techniques for approximate computing. ACM Comput. Surv. 48(4), 62:1–62:33 (2016)
31. Pauck, F.: Generierung von Eigenschaftsprüfern in einem Hardware/Software-Co-Verifikationsverfahren. Bachelor thesis, Paderborn University (2014)
32. Podelski, A., Rybalchenko, A.: Transition invariants. In: Proceedings of the LICS, pp. 32–41. IEEE Computer Society (2004)
33. Sampson, A., Dietl, W., Fortuna, E., Gnanapragasam, D., Ceze, L., Grossman, D.: EnerJ: approximate data types for safe and general low-power computation. In: Proceedings of the PLDI, pp. 164–174. ACM (2011)
34. Sery, O., Fedyukovich, G., Sharygina, N.: Interpolation-based function summaries in bounded model checking. In: Eder, K., Lourenço, J., Shehory, O. (eds.) HVC 2011. LNCS, vol. 7261, pp. 160–175. Springer, Heidelberg (2012). https://doi.org/10.1007/978-3-642-34188-5_15
35. Shafique, M., Ahmad, W., Hafiz, R., Henkel, J.: A low latency generic accuracy configurable adder. In: Proceedings of the DAC, pp. 86:1–86:6. ACM (2015)
36. Verma, A.K., Brisk, P., Ienne, P.: Variable latency speculative addition: a new paradigm for arithmetic circuit design. In: Proceedings of the DATE, pp. 1250–1255. ACM (2008)
37. Wolf, C.: Yosys open synthesis suite. http://www.clifford.at/yosys/
38. Ye, R., Wang, T., Yuan, F., Kumar, R., Xu, Q.: On reconfiguration-oriented approximate adder design and its application. In: Proceedings of the CAD, pp. 48–54. IEEE Press (2013)
39. Zhu, N., Goh, W.L., Yeo, K.S.: An enhanced low-power high-speed adder for error-tolerant application. In: Proceedings of the International Symposium on Integrated Circuits, pp. 69–72. IEEE (2009)

Testing Robots Using CSP

Ana Cavalcanti[1]([✉]), James Baxter[1], Robert M. Hierons[2],
and Raluca Lefticaru[2]

[1] Department of Computer Science, University of York, York YO10 5GH, UK
Ana.Cavalcanti@york.ac.uk
[2] Department of Computer Science, University of Sheffield, Sheffield S1 4DP, UK

Abstract. This paper presents a technique for automatic generation
of tests for robotic systems based on a domain-specific notation called
RoboChart. This is a UML-like diagrammatic notation that embeds a
component model suitable for robotic systems, and supports the definition of behavioural models using enriched state machines that can feature
time properties. The formal semantics of RoboChart is given using tock-
CSP, a discrete-time variant of the process algebra CSP. In this paper,
we use the example of a simple drone to illustrate an approach to generate tests from RoboChart models using a mutation tool called Wodel.
From mutated models, tests are generated using the CSP model checker
FDR. The testing theory of CSP justifies the soundness of the tests.

1 Introduction

RoboChart [38] is a domain-specific language for the design of robotic systems. Typically, robotic systems are described in the literature using state
machines [39,44,45,50] specified informally, with a notation that does not have
even a precise syntax. Recently, a number of domain-specific notations have been
proposed to enable tool support in the development of models, and automatic
generation of code. RoboChart is distinctive in its support to specify timed
properties, and in its formal semantics based on the process algebra CSP [32].

We can think of RoboChart as a profile for UML component and state-
machine diagrams. It is, however, enriched with facilities to specify time bud-
gets and deadlines. In RoboChart, a system is specified by a module, whose
components identify a robotic platform and one or more controllers. The robotic
platform identifies just the sensor and actuator functionality required for the
system. These requirements are modelled by variables, operations, and atomic
and instantaneous events that can communicate data.

Previous work on RoboChart has concentrated on verification by model
checking [37] and theorem proving [21]. RoboTool[1] provides support for modelling and automatic generation of a CSP model of a RoboChart module. Extensive work has also been carried out in the verification of simulations of RoboChart

---

[1] https://www.cs.york.ac.uk/robostar/.

© Springer Nature Switzerland AG 2019
D. Beyer and C. Keller (Eds.): TAP 2019, LNCS 11823, pp. 21–38, 2019.
https://doi.org/10.1007/978-3-030-31157-5_2

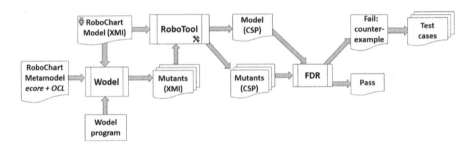

Fig. 1. Overview of our testing approach

models [17]. Extensions of RoboChart deal with collections [16] involving robots defined as instances of various modules, and with probabilistic properties [20].

A formal semantics also creates the opportunity for automatic generation of sound tests from RoboChart models. In this paper, we present an approach via a simple rescue application that uses a drone. The approach uses mutation testing as supported by the tool Wodel [24,26]. We describe a few mutation operators for RoboChart and the results of their application to our running example.

A high level overview of the approach is presented in Fig. 1. The input to Wodel is an XMI representation of a RoboChart model (developed using RoboTool), the RoboChart metamodel, and Wodel programs that implement RoboChart mutation operators. Wodel applies the RoboChart mutation operators to generate mutants, and eliminates ill-formed mutants, that is, those that do not satisfy the well-formedness rules of RoboChart. For that, we use OCL definitions of the RoboChart rules, which we briefly describe here. The valid mutants can be loaded in RoboTool for analysis.

As already said, RoboTool generates CSP scripts for valid RoboChart models. For each mutant, using the CSP model checker FDR [23], we compare its CSP specification to that of the original model. If the mutant is not a refinement of the original model, FDR generates a trace of interactions common to both models and a continuation that is forbidden by the original model. This is what is needed to define a test for traces refinement as identified in the CSP testing theory [11]. We illustrate this approach for our drone mutants.

The structure of this paper is as follows. Section 2 gives an overview of RoboChart and introduces our running example. Wodel is presented in Sect. 3, and CSP and FDR in Sect. 4. Our testing approach is the subject of Sect. 5. Finally, we discuss related work in Sect. 6, and future work in Sect. 7.

2   RoboChart

Our example is a simple rescue application that uses a drone to deliver some relief (water, mask, and so on) to a given target location identified via some feature (a person or a vehicle, for instance) in a particular direction. Figure 2

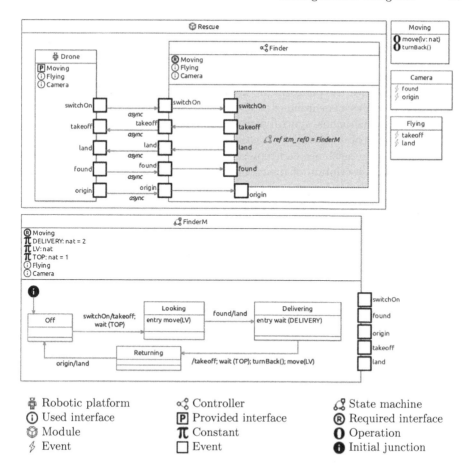

Fig. 2. RoboChart model of a simple rescue drone

presents the RoboChart model. The module, called Rescue, includes the definition of a robotic platform Drone and a controller Finder. In general, a module
can have several controllers running in parallel; in our example we have just one.

The platform provides two operations: move(lv: nat) and turnBack(), and
defines five events: switchOn, takeoff, land, found, and origin. They are abstractions for sensors and actuators. We have an on/off button, represented by the
event switchOn, and a motor that can be used to raise the drone off the ground,
abstracted by the event takeoff. Using the motor, we can also request that the
drone lands, moves forward with a particular speed, or turns back to return to
its origin: this is abstracted by the events land, and operations move(lv: nat) and
turnBack(). Finally, a camera can be used to identify the target of the rescue
operation, abstracted by the event found, or the origin.

Operations and events can be declared in interfaces. In the example, we have
interfaces Flying, Moving, and Camera also in the controller to define that it

requires all of the operations provided by the platform, and that it has the same events. Connections between events define the dataflow. In general, connections can be between events of different names, but of the same type. In our simple example, we use the same event names in every component.

Connections with the platform are asynchronous. Connections between controllers can be either synchronous or asynchronous. Although implementations are typically asynchronous, synchronicity can be defined for abstraction.

The behaviour of a controller is defined by one or more state machines. The use of several state machines can represent different threads of computation or provide modular description of functionality. In our example, we have just one state machine FinderM. The notation is, by and large, standard.

Of note in the state machine notation is the fact that it is a self-contained component that declares all the required variables and operations, and events that it uses. In our example, these are all those provided by the platform (and required by the controller for use in the machine). This means that a state machine can be treated independently in verification, simulation, and testing.

A machine can also declare local variables, constants, and clocks. In our example, we have three constants DELIVERY, LV, and TOP, which define the amount of time that the drone stays on the ground once it finds its target, the speed with which it moves, and the time it takes to take off.

The RoboChart notation to specify entry, during, exit, and transition actions is well defined. It is a language with assignments, operation calls, sequence, conditional, and inputs or outputs via events. Of note is the availability of time primitives. For instance, wait(TOP) is an action that pauses for TOP time units. In the example, it is used in the transition from the state Off to the state Looking.

The behaviour of the Rescue system is as follows. In the initial state Off, indicated by the initial junction, it accepts a request to switchOn, and, as a result, there is a takeoff. After that, the drone waits for TOP time units before it moves to the state Looking. Upon entry in Looking, the operation move(LV) is called and the drone proceeds until the target is reached as signalled by the input event found. When that happens, the controller issues a command to land. The drone moves to the state Delivering, whose entry action forces a pause of DELIVERY time units. Afterwards, the transition to the state Returning is taken, which causes the drone to takeoff, turnBack, and move again. In Returning, the transition back to Off is taken when the origin is found, and then the drone lands.

A full account of RoboChart, including its semantics, can be found in [38]. Several other examples are available at https://www.cs.york.ac.uk/robostar/, where the project files for this example can also be found.

3   Mutation Testing and Wodel

The idea behind mutation testing is that we take an entity p, such as a piece of code or a model, and use *mutation operators* to change (mutate) p in order to simulate potential faults. If we have an initial entity p and a set M of mutants, then a test suite T is assessed by determining what proportion of the (non-equivalent) elements of M are distinguished from p by T (are *killed* by T).

The essential concept is that if a test suite T is good at distinguishing p from its mutants, then T is also good at distinguishing p from some unknown correct version of p (if p is faulty). In addition, mutation testing can be used to drive test-case generation: given a non-equivalent mutant m of p, one might aim to generate a test case that kills m. This is the use of mutation testing that we discuss here, although we use refinement rather than equivalence.

There is potential to automate many parts of mutation testing, such as the generation of mutants and the execution of test cases on the mutants. As a result, the application of mutation testing is typically supported by a tool. However, mutation testing tools are normally language specific, leading to the need to develop a new tool whenever we consider a new language.

This has motivated the development of Wodel, which is a domain-specific language and tool for model-based mutation [24,26]. Wodel has been used in a range of case studies, for example, automatic generation of exercises for automata training [25] or mutation of security policies [26]. Wodel is metamodel independent, which means that users can define their own mutation operators for arbitrary metamodels – Wodel comes with some predefined examples: finite automata, probabilistic automata, and UML class diagrams.

Wodel is based on Eclipse Modelling Framework (EMF) and is available as an Eclipse plugin. The framework provides an editor to define the mutation operators, a compiler that transforms Wodel programs into Java code, metrics for mutation footprints, which provide information about the static and dynamic coverage of a metamodel and models used, a seed model synthesizer, and an extensibility mechanism that allows pipelining external applications.

Wodel provides high-level mutation primitives, such as, creation, deletion, reference reversal, attribute modification, object retyping, and object cloning, together with strategies for their customization and support for composition of mutation operators. The Wodel IDE provides an easy way for adding extension points, which allows users to register domain-specific post-processors to be executed upon mutant generation, for instance, to identify mutant equivalence.

Section 5 gives example of Wodel statements to implement operators.

4   CSP and FDR

Communicating Sequential Processes (CSP) [46] is a process algebra. Computation is modelled by processes, whose behaviour, in its simplest form, is described in terms of traces, that is, sequences of events. A CSP event is an atomic and instantaneous communication on a channel that may be represented by a simple flag, or carry values of particular types as parameters.

Processes can be defined using the basic processes *Stop*, representing deadlock, *Skip*, representing termination, and *DIV*, representing divergence (that is, livelock). Events can be prefixed to a process P. For example, $c.e \rightarrow P$ is a process that is ready to engage in the event $c.e$ and then behave like P.

CSP events are defined by a channel name and, optionally, parameters. As illustrated, a parameter e can be appended to a channel name c using a dot $(c.e)$. This represents a communication of e via c. An exclamation mark can be used $(c!e)$ to indicate that e is output on c. Use $c?x$ of a question mark indicates that the parameter is accepted as input and bound to the variable name x.

Processes P and Q can be combined using various operators, such as, internal (nondeterministic) choice $(P \sqcap Q)$ for the process, external choice $(P \square Q)$ made by the environment, parallel interleaving $(P \mathbin{|||} Q)$, parallel composition with synchronisation on an alphabet of events A $(P \mathbin{|[\,A\,]|} Q)$, and interrupt $(P \triangle Q)$.

A process Q is said to refine another process P, written $P \sqsubseteq Q$, if every behaviour of Q is a possible behaviour of P. This allows for incremental development of a correct program from a specification of how it should behave. In our work, refinement is the conformance relation used in testing. So, a mutant that merely refines the original model is not useful: it does not identify a fault.

CSP has various semantic models that permit reasoning about processes. These models vary in the aspects of behaviour that they can capture, and, therefore, in the processes they can distinguish. The most commonly used semantic models for CSP are the traces model, the stable failures model, and the failures-divergences model. Here, we consider just the traces model, and traces-refinement. We say that P is traces refined by Q, written $P \sqsubseteq_T Q$ if the set of traces of Q is included in that of P. This is our notion of conformance here.

To capture the timed behaviour of RoboChart models, we use a variant of CSP that includes a special event $tock$ to mark the passage of time. The testing theory for this version of CSP is ongoing work, based on the testing theory for the refusal-testing semantics of CSP. Here, as already mentioned, we consider just traces refinement. We note, however, that testing in CSP-based theories can consider traces refinement [11,12] in isolation, and use an additional conformance relation $conf$ to deal with refusals. Exhaustive test sets for the richer notions of refinement include the exhaustive test sets for traces refinement and $conf$. We expect that the same approach works for tock-CSP and its notion of refinement.

Using their semantic models, CSP processes can be reasoned about using mathematical proof, but automatic analysis of finite-state CSP processes can be performed using model checking. This is implemented by the tool FDR [23], which checks whether one process refines another, and can produce counterexamples when a refinement does not hold. The semantics for RoboChart models is calculated in RoboTool using the ASCII syntax for CSP (called CSP-M) that enables checking of RoboChart models using FDR. We use checking of RoboChart models in FDR as part of the testing strategy described next.

5 Mutation-Driven Testing

In this section, we present our approach to test generation using Wodel and FDR. First, we present in Sect. 5.1 a few mutation operators and their implementation in Wodel. We then discuss how ill-formed mutants are discarded in Sect. 5.2. Finally, in Sect. 5.3, we explain how we generate tests.

Table 1. Example of mutations used and corresponding Wodel blocks

Mutation	Wodel blocks	#
mStActEnDu	**retype one** EntryAction **as** DuringAction // modifies a state by changing an entry action into a during action	2
mStActEnEx	**retype one** EntryAction **as** ExitAction // modifies entry into exit action	2
mTransSource	tr = **select one** Transition **where** {^source ⬦ **one** Initial} **modify target** ^source **from** tr **to other** State // changes the start state of a transition, except the one from the initial junction	12
mTransTarget	**modify target** ^target **from one** Transition **to other** State // changes the ending state of a transition	15
mTransTrigger	interf = **select one** Interface **where** {events ⬦ **null**} ev = **select one** Event **in** interf–>events tg = **create** Trigger **with** {event = ev} **modify one** Transition **with** {trigger = tg} // modifies a transition by replacing its trigger with another event	6
rSeqStatement	ss = **select one** SeqStatement **remove one** Statement **from** ss–>statements [1..5] **remove all** SeqStatement **where** {statements = **null**} // randomly deletes 1–4 statements from a sequence and all empty sequences	12
rState	st = **select one** State **remove all** Transition **where** {^source = st} **remove all** Transition **where** {^target = st} **remove** st // removes a non initial state and all transitions from or to that state	3
rTran	**remove one** Transition **where** {^source ⬦ **one** Initial} // deletes one transition, except the one from initial junction	4
rTranAction	tr = **select one** Transition **where** {action ⬦ **null**} **remove one** Call **from** tr–>action **remove one** SendEvent **from** tr–>action **remove one** Action **from** tr // removes the action associated with a transition (call or send event)	2
Total		**58**

5.1   Mutation Operators

To generate tests from RoboChart models, we have used a number of mutation operators inspired by other works that use Wodel [24–26], and that consider mutations for UML class diagrams [27], state models [49], or interfaces [19]. We have adapted the operators to the particularities of the RoboChart metamodel. Many of them apply to elements of state machines.

Some operators that we have applied to the example from Fig. 2 are given in Table 1. In the first column, we give the name we have assigned to the mutation operator. The second column gives a block of Wodel statements that implements the operator. The third column gives the number of different valid mutants generated using the mutation operator. In total, for the example in Fig. 2, we have used 9 mutation operators and generated 58 valid mutants.

In RoboChart, a state can have associated actions identified in the metamodel as `EntryAction`, `DuringAction`, or `ExitAction`, all having as super type `Action`. We can use the Wodel statement **retype** to change one object type with another – the implementations of the mutation operators mStActEnDu and mStActEnEx use **retype** to change the type of a state action.

Wodel provides flexible statements such as **remove**, **create** or **clone**, which make it possible to delete or create new objects. These statements can be used in conjunction with different selection strategies, such as **select one**, or **all**, or as specified by a clause **where** *criteria*. Also, it is possible to change objects using a statement **modify** *object selection strategy* **with** *attribute set*.

We can redirect the **source** or **target** of a reference to another object, as illustrated by the implementation of the operators mTransSource and mTransTarget. A RoboChart `Transition` has the source and target states specified by attributes called `source` and `target` in the RoboChart metamodel. These attribute names, however, are also Wodel keywords. To differentiate between Wodel syntax and RoboChart metamodel elements, the latter are preceded by a caret symbol ^ (a special notation used in the Xtext[2]-based editor for Wodel programs in order to avoid this duplicity). This is illustrated by the implementation of the mutation operators mTransSource, mTransTarget, and rState.

In Wodel, it is possible to compose statements, as shown in the implementation of rSeqStatement, where a **remove** statement is repeated a random number of times between [1..5], to delete an action from a sequence. If all the statements have been deleted, then the empty `SeqStatement` element is further removed. Similarly, elements that would become invalid (having null attributes) are deleted from the model. For instance, the incoming or outgoing transitions from a state that is removed are also removed – see the rState operator.

The output of Wodel consists in XMI files; they have the same structure as the initial model, and describe mutants that conform to the metamodel and well-formedness rules of RoboChart. For Wodel validation of the mutants we have embedded in the metamodel the RoboChart well-formedness rules using the OCLinEcore language. They are further discussed in the next section.

---

[2] https://www.eclipse.org/Xtext/.

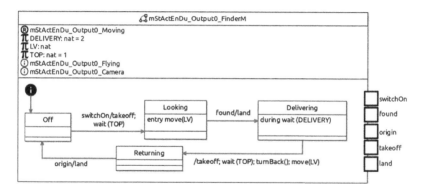

Fig. 3. Mutant for RoboChart model in Fig. 2 – the Delivering state has its entry action changed into a during action (mStActEnDu operator)

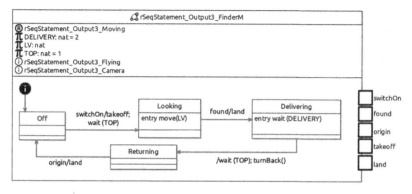

Fig. 4. Mutant for RoboChart model in Fig. 2 – two actions are removed from the sequence in the transition from the Delivering state (rSeqStatement operator)

For illustration, we include in Figs. 3 and 4 the state machines for two mutants of the model in Fig. 2. The module and controller of the mutants are the same, except that their names are changed to make them unique in a context (like a RoboChart package, for example) that includes both the original model and the mutant. We explain below why this is important.

The machines in the mutants, on the other hand, are obtained by applying two different mutation operators. For the mutant in Fig. 3, we have used the operator mStActEnDu that changes the entry action of a state to a during action. We have applied it to the Delivering state in Fig. 2. To obtain the mutant in Fig. 4, we have used rSeqStatement. We have applied this operator to the action in the transition from Delivering, and it has removed two basic RoboChart actions: the event takeoff and the call move(LV).

```
context Connection
  inv Cn9: (not self.bidirec
    and ControllerDef.allInstances()
      ->exists(c | c.connections->includes(self))
    and self.from.oclIsKindOf(StateMachine)
  ) implies self.from.oclAsType(StateMachine).stmDef()
      .ncInputEvents()->excludes(self.efrom)
```

Fig. 5. OCL constraint for RoboChart well-formedness condition Cn9

5.2 OCL Constraints

Application of some operators may lead to an invalid mutant, that is, a mutant that does not satisfy the RoboChart well-formedness conditions. An example of such an operator is mTransTrigger, which changes the event in a transition trigger. An application of mTransTrigger may give rise to a transition whose trigger event is associated with an outgoing (non-bidirectional) connection from the state machine. In this case, the result is an event that is used as an input, but associated with a connection that indicates it is used as an output. This violates the RoboChart well-formedness condition called Cn9 stating that events connected by such connections must not be used as inputs.

To exclude invalid mutants, we have translated the well-formedness conditions of RoboChart into Object Constraint Language (OCL), a language for specifying constraints on the structure of a metamodel. This allows the conditions to be considered by Wodel along with the RoboChart metamodel. Wodel then eliminates mutants that are not valid according to the constraints.

As an example, we provide in Fig. 5 the OCL constraint for the RoboChart well-formedness condition just described. The **context** declaration at the start indicates it is a constraint on a Connection, the RoboChart metamodel element representing connections. The constraint Cn9 is specified as an **invariant** for this model element. It is formalised as an implication (**implies**), where the antecedent identifies the connections to which the constraint applies. Specifically, it applies when self, the initial connection being considered, is **not** bidirectional, is contained in the connections of some ControllerDef (that is, it is a connection of a controller rather than a module), and has a source (self.from) of type (oclIsKindOf) StateMachine (that is, it does not connect from the boundary of the containing controller). ControllerDef.allInstances() identifies all controllers in the model, and exists(c | c.connections->includes(self)) requires that there exists such a controller c whose connections includes self.

Where these conditions are met, the constraint checks the source, from, of self, casting it to the StateMachine type and applying a function stmDef() to obtain the definition of the state machine. The events used as inputs by the state machine are then identified by another function ncInputEvents(), and the event that self connects from (efrom) is required to not be among them.

The full set of OCL constraints can be found in the RoboChart reference manual [52]. These constraints cover most of the well-formedness conditions of

RoboChart, but there are three that are not possible to define in OCL without an impractical amount of effort. The first is Cn4, which requires types of the source and target events of a connection to agree. Checking this would involve an implementation of a large part of the RoboChart type system within OCL.

The second condition not included in our OCL constraints is V1, which requires that the initial value of a variable must agree with those of the declarations of that variable in outer scopes. Since the initial value may be given by an arbitrarily complex expression, this requires an evaluator for RoboChart expressions. Due to the complexity of the RoboChart expression language, this is non-trivial.

The final such well-formedness condition is J2, which states that the guards of the outgoing transitions of a junction must form a cover. Since these guards are arbitrary expressions that need to be checked for all instantiations of the variables within them, this is a condition that can, in general, only be checked by a theorem prover. It is beyond the capacity of OCL to express such a constraint.

The files with the Wodel mutants can be imported back into RoboTool, so that their tock-CSP model is generated. Mutants that are not well formed, because they do not satisfy Cn4 or V1, are identified by RoboTool. For those, no CSP model is generated. For those that do not satisfy J2, a CSP model is generated, but a deadlock check can be used to identify the issue.

So, there is no real problem in importing potentially invalid mutants into RoboTool. Only tests based on valid mutants are generated, as explained next.

5.3   Test Generation

With the CSP models for both the original model and for a mutant (automatically generated by RoboTool), we can use the FDR model checker to generate tests (for traces refinement). This is achieved by checking whether the original model is traces-refined by the mutant. If it is, the check passes, and in this case, the mutant does not identify a fault. No test is generated. Of the 58 mutants in our example, five do not identify a fault and so are not useful.

If the mutant does identify a fault, FDR provides a counterexample for the check. This is a trace that is common to both models, except for its last event, which is allowed by the mutant, but not the original model. This last event is, therefore, a forbidden continuation for the preceding trace. For example, for the mutant in Fig. 3, the check raises the following counterexample.

```
Rescue_switchOn.in -> Rescue_takeoff.out -> tock ->
moveCall.1 -> moveRet -> Rescue_found.in -> Rescue_land.out ->
Rescue_takeoff.out
```

This indicates that, for the Rescue module, if we observe interactions characterised by the events switchOn and takeoff, and, after one time unit, the time required for taking off, we observe a call and return of the operation move with parameter 1, and then the events found and land, there should not be an immediate takeoff. This would not allow time for the delivery of relief. Such undesirable behaviour arises in the mutant, because the change of the entry action of Delivering to a during action allows it to be interrupted by takeoff.

For the mutant in Fig. 4, the check raises the following counterexample.

```
Rescue_switchOn.in -> Rescue_takeoff.out -> tock ->
moveCall.1 -> moveRet -> Rescue_found.in -> Rescue_land.out ->
tock -> tock -> tock ->
turnBackCall
```

Here, the forbidden continuation is the call of turnBack after the delivery and take off time (three time units), but without the actual takeoff. In this case, we have an attempt to turn the drone on the floor, which may damage it. The mutant captures this fault because its takeoff event has been removed.

These traces and forbidden continuations are exactly the data that we need to construct a test for traces refinement. In the CSP testing theory [11], a test is characterised by a function $T_T(t, e)$ for a trace t and a forbidden continuation. In the first example above, the trace is shown below.

$$\langle\, Rescue\_switchOn.in, Rescue\_takeoff.out, tock,$$
$$moveCall.1, moveRet, Rescue\_found.in, Rescue\_land.out \,\rangle$$

The forbidden continuation is $Rescue\_takeoff.out$. As may be expected, the use of the RoboChart events and operations of the robotic platform of a module are captured in the CSP model as CSP events. The CSP events for RoboChart events are tagged to indicate whether they are *in*puts or *out*puts, and the CSP events for operation calls are tagged with the arguments.

The test corresponding to this trace and forbidden continuation is characterised as a CSP process and it is shown below. It uses special events to indicate whether the verdict of the test execution is *in*conclusive, *fail* or *pass*.

$$inc \rightarrow Rescue\_switchOn.in \rightarrow inc \rightarrow Rescue\_takeoff.out \rightarrow inc \rightarrow tock \rightarrow$$
$$inc \rightarrow moveCall.1 \rightarrow inc \rightarrow moveRet \rightarrow$$
$$inc \rightarrow Rescue\_found.in \rightarrow inc \rightarrow Rescue\_land.out \rightarrow$$
$$pass \rightarrow$$
$$Rescue\_takeoff.out \rightarrow fail \rightarrow Stop$$

The verdict is given by the last (special) event observed before a deadlock. So, the test first raises the *inc* event, and then offers the input to switchOn the drone. If it is refused, we have a deadlock, and the verdict is *in*conclusive as it has not been possible to drive the drone through the trace of events of interest for this test. If it is accepted, an additional *inc* event is raised, and the output takeoff is expected. This goes on, until the last event land of the trace is observed, when the test raises the verdict event *pass*. If there is now a deadlock, the test passes. If, however, we observe the forbidden event takeoff, then there is a fault, and the verdict event *fail* is finally raised, before the test deadlocks.

The testing theory of CSP guarantees that this is a sound test. Any fault identified is indeed a fault. The testing theory also guarantees exhaustiveness: if all traces of the original model and all their forbidden continuations are considered, then we can uncover all faults if we can reveal all behaviours under testing. These are, however, too many tests. Mutation helps us to select some.

6   Related Work

Mutation has been used in connection with several notations to guide test-generation or assess the quality of a test suite [1,3,48]. As said above, it tackles the explosion of test cases by selecting on which errors to concentrate [3,22,33].

Budd and Gopal [10] have pioneered work on mutation testing with specifications based on predicate calculus. Mutation has been widely studied, and applied using model checking [8,29] like here, and in the context of Simulink [9], whitebox testing [43], contracts [34], and security properties [48,54]. Other related works specifically for diagrammatic models, include mutation testing for state and activity models [49], UML class diagrams [27], interfaces [19], or component-based real-time systems described using a graph notation [28].

Aichernig et al. have considered various formalisms [1–3,5]. In those works, a test case is an abstraction according to traces refinement of the specification, and so an implementation should refine the test case if it passes the test. Test-case generation is, therefore, a reverse-refinement problem. We adopt a more standard approach and use (failed) traces-refinement checks to identify tests.

For CSP, Clark et al. [48] presents mutant operators and uses mutation testing for checking system security; the goal is to validate the specifications rather than generate tests. For *Circus*, a data-rich extension of CSP, mutation is considered in [7] for test generation. In practical experiments, *Circus* [18] models are translated to CSP for use of model checking via FDR as illustrated here. Our mutation operators, however, are for a language whose semantics is given in CSP, rather than CSP directly. Still, it would be interesting to explore the value of mutating the semantics of the RoboChart models.

A recent overview paper [53] focusses on model-based mutation testing for timed systems. It presents a taxonomy of the mutation operators and discusses their usages on various formalisms, such as timed automata or synchronous languages. For timed systems initial works focused on timeliness (the ability of a system to meet its deadlines) and introduced mutation operators for timed automata with tasks (TAT) [40–42], or timed automata similar to the UPPAAL format [6,51]. We plan to use these works as a starting point for developing additional mutation operators for RoboChart time features.

There are several research groups working on mutation testing for timed automata, developing tools such as MoMuT::TA [4,6], Ecdar [35,36] and using model-checking or refinement-check approaches to generate test data. The mutation tool μUTA for UPPAAL timed automata is presented in [47] where the authors introduce three new operators compared to previous works [6,51]. In contrast to this work, our approach is based on a domain-specific language similar to those used by practitioners. In addition, by basing the semantics on CSP we introduce the potential to include richer types of observations such as failures and refusal traces; future work will explore the use of such observations within the mutation-testing framework presented here.

7   Conclusions

This paper presents an approach to apply the well-established technique of mutation testing to a domain-specific notation for robotics: RoboChart. It uses generic tools: Wodel, for generation of mutants, and FDR, for generation of traces and forbidden continuations. The conformance relation is traces refinement.

This experience has raised some interesting issues. First of all, we are definitely interested in testing for stronger conformance relations. More specifically, we will ultimately define a testing theory for tock-CSP and adopt timed refinement as a conformance relation. In that work, we will also take advantage of results on testing with inputs and outputs [14,15]. Experience shows that testing for traces refinement, as considered here, is an important common step to consider all the stronger conformance relations.

With the automation that we have in place, we will consider additional case studies, completing a comprehensive implementation of mutation operators. We are interested in assessing the performance of the approach in terms of generation of useless mutants. Another aspect of performance to be investigated is the trade off between more complex implementations of mutation operators that do not generate invalid mutants, and simpler implementations that rely on the OCL constraints to eliminate invalid mutants.

More interestingly, even for our simple example, we note the generation of tests that are not feasible or not typical of execution in realistic environments. Of particular note here is the issue of time. In our example tests, because FDR generates the shortest traces that lead to a counterexample, as soon as the drone takes off it finds the target. In typical environments, this is not going to be the case; the target is going to be some distance away from the origin. The RoboChart model, however, simply states that control software is ready to react to a detection at any time, including immediately. It is in our plan for future work to enrich RoboChart with features to model environments. The richer language will discard such unlikely or even infeasible scenarios for tests.

Finally, the work described in this paper has assumed that there is a single robotic systems, and tests apply inputs and observe outputs. Swarm robotic systems, however, are formed by a collection of robots and has many interesting and important applications. Swarms carry out tasks via collaboration between robots, and are resilient to faults. In this case, the system interacts with its environment at a number of physically distributed locations, namely, via a number of robotic platforms. In such situations, there may be independent local testers and this scenario alters how testing proceeds and the conformance relations used [30,31]. There has been some work within the context of refinement and CSP [13], but there does not yet appear to be research that uses mutation.

Acknowledgements. This work is funded by the EPSRC grants EP/M025756/1 and EP/R025479/1, and by the Royal Academy of Engineering. We have benefited from discussions with Pablo Gómez-Abajo and Mercedes Merayo with regards to Wodel implementation, and Sharar Ahmadi, Alvaro Miyazawa, and Augusto Sampaio with regards to our example and its simulation.

References

1. Aichernig, B., Jifeng, H.: Mutation testing in UTP. Formal Aspects Comput. **21**(1–2), 33–64 (2008)
2. Aichernig, B.K.: Mutation testing in the refinement calculus. Formal Aspects Comput. **15**(2), 280–295 (2003)
3. Aichernig, B.K.: Model-based mutation testing of reactive systems. In: Liu, Z., Woodcock, J., Zhu, H. (eds.) Theories of Programming and Formal Methods. LNCS, vol. 8051, pp. 23–36. Springer, Heidelberg (2013). https://doi.org/10.1007/978-3-642-39698-4_2
4. Aichernig, B.K., Hörmaier, K., Lorber, F.: Debugging with timed automata mutations. In: Bondavalli, A., Di Giandomenico, F. (eds.) SAFECOMP 2014. LNCS, vol. 8666, pp. 49–64. Springer, Cham (2014). https://doi.org/10.1007/978-3-319-10506-2_4
5. Aichernig, B.K., Jöbstl, E., TiranStefan, S.: Model-based mutation testing via symbolic refinement checking. Sci. Comput. Program. **97**(P4), 383–404 (2015)
6. Aichernig, B.K., Lorber, F., Ničković, D.: Time for mutants—model-based mutation testing with timed automata. In: Veanes, M., Viganò, L. (eds.) TAP 2013. LNCS, vol. 7942, pp. 20–38. Springer, Heidelberg (2013). https://doi.org/10.1007/978-3-642-38916-0_2
7. Alberto, A., Cavalcanti, A.L.C., Gaudel, M.-C., Simao, A.: Formal mutation testing for Circus. Inf. Softw. Technol. **81**, 131–153 (2017)
8. Ammann, P.E., Black, P.E., Majurski, W.: Using model checking to generate tests from specifications. In: 2nd International Conference on Formal Engineering Methods, pp. 46–54. IEEE (1998)
9. Brillout, A., et al.: Mutation-based test case generation for simulink models. In: de Boer, F.S., Bonsangue, M.M., Hallerstede, S., Leuschel, M. (eds.) FMCO 2009. LNCS, vol. 6286, pp. 208–227. Springer, Heidelberg (2010). https://doi.org/10.1007/978-3-642-17071-3_11
10. Budd, T.A., Gopal, A.S.: Program testing by specification mutation. Comput. Lang. **10**(1), 63–73 (1985)
11. Cavalcanti, A., Gaudel, M.-C.: Testing for refinement in CSP. In: Butler, M., Hinchey, M.G., Larrondo-Petrie, M.M. (eds.) ICFEM 2007. LNCS, vol. 4789, pp. 151–170. Springer, Heidelberg (2007). https://doi.org/10.1007/978-3-540-76650-6_10
12. Cavalcanti, A.L.C., Gaudel, M.-C.: Testing for refinement in Circus. Acta Informatica **48**(2), 97–147 (2011)
13. Cavalcanti, A.L.C., Gaudel, M.-C., Hierons, R.M.: Conformance relations for distributed testing based on CSP. In: Wolff, B., Zaïdi, F. (eds.) ICTSS 2011. LNCS, vol. 7019, pp. 48–63. Springer, Heidelberg (2011). https://doi.org/10.1007/978-3-642-24580-0_5
14. Cavalcanti, A.L.C., Hierons, R.M.: Testing with inputs and outputs in CSP. In: Cortellessa, V., Varró, D. (eds.) FASE 2013. LNCS, vol. 7793, pp. 359–374. Springer, Heidelberg (2013). https://doi.org/10.1007/978-3-642-37057-1_26

15. Cavalcanti, A.L.C., Hierons, R.M., Nogueira, S., Sampaio, A.C.A.: A suspension-trace semantics for CSP. In: International Symposium on Theoretical Aspects of Software Engineering, pp. 3–13 (2016). Invited paper

16. Cavalcanti, A., Miyazawa, A., Sampaio, A., Li, W., Ribeiro, P., Timmis, J.: Modelling and verification for swarm robotics. In: Furia, C.A., Winter, K. (eds.) IFM 2018. LNCS, vol. 11023, pp. 1–19. Springer, Cham (2018). https://doi.org/10.1007/978-3-319-98938-9_1

17. Cavalcanti, A.L.C., et al.: Verified simulation for robotics. Sci. Comput. Program. **174**, 1–37 (2019)

18. Cavalcanti, A.L.C., Sampaio, A.C.A., Woodcock, J.C.P.: A refinement strategy for Circus. Formal Aspects Comput. **15**(2–3), 146–181 (2003)

19. Delamaro, M.E., Maldonado, J.C., Mathur, A.P.: Interface mutation: an approach for integration testing. IEEE Trans. Softw. Eng. **27**(3), 228–247 (2001)

20. Conserva Filho, M.S., Marinho, R., Mota, A., Woodcock, J.: Analysing RoboChart with probabilities. In: Massoni, T., Mousavi, M.R. (eds.) SBMF 2018. LNCS, vol. 11254, pp. 198–214. Springer, Cham (2018). https://doi.org/10.1007/978-3-030-03044-5_13

21. Foster, S., Baxter, J., Cavalcanti, A.L.C., Miyazawa, A., Woodcock, J.C.P.: Automating verification of state machines with reactive designs and Isabelle/UTP. In: Bae, K., Ölveczky, P.C. (eds.) FACS 2018. LNCS, vol. 11222, pp. 137–155. Springer, Cham (2018). https://doi.org/10.1007/978-3-030-02146-7_7

22. Fraser, G., Wotawa, F., Ammann, P.E.: Testing with model checkers: a survey. Softw. Test. Verif. Reliab. **19**(3), 215–261 (2009)

23. Gibson-Robinson, T., Armstrong, P., Boulgakov, A., Roscoe, A.W.: FDR3—a modern refinement checker for CSP. In: Ábrahám, E., Havelund, K. (eds.) TACAS 2014. LNCS, vol. 8413, pp. 187–201. Springer, Heidelberg (2014). https://doi.org/10.1007/978-3-642-54862-8_13

24. Gómez-Abajo, P., Guerra, E., de Lara, J.: Wodel: a domain-specific language for model mutation. In: Ossowski, S. (ed.) Proceedings of the 31st Annual ACM Symposium on Applied Computing, Pisa, Italy, 4–8 April 2016, pp. 1968–1973. ACM (2016)

25. Gómez-Abajo, P., Guerra, E., de Lara, J.: A domain-specific language for model mutation and its application to the automated generation of exercises. Comput. Lang. Syst. Struct. **49**, 152–173 (2017)

26. Gómez-Abajo, P., Guerra, E., de Lara, J., Merayo, M.G.: A tool for domain-independent model mutation. Sci. Comput. Program. **163**, 85–92 (2018)

27. Granda, M.F., Condori-Fernández, N., Vos, T.E.J., Pastor, O.: Mutation operators for UML class diagrams. In: Nurcan, S., Soffer, P., Bajec, M., Eder, J. (eds.) CAiSE 2016. LNCS, vol. 9694, pp. 325–341. Springer, Cham (2016). https://doi.org/10.1007/978-3-319-39696-5_20

28. Guan, J., Offutt, J.: A model-based testing technique for component-based real-time embedded systems. In: Eighth IEEE International Conference on Software Testing, Verification and Validation, ICST 2015 Workshops, Graz, Austria, 13–17 April 2015, pp. 1–10. IEEE Computer Society (2015)

29. Herzner, W., Schlick, R., Brandl, H., Wiessalla, J.: Towards fault-based generation of test cases for dependable embedded software. Softwaretechnik-Trends **31**(3) (2011)

30. Hierons, R.M., Merayo, M.G., Núñez, M.: Implementation relations and test generation for systems with distributed interfaces. Distrib. Comput. **25**(1), 35–62 (2012)

31. Hierons, R.M., Ural, H.: The effect of the distributed test architecture on the power of testing. Comput. J. **51**(4), 497–510 (2008)

32. Hoare, C.A.R.: Programming: sorcery or science? IEEE Trans. Softw. Eng. **4** (1984)
33. Jia, Y., Harman, M.: An analysis and survey of the development of mutation testing. IEEE Softw. Eng. **37**(5), 649–678 (2011)
34. Krenn, W., Aichernig, B.K.: Test case generation by contract mutation in Spec#. Electron. Notes Theor. Comput. Sci. **253**(2), 71–86 (2009)
35. Larsen, K.G., Lorber, F., Nielsen, B., Nyman, U.: Mutation-based test-case generation with Ecdar. In: 2017 IEEE International Conference on Software Testing, Verification and Validation Workshops, ICST Workshops 2017, Tokyo, Japan, 13–17 March 2017, pp. 319–328. IEEE Computer Society (2017)
36. Lorber, F., Larsen, K.G., Nielsen, B.: Model-based mutation testing of real-time systems via model checking. In: 2018 IEEE International Conference on Software Testing, Verification and Validation Workshops, ICST Workshops, Västerås, Sweden, 9–13 April 2018, pp. 59–68. IEEE Computer Society (2018)
37. Miyazawa, A., Ribeiro, P., Li, W., Cavalcanti, A.L.C., Timmis, J.: Automatic property checking of robotic applications. In: IEEE/RSJ International Conference on Intelligent Robots and Systems, pp. 3869–3876 (2017)
38. Miyazawa, A., Ribeiro, P., Li, W., Cavalcanti, A.L.C., Timmis, J., Woodcock, J.C.P.: RoboChart: modelling and verification of the functional behaviour of robotic applications. Softw. Syst. Model. **18**, 3097–3149 (2019)
39. Naylor, B., Read, M., Timmis, J., Tyrrell, A.: The Relay Chain: A Scalable Dynamic Communication link between an Exploratory Underwater Shoal and a Surface Vehicle (2014)
40. Nilsson, R., Offutt, J.: Automated testing of timeliness: a case study. In: Zhu, H., Wong, W.E., Paradkar, A.M. (eds.) Proceedings of the Second International Workshop on Automation of Software Test, AST 2007, Minneapolis, MN, USA, 26–26 May 2007, pp. 55–61. IEEE Computer Society (2007)
41. Nilsson, R., Offutt, J., Andler, S.F.: Mutation-based testing criteria for timeliness. In: Proceedings of the 28th International Computer Software and Applications Conference (COMPSAC 2004), Design and Assessment of Trustworthy Software-Based Systems, Hong Kong, China, 27–30 September 2004, pp. 306–311. IEEE Computer Society (2004)
42. Nilsson, R., Offutt, J., Mellin, J.: Test case generation for mutation-based testing of timeliness. Electr. Notes Theor. Comput. Sci. **164**(4), 97–114 (2006)
43. Papadakis, M., Malevris, N.: Searching and generating test inputs for mutation testing. SpringerPlus **2**(1), 1–12 (2013)
44. Park, H.W., Ramezani, A., Grizzle, J.W.: A finite-state machine for accommodating unexpected large ground-height variations in bipedal robot walking. IEEE Trans. Rob. **29**(2), 331–345 (2013)
45. Rabbath, C.A.: A finite-state machine for collaborative airlift with a formation of unmanned air vehicles. J. Intell. Rob. Syst. **70**(1), 233–253 (2013)
46. Roscoe, A.W.: Understanding Concurrent Systems. Texts in Computer Science. Springer, London (2011). https://doi.org/10.1007/978-1-84882-258-0
47. Siavashi, F., Truscan, D., Vain, J.: Vulnerability assessment of web services with model-based mutation testing. In: 2018 IEEE International Conference on Software Quality, Reliability and Security, QRS 2018, Lisbon, Portugal, 16–20 July 2018, pp. 301–312 (2018)
48. Srivatanakul, T., Clark, J.A., Stepney, S., Polack, F.: Challenging formal specifications by mutation: a CSP security example. In: 10th Asia-Pacific Software Engineering Conference, pp. 340–350. IEEE Press (2003)
49. Swain, S.K., Mohapatra, D.P., Mall, R.: Test case generation based on state and activity models. J. Object Technol. **9**(5), 1–27 (2010)

50. Tomic, T., et al.: Toward a fully autonomous UAV: research platform for indoor and outdoor urban search and rescue. IEEE Rob. Autom. Mag. **19**(3), 46–56 (2012)
51. Trab, M.S.A., Counsell, S., Hierons, R.M.: Specification mutation analysis for validating timed testing approaches based on timed automata. In: 36th Annual IEEE Computer Software and Applications Conference, COMPSAC 2012, Izmir, Turkey, 16–20 July 2012, pp. 660–669 (2012)
52. University of York. RoboChart Reference Manual. `www.cs.york.ac.uk/circus/RoboCalc/robotool/`
53. Vega, J.J.O., Perrouin, G., Amrani, M., Schobbens, P.-Y.: Model-based mutation operators for timed systems: a taxonomy and research agenda. In: 2018 IEEE International Conference on Software Quality, Reliability and Security, QRS 2018, Lisbon, Portugal, 16–20 July 2018, pp. 325–332 (2018)
54. Wimmel, G., Jürjens, J.: Specification-based test generation for security-critical systems using mutations. In: George, C., Miao, H. (eds.) ICFEM 2002. LNCS, vol. 2495, pp. 471–482. Springer, Heidelberg (2002). https://doi.org/10.1007/3-540-36103-0_48

Regular Contributions

Constraints in Dynamic Symbolic Execution: Bitvectors or Integers?

Timotej Kapus, Martin Nowack$^{(\boxtimes)}$, and Cristian Cadar

Imperial College London, London, UK
{t.kapus,m.nowack,c.cadar}@imperial.ac.uk

Abstract. Dynamic symbolic execution is a technique that analyses programs by gathering mathematical constraints along execution paths. To achieve bit-level precision, one must use the theory of bitvectors. However, other theories might achieve higher performance, justifying in some cases the possible loss of precision.

In this paper, we explore the impact of using the theory of integers on the precision and performance of dynamic symbolic execution of C programs. In particular, we compare an implementation of the symbolic executor KLEE using a partial solver based on the theory of integers, with a standard implementation of KLEE using a solver based on the theory of bitvectors, both employing the popular SMT solver Z3. To our surprise, our evaluation on a synthetic sort benchmark, the ECA set of Test-Comp 2019 benchmarks, and GNU Coreutils revealed that for most applications the integer solver did not lead to any loss of precision, but the overall performance difference was rarely significant.

1 Introduction

Dynamic symbolic execution is a popular program analysis technique that aims to systematically explore all the paths in a program. It has been very successful in bug finding and test case generation [3,4]. The research community and industry have produced many tools performing symbolic execution, such as CREST [5], FuzzBALL [9], KLEE [2], PEX [14], and SAGE [6], among others.

To illustrate how dynamic symbolic execution works, consider the program shown in Fig. 1a. Symbolic execution runs the program similarly to native execution, but it introduces the notion of symbolic variables. These denote variables that are initially allowed to take any value. In our example, variable x is marked as symbolic. As we start execution, we immediately hit the branch if (x < 3). Since x is symbolic, we cannot directly evaluate the branch condition but have to treat it as a symbolic expression in terms of x. At this point, we can ask an SMT solver if $x < 3$ can be *true* under the current path constraints. Since we do not have any path constraints yet, $x < 3$ can be *true*, e.g. by setting it to 1. Therefore, we explore the then branch, add $x < 3$ to our path constraints, and continue execution along that path. In our example, we simply **return** 1. To handle the else branch, we similarly consider the path where $x \geq 3$.

© Springer Nature Switzerland AG 2019
D. Beyer and C. Keller (Eds.): TAP 2019, LNCS 11823, pp. 41–54, 2019.
https://doi.org/10.1007/978-3-030-31157-5_3

```
int lessThanThree() {      array x[2] : w32->w8      array x[1] : i->i
  short x = sym();          (SignedLessThan           (< (Read 0 x) 32768)
  if (x < 3) {                (Concat                 (> (Read 0 x) -32769)
    return 1;                     (Read 1 x)
  } else {                        (Read 0 x)          (<
    return 0;                 )                            (Read 0 x)
  }                           3                            3
}                           )                         )

(a) Simple program         (b) BV constraints         (c) Int constraints
```

Fig. 1. Constraints KLEE gathers when symbolically executing a simple function.

To accurately model the semantics of machine integers that have a finite number of bits, one has to use the theory of bitvectors, and tools such as Angr [13] and KLEE [2] do so. However, using the theory of mathematical integers, as tools like CREST [5] and CUTE [12] do, has the potential of improving performance, justifying in some cases the possible loss of precision. This performance/precision trade-off between the bitvector and integer theories has been documented before. For instance, He and Rakamarić discuss that *"On one end of the spectrum, verifiers opt for exclusively bit-precise reasoning, which often becomes a performance and/or scalability bottleneck. On the other end, verifiers opt for imprecise modelling using integers and uninterpreted functions, which often leads to a large number of false alarms"* [7]. However, while this trade-off has been studied in the context of static verification, we are not aware of any similar study for dynamic symbolic execution.

In this paper, we examine how gathering and solving constraints in the two theories impacts symbolic execution. We build a partial integer solver on top of KLEE [2] and Z3 [10] that aims to determine which queries can be easily expressed in the theory of integers and solve them with an integer solver, while delegating all others to a bitvector solver. In particular, we delegate to a bitvector solver queries involving bitwise operations and casts, which are not easily modelled in the theory of integers.[1]

We compare a version of KLEE using this partial integer solver to a standard version of KLEE using a bitvector solver on three different sets of benchmarks: a synthetic sort benchmark involving mostly inequalities, the ECA benchmark suite from Test-Comp involving mostly equalities, and the Coreutils application suite of 105 UNIX utilities, focusing on whether the two solvers produce identical results and how performance differs between the two configurations.

Surprisingly, our results show that the integer solver disagrees with the bitvector solver for only 32 Coreutils applications, the integer solver can be up to 40% faster and 16% slower, but the overall performance differences are not significant.

---

[1] Symbolic execution tools that use integer solvers typically do not handle such operations, e.g. CREST reverts to the concrete case when encountering a bitwise operation.

2 Partial Integer Solver

We chose to implement our partial integer solver in KLEE [2], a popular symbolic execution engine for LLVM [8] bitcode. KLEE gathers constraints in the theory of bitvectors and arrays. Therefore, we need to translate queries from this theory into the theory of integers and arrays.

While translating some constructs from bitvectors to integers is trivial—for example replacing bitvector addition with integer addition—there are two major challenges: translating arrays of bytes into mathematical integers and handling sign. Before we can show how we address these challenges, we need to describe precisely how KLEE gathers constraints.

Based on the symbolic execution of `lessThanThree` in Fig. 1a, consider the bitvector query that KLEE generates in Fig. 1b. KLEE represents each memory object as an array of bytes. So the variable x in our example is a two-byte memory object. This memory object is presented to the solver as `array x`. Arrays have a domain (type of index, `w32`) and range (type of value, `w8`). In KLEE, all arrays map 32-bit bitvector indices to 8-bit bitvector values.

The expression `x < 3` is then represented by the `SignedLessThan` construct, with a concatenation of two read expressions and the constant 3 as arguments. Because KLEE has a byte-level view of memory, it has to construct wider types such as `short` or `int` as a concatenation of byte-level reads.

2.1 Translating Queries to the Integer Theory

To translate the query in Fig. 1b to integers as shown in Fig. 1c, we first change `array x` from a two-byte array to an array containing a single integer, which reflects the fact there is a single integer in the program. We could have opted to keep the byte-level view in integer constraints, but that would have led to a large amount of expensive non-linear constraints due to concatenate operations.

We infer the type of `array x` from LLVM's type information of the allocation site of the memory object that `array x` refers to. In our example, we would know x is an array of `short`, therefore we obtain a solver array with a single integer. We also constrain each element of the array to the numerical limits of the type (in our case [-32768, 32767]).

During execution, we collapse the concatenation of stridden read expression into a single read expression by pattern matching. This strategy is already employed by KLEE and its solver component Kleaver to print expressions in a more human-friendly form.

LLVM type information can be imprecise due to casting, which can occur for multiple reasons, such as viewing memory both as a struct and an array of chars (in a `memcpy`); or casting to the "correct" type only after allocation, which would be the case if the program has a special allocation function. Since we choose to view the memory as having only a single type, we can detect this case by comparing the width of the (collapsed) read with the type of the array. If there is a mismatch, we delegate the query to the bitvector solver.

2.2 Sign of Variables

In the theory of bitvectors, variables do not have a sign. The sign is only inferred through operations on variables (i.e. `SignedLessThan` vs `UnsignedLessThan`). When translating to integers, we need to know the sign of variables to infer their ranges.

We first considered inferring the sign from the operations performed on the variable. While this can be done in some cases for a single expression, it is hard to keep it consistent across multiple expressions. Since KLEE queries the solver with a set of expressions representing the current path constraints, the variables common across expressions need to have a consistent sign. Unfortunately, inferring the sign from the operations performed can lead to contradictions across expressions.

Therefore, we had to decide whether to keep all variables signed or unsigned. Since mistakenly treating signed variables as unsigned can lead to more problems in practice (e.g. it causes -1 to be greater than 0), we decided to treat all variables as signed.

2.3 Operations Delegated to the Bitvector Solver

As first discussed in Sect. 1, operations that cannot be easily translated to the theory of integers are delegated to the bitvector solver. We discuss each operation type below:

1. *Bitwise and, not, or, xor, shift.* Encoding them in the theory of integers would produce a large amount of non-linear constraints. We still keep any boolean versions of these operations.
2. *Extract expressions* arise due to casting (i.e. from `int` to `short`). Encoding them in the theory of integers would involve a lot of expensive division and module operations.
3. *Type mismatches*, which were described in Sect. 2.1.

2.4 Extending KLEE's Solver Chain

One of KLEE's strengths is its extensibility. For example, a set of solvers form a chain that is typically ordered from the most lightweight to the most expensive solver [2,11]. Each solver chain element tries to solve a query. If this is unsuccessful, the next chain element is queried. While the first elements in the chain contain simple optimisation and independent-set calculations, further elements cache queries and their solutions. The final element is the actual solver, e.g. Z3.

We added a new chain element before the final solver, which consists of an expression analyser and our integer-based solver. The analyser, as discussed in Sect. 2.3, decides if the integer solver should handle the query. If so, the query is delegated to the Z3-based integer solver, which can use solving tactics specific to the integer theory. If not, the query is forwarded to the bitvector solver.

3   Evaluation

We evaluated our partial solver on several benchmarks: a synthetic sort benchmark, which produces inequality constraints (Sect. 3.1); the ECA set of benchmarks from the Test-Comp 2019 competition, which produces equality constraints (Sect. 3.2), and GNU Coreutils, a set of UNIX utilities, which produces a wide mix of constraints (Sect. 3.3).

Our implementation[2] was based on top of KLEE commit 44325801, built with LLVM 3.8. For the ECA set of benchmarks, we also rebased the commits with which KLEE participated in Test-Comp 2019 to be reasonably competitive on that benchmark suite.[3]

In all our experiments, we used Z3 version 4.8.4 as the backend for both the integer and bitvector theories, as we felt it makes more sense to compare within a single solver than across multiple solvers.

3.1   Synthetic Sort Benchmark

Our synthetic sort benchmark crosschecks an implementation of insertion sort with one of bubble sort on a small array of N symbolic integers, as shown in Fig. 2a. This benchmark generates mostly inequalities, making it a favourable benchmark for solving in the theory of integers.

Figure 2b shows the results of running the simple sort benchmark as we increase N up to 8 on a machine with Intel i7-6700 @ 3.60 GHz CPU and 16 GB RAM running Ubuntu 16.04. For each N we run KLEE twice, once with the default bitvector solver and once with our partial integer solver. We then plot the time it takes KLEE to fully explore all the paths in each case. We omit the runs for N between 1 and 4 as they terminate in under a second for both solvers.

Over the four array sizes shown, the integer solver makes KLEE explore all the paths between 49% and 90% faster, with a median of 77%. The integer solver causes no loss of precision in these experiments.

3.2   ECA Set

The ECA set, part of the SV-COMP/Test-Comp benchmark suite,[4] consists of benchmarks that represent event condition action systems. We picked the ECA set because it contains fairly large programs (several thousand lines of code) that mostly consist of simple int assignments and conjunctions of equalities. Therefore, the ECA set illustrates the performance of the integer solver on a distinct set of constraints when compared to the synthetic sort benchmark. We used the same hardware as in Sect. 3.1 for this experiment.

---

[2] Available at https://github.com/kren1/klee/tree/int_constraints.

[3] Available at https://github.com/kren1/klee/commits/int_testcomp.

[4] https://github.com/sosy-lab/sv-benchmarks.

```
int buf1[N] = sym();
int buf2[N] = sym();
for (int i = 0; i < N; i++)
    assume(buf1[i] == buf2[i]);


insertion_sort(buf1, N);
bubble_sort(buf2, N);


for (int i = 0; i < N; i++)
    assert(buf1[i] == buf2[i]);
```

(a) Pseudo code for the sort benchmark: two identical arrays of size N are sorted via insertion and bubble sort respectively and their results are crosschecked.

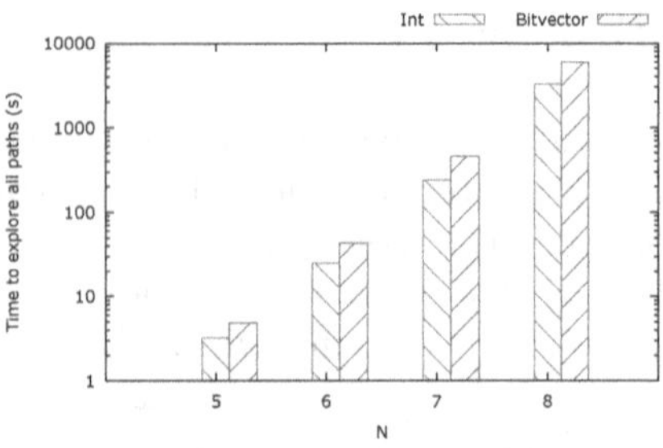

(b) Runtime of KLEE to fully explore the sort benchmark with integer and bitvector solvers for different number of elements (log scale).

Fig. 2. Synthetic sort benchmark and its KLEE runtime.

We performed a preliminary run of the whole ECA set of 412 benchmarks and excluded those for which KLEE times out with both solvers. That left us with 247 benchmarks. We ran each one 14 times with both the integer and the bitvector solvers. The relative performance difference between the two solvers, with 95% confidence intervals included, is shown in Fig. 3. The benchmarks are sorted by the performance difference between the two solvers. There are more programs that are faster with the integer solver, but the average speedup is only 0.37%, which is quite negligible (however, using a t-test gives us a p-value of 0.00, showing that the difference is statistically significant). The integer solver causes no loss of precision in these experiments either.

3.3 GNU Coreutils

Our main evaluation was performed on GNU Coreutils,[5] a popular application suite for evaluating symbolic execution-based techniques. We used version 8.29, which consists of 105 utilities. In our experiments, we exclude those runs for which KLEE did not terminate successfully (e.g., due to resource limitations or imprecision of the integer solver).

We pose four research questions. We first analyse the performance impact of our partial integer solver (RQ1) and if it can be explained by the proportion of inequality queries a benchmark produces (RQ2). We then evaluate what proportion of queries our partial solver handles (RQ3) and look into the imprecision of our solver (RQ4).

We ran all experiments in a Docker container, on a cluster of 14 identical machines with Intel i7-4790 @ 3.60 GHz CPU with 16 GB of RAM running Ubuntu 18.04. We used the same flags for all Coreutils, as discussed on the KLEE website;[6] in particular each utility was run for one hour.

---

[5] https://www.gnu.org/software/coreutils/.
[6] http://klee.github.io/docs/coreutils-experiments/.

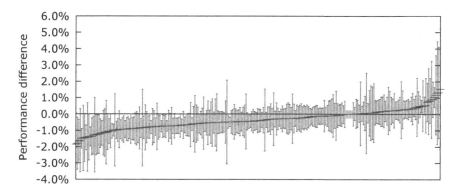

Fig. 3. Speedups (negative values) and slowdowns (positive values) recorded when using the integer solver instead of the bitvector solver on the ECA benchmarks (with 95% confidence intervals).

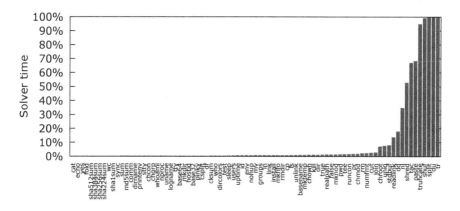

Fig. 4. Percentage of execution time spent in the bitvector solver for Coreutils.

RQ1: What is the performance impact of our partial integer solver on the symbolic execution of Coreutils?

To answer this question, we first run KLEE with the bitvector solver for one hour, recording the number of instructions executed. We then rerun KLEE with the integer solver for the same number of instructions and record the time taken. To ensure deterministic execution, we configure KLEE to use the DFS heuristic.

Figure 4 shows the time spent by each benchmark in the solver, when using the bitvector theory. These numbers indicate the extent to which optimising the solver can affect the overall runtime of KLEE. As can be seen, most benchmarks are not solver-bound in these experiments, but in several cases, the solver time dominates the execution time (note however that KLEE performs several other constraint-solving activities such as caching, but here we are only interested in the time spent in the SMT solver).

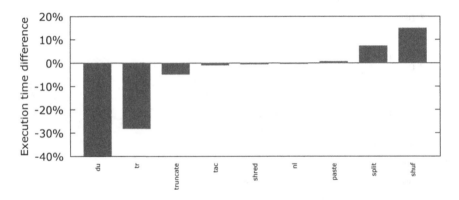

Fig. 5. Speedups (negative values) and slowdowns (positive values) for the whole execution when using the integer solver instead of the bitvector solver for the Coreutils benchmarks.

Based on the results, we select for investigation the applications that spend significant time in the solver—we choose 30% as our lower bound. Figure 5 shows for each utility the speedup or slowdown for the whole execution when the partial integer solver is used instead of the bitvector one for these applications. There are notable improvements in du and tr utilities, which see a 39.7% and 28.0% speedup respectively when using the integer solver. On the other end of the spectrum, shuf and split experience slowdowns of 14.8% and 7.3% respectively.

Figure 6 shows the speedups or slowdowns achieved for the solver time only. In broad strokes, the results match those in the previous figure, which makes sense, given that the utilities experiencing larger speedups or slowdowns spend most of their time in the solver.

From these results, we can conclude that there can be significant performance differences when symbolically executing GNU Coreutils in DFS mode with an integer vs a bitvector solver, but for most applications the impact is negligible.

RQ2: Does the proportion of inequality queries explain the performance differences?

The results from Sect. 3.1 indicate that the integer solver seems to perform significantly better when solving inequality ($<$, $>$, $\leq$, $\geq$) queries.

To explore this, we measured the proportion of inequality constructs in the queries. For this, we inspected the type of each node of every expression in the queries solved by the integer solver. To answer our research question, we computed the ratio of the number of inequalities over the number of all other constructs.

The results are shown in Fig. 7. As one can see, there is no correlation between the proportion of inequalities shown in this figure and the performance numbers of Fig. 6. For example, a significant fraction of inequalities are generated by shred and paste, but their performance changes are minor. In contrast, du and shuf also have a significant fraction of inequalities, and their performance

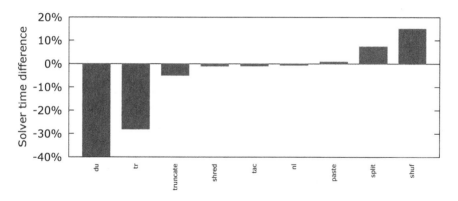

Fig. 6. Speedups (negative values) and slowdowns (positive values) for the solver time only when using the integer solver instead of the bitvector solver for the Coreutils benchmarks.

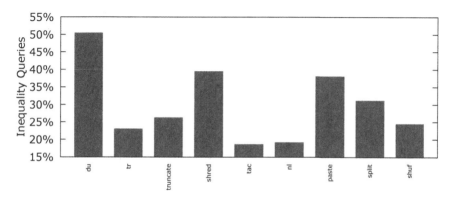

Fig. 7. Proportion of inequalities for the Coreutils experiments.

changes are also significant—but du experiences a speedup, while shuf experiences a slowdown.

RQ3: What portion of the queries can the partial integer solver handle and what are the reasons for delegating queries to the bitvector solver?

For this research question and RQ4, we also configure KLEE with its default search heuristic. This is because to answer these research questions, we do not require deterministic execution, and KLEE's default heuristic matches better how KLEE is used in practice. We run all utilities for one hour each again.

To answer RQ3, we collect the number of queries handled by our partial integer solver and the number of queries delegated to the bitvector solver. Figure 8 shows the proportion of queries that are solved by the integer solver. The proportion varies significantly, from only 2% for expr to 93% for link, with the average across all Coreutils of 37% queries solved by the integer solver. There-

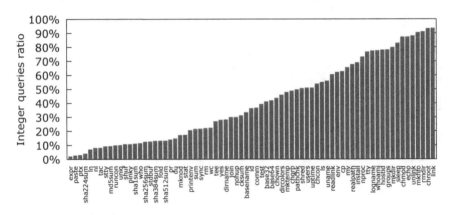

Fig. 8. Proportion of queries solved by the integer solver with default search heuristic.

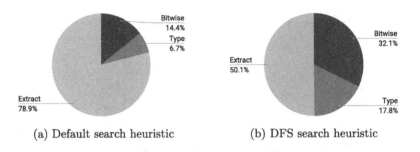

(a) Default search heuristic   (b) DFS search heuristic

Fig. 9. Reasons for delegation to the bitvector solver in Coreutils, for the DFS and default heuristics.

fore, a significant proportion of queries for Coreutils can indeed be solved in the theory of integers.

For each query that is delegated to the bitvector solver, we record the first reason for which it is delegated. For example, if a query has both an Extract operation and a bitwise And, but the Extract is closer to the root of the parse tree, we would only report the reason for delegation as Extract. Figure 9a shows the results averaged across Coreutils. The vast majority of 79% is due to Extract operations. 14% of queries are delegated due to bitwise operations and only 7% due to type mismatches. Shift operations form an insignificant proportion of delegation reasons, only occurring in three Coreutils.

For comparison, we also report the proportion of integer queries and the reasons for delegation when using the DFS searcher in Figs. 10 and 9b respectively. In this setup, there seem to be fewer queries eligible for solving with our integer solver. In terms of reasons for delegation, Extract is still the dominant reason, however less so than with the default search heuristic.

RQ4: How many queries does the integer solver handle correctly with respect to the theory of bitvectors?

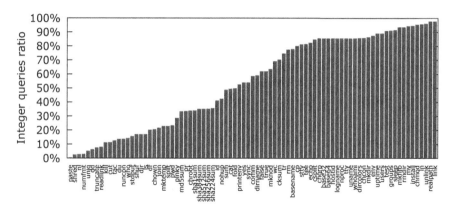

Fig. 10. Proportion of queries solved by the integer solver with DFS heuristic.

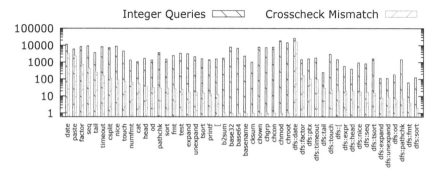

Fig. 11. Number of integer queries and their mismatches for the Coreutils experiments (log scale). Utilities with no mismatches are omitted.

We run another full set of Coreutils experiments for one hour per utility, with the integer solver being crosschecked by the bitvector solver. If they disagree, we record a mismatch and use the result of the bitvector solver to continue. We run this experiment with both the default heuristic and the DFS heuristic.

To our surprise, only 32 Coreutils have any mismatches with the default search heuristic, and only 18 with DFS (for a total of 34 distinct utilities). Figure 11 shows the number of mismatches for these programs; some programs appear twice if they had mismatches in runs with both the default search heuristic and DFS. We also show the number of queries solved by the integer solver in those programs for context. Since the number of mismatches is vastly different, we use a log scale. For the 32 programs where mismatches are present with the default search heuristic, they are relatively scarce. **paste** and **date** are notable exceptions where almost one third of the queries solved by the integer solver are wrong. However, we note that even a single divergence can lead to the exploration of many infeasible paths if it occurs early in the execution. For DFS, the results look similar, with the one notable exception in `date`, where almost two thirds of the queries are not solved correctly in theory of integers.

Furthermore, note that in the experiments where we do not perform this crosschecking step, mismatches often manifest themselves as crashes in KLEE, because wrong solver results can break KLEE's internal invariants. As mentioned before, we exclude from the figures the experiments for which KLEE did not terminate successfully.

4   Threats to Validity

Our preliminary study comparing the bitvector and integer theories in dynamic symbolic execution has a number of threats to validity. We highlight the most important ones below.

Design decisions. Our results may be influenced by several design decisions we made when developing our partial integer solver. For example, while we send all the queries involving bitwise operations to the bitvector solver, constraints involving division, modulo and multiplications are still sent to the integer solver (unless other operations prevent this). This means that we use more than the theory of integer linear arithmetic.

KLEE dependencies. Some design decisions are inherited from KLEE, and may also influence results. For example, KLEE does not explicitly choose a tactic to use and leaves Z3 to choose one itself. We use the same approach.

Z3 dependencies. Our study is limited to the Z3 solver, and results may differ for other solvers. We chose Z3 as it is one of the most popular SMT solvers implementing all of the bitvector, integer and array theories. Moreover, Z3 decides on theory and solving tactics for the query it receives automatically. Unfortunately, sometimes Z3 can choose a suboptimal tactic. However, the modular design of the solver chain (see Sect. 2.4) means that the integer expression analyser is independent of Z3 and could be reused with other solvers as well, e.g. with CVC4 [1].

Benchmark selection. As for all empirical studies, the conclusion of our study is dependent on our choice of benchmarks. We decided to study two types of synthetic benchmarks—one using mostly inequalities and the other mostly equalities—and GNU Coreutils, which is one of the most popular benchmarks used to evaluate symbolic execution tools.

We make our artefact available at https://srg.doc.ic.ac.uk/projects/klee-z3-int-vs-bv, in order to facilitate future exploration of alternative design decisions.

5   Conclusion

In this paper, we have investigated the impact of using the theory of integers instead of the theory of bitvectors on the precision and performance of dynamic symbolic execution. In particular, we have conducted experiments based on KLEE and Z3, applied to several benchmarks, including GNU Coreutils.

Our results show that an integer solver can be applied to a large proportion of queries and that many benchmarks are not affected by the imprecision of the integer solver. While the performance differences can be sometimes significant—with Coreutils applications experiencing slowdowns of up to 14.8% and speedups of up to 39.7%—in most cases they are negligible.

Acknowledgements. We would like to thank Yannick Moy for challenging us at the Dagstuhl Seminar 19062 to pursue this direction of research, and Frank Busse and the anonymous reviewers for their valuable feedback. This research was generously sponsored by the UK EPSRC via grant EP/N007166/1 and a PhD studentship.

References

1. Barrett, C., Conway, C., Deters, M., Hadarean, L., Jovanovic, D., King, T., Reynolds, A., Tinelli, C.: CVC4. In: Gopalakrishnan, G., Qadeer, S. (eds.) CAV 2011. LNCS, vol. 6806, pp. 171–177. Springer, Heidelberg (2011). https://doi.org/10.1007/978-3-642-22110-1_14
2. Cadar, C., Dunbar, D., Engler, D.: KLEE: unassisted and automatic generation of high-coverage tests for complex systems programs. In: Proceedings of the 8th USENIX Symposium on Operating Systems Design and Implementation (OSDI 2008), December 2008
3. Cadar, C., Godefroid, P., Khurshid, S., Pasareanu, C., Sen, K., Tillmann, N., Visser, W.: Symbolic execution for software testing in practice-preliminary assessment. In: Proceedings of the 33rd International Conference on Software Engineering, Impact Track (ICSE Impact 2011), May 2011
4. Cadar, C., Sen, K.: Symbolic execution for software testing: three decades later. Commun. Assoc. Comput. Mach. (CACM) **56**(2), 82–90 (2013)
5. CREST: Automatic Test Generation Tool for C. https://github.com/jburnim/crest
6. Godefroid, P., Levin, M.Y., Molnar, D.A.: Automated whitebox fuzz testing. In: Proceedings of the 15th Network and Distributed System Security Symposium (NDSS 2008), February 2008
7. He, S., Rakamarić, Z.: Counterexample-guided bit-precision selection. In: Chang, B.-Y.E. (ed.) APLAS 2017. LNCS, vol. 10695, pp. 534–553. Springer, Cham (2017). https://doi.org/10.1007/978-3-319-71237-6_26
8. Lattner, C., Adve, V.: LLVM: a compilation framework for lifelong program analysis & transformation. In: Proceedings of the 2nd International Symposium on Code Generation and Optimization (CGO 2004), March 2004
9. Martignoni, L., McCamant, S., Poosankam, P., Song, D., Maniatis, P.: Path-exploration lifting: hi-fi tests for lo-fi emulators. In: Proceedings of the 17th International Conference on Architectural Support for Programming Languages and Operating Systems (ASPLOS 2012), March 2012
10. de Moura, L., Bjørner, N.: Z3: an efficient SMT solver. In: Ramakrishnan, C.R., Rehof, J. (eds.) TACAS 2008. LNCS, vol. 4963, pp. 337–340. Springer, Heidelberg (2008). https://doi.org/10.1007/978-3-540-78800-3_24
11. Palikareva, H., Cadar, C.: Multi-solver support in symbolic execution. In: Proceedings of the 25th International Conference on Computer-Aided Verification (CAV 2013), July 2013. http://srg.doc.ic.ac.uk/files/papers/klee-multisolver-cav-13.pdf

12. Sen, K., Marinov, D., Agha, G.: CUTE: a concolic unit testing engine for C. In: Proceedings of the Joint Meeting of the European Software Engineering Conference and the ACM Symposium on the Foundations of Software Engineering (ESEC/FSE 2005), September 2005
13. Shoshitaishvili, Y., Wang, R., Salls, C., Stephens, N., Polino, M., Dutcher, A., Grosen, J., Feng, S., Hauser, C., Kruegel, C., Vigna, G.: SoK: (state of) the art of war: offensive techniques in binary analysis. In: Proceedings of the IEEE Symposium on Security and Privacy (IEEE S&P 2016), May 2016
14. Tillmann, N., de Halleux, J.: Pex–white box test generation for .NET. In: Beckert, B., Hähnle, R. (eds.) TAP 2008. LNCS, vol. 4966, pp. 134–153. Springer, Heidelberg (2008). https://doi.org/10.1007/978-3-540-79124-9_10

Fast, Automatic, and Nearly Complete Structural Unit-Test Generation Combining Genetic Algorithms and Formal Methods

Eric Lavillonnière[✉], David Mentré[✉], and Denis Cousineau[✉]

Mitsubishi Electric R&D Centre Europe, Rennes 35708, France
{e.lavillonniere,d.mentre,d.cousineau}@fr.merce.mee.com

Abstract. Software testing is a time consuming and error prone activity, mostly manual in most industries. One approach to increase productivity is to automatically generate tests. In this paper, we focus on automatic generation of structural unit tests of safety-critical embedded software. Our purpose is to make a tool that integrates seamlessly with existing test processes in industry. We use genetic algorithms and automatic stub generation to quickly and automatically produce test cases satisfying test objectives of a given coverage criteria, using only the software under test as input. Moreover, we combine those genetic algorithms with formal methods to determine unfeasible test objectives and help on the coverage of difficult test objectives. We implemented our approach in a tool and tested it on a real-world industrial project, demonstrating that our approach can reliably generate test cases when feasible or demonstrate they are unfeasible for 99% of the MC/DC test objectives in about half an hour for 82,000 lines of C code with integer data.

Keywords: Structural unit test · Automatic stub generation ·
Genetic algorithms · Abstract Interpretation ·
Concolic test generation · Bounded Model Checking

1 Introduction

Quality checking of software and more specifically safety critical software relies on review and testing. Software testing is a time consuming and error-prone activity, mostly manual. On a typical safety critical industrial project, total testing amounts to 65% of total development time. Beyond cost, such long testing time impacts time-to-market and project agility. One approach to increase productivity is to automatically generate tests. In this paper, we focus on automatic generation of structural unit tests of safety-critical embedded software in the C language with integers data types. Our purpose is to make a tool that integrates seamlessly with existing test processes in industry. In particular, we do not want to change the existing testing process but make a tool that takes as input

© Springer Nature Switzerland AG 2019
D. Beyer and C. Keller (Eds.): TAP 2019, LNCS 11823, pp. 55–63, 2019.
https://doi.org/10.1007/978-3-030-31157-5_4

unmodified source code and produces as output ready-to-use test spreadsheets in both human and machine-readable formats.

To this end, Mitsubishi Electric R&D Centre Europe (MERCE), the advanced European research laboratory of Mitsubishi Electric group, developed, in collaboration with CEA-List, a first proof of concept tool [4] using PathCrawler/LTest [2,5,14] concolic test generation tool. This tool takes as input unmodified C language source code. It automatically adds to source code *labels* stating test objectives defined by some simple business unit coverage criterion. It automatically produces stubs suitable for unit testing. Given those labels and stubs, it finds test cases satisfying test objectives, using PathCrawler/LTest. And it finally produces test spreadsheets and stubs for human and machine use in the remaining part of the test process. The results were encouraging with 86% of the test objectives covered, but several points could be improved like the tool speed, the detection of unfeasible test objectives and the global number of solved test objectives.

In this paper, we present a new version of the tool, built on a new architecture combining several formal methods tools and a non-formal approach, namely Genetic Algorithms. This new version of the tool additionally targets MC/DC (Modified Condition/Decision Coverage) [10] criterion, which is more complicated than the previously targeted criterion. Nevertheless, thanks to the smart combination of formal methods and genetic algorithms, we could improve drastically speed and coverage of the tool. We eventually obtained a fully automatic, almost complete in practice and very fast structural unit test generation tool.

2   Technological Context

Industrial process. We focus on unit testing, *i.e.* testing individually each function independently of other functions. This implies the necessity to develop *stubs*: replacement functions for each function that is called in the body of the function under test.

We consider structural tests, *i.e.* test objectives defined by the control structure of the code: on a given control statement (*e.g.* if, while, *etc...*), the structural coverage criterion defines, from the associated condition, one or more test objectives, *i.e.* specific values that variables should have at this location at execution. The goal of our tool is to find test cases that fulfill those test objectives, *i.e.* initial values of variables which lead, during execution, to expected values defined by the test objectives, when given to the function under test.

As for our previous version of the tool, our goal is to build a tool that could integrate seamlessly into existing industrial test processes. So we target a fully automatic tool that processes unmodified C source code and produces ready-to-use test spreadsheets, filled with input values for each test case. According to the test process, expected output values (*oracles*) should then be filled by the test engineer, and later checked by executing the code in an external tool.

MC/DC coverage criterion. Additionally to the specific business unit criterion handled by the previous version of our tool, this version also targets

MC/DC coverage criterion. MC/DC criterion exercises every atomic condition (called *condition*) of a control statement in turn, to check that each of those conditions has influence on the statement entire condition (called *decision*) hence on the program control flow. More precisely, we target Masking MC/DC [10] criterion that takes into account the logical dependencies between conditions of a control statement decision.

Genetic algorithms. Genetic algorithms have been widely used for generating test cases [1,12]. The idea of genetic algorithms is to model Natural Selection. First it *selects*, from individuals (defined by their *genes*), the ones that fit best for solving some problem, given their scores on a *fitness* function. Then it mixes the solutions candidates by combining their genes, during the *cross-over* phase, for creating new individuals. And it also *mutates* some individuals' genes for avoiding being stuck in local optimums. Finally it iterates this whole process, improving individuals' scores generation after generation, hopefully reaching a solution of the initial problem at the end of the process.

Formal methods tools. Genetic algorithms are known to have very good performances for finding test cases, but they also have drawbacks. In particular, they cannot detect unfeasible test objectives (typically a variable value target that is impossible at some location of the code, due to the control flow of the program), hence they can waste a lot of time trying to find solutions to problems that cannot be solved. Another limitation concerns the fact that they do not exhaustively consider the candidates test cases, hence sometimes do not find a solution for problems that can be solved. In our development, we used several formal methods tools to alleviate those drawbacks.

- **Value Analysis** [6] is a plug-in of Frama-C framework [11]. Value Analysis implements Abstract Interpretation [8] technique to determine an over-approximation of the set of values that each variable can have at each point of the program and for all possible executions. For this purpose it uses fixed point computation on abstract domains related to the concrete domain through sound abstraction and concretization functions. The Value Analysis plug-in is sound, it applies directly on C source code and is quite fast.

- **PathCrawler/LTest** [2,5,14] is also a plug-in of Frama-C framework [11]. It is a test generation tool using Concolic technique. PathCrawler mixes concrete execution of instrumented code to determine covered path and symbolic execution of code to determine constraints needed to satisfy a given path and thus needed input values to cover new paths. PathCrawler is sound, and it is of medium speed due to several calls to constraint solving.

- **CBMC** [7] is a Bounded Model Checker for C and C++. CBMC transforms C code into Static Single Assignment form and then into equations that can be given to an SMT solver to check a logical formula. Loops are unrolled up to a user-defined bound. CBMC is sound and it is of medium speed, the SMT solver possibly being called several times during its execution.

3   Tool Architecture

Our test generation tool architecture is organized into a six-step pipeline toolchain. Step 1 pre-processes source files, generates (distinct) stubs for the following steps, and computes labels for expressing test objectives for MC/DC criterion. Each of steps 2 to 5 tries to identify unfeasible test objectives and/or find new test cases satisfying test objectives. At each step, the remaining unsolved test objectives are forwarded to the next step. Finally, step 6 optimizes the produced test suite, by reducing the total number of test cases and disambiguating them.

Step 1: Pre-processing. This step first substitutes definitions and macros in C source code. Then, for each function under test, it identifies called functions (hence stubs to be defined), and the parameters (global variables, function inputs, *etc...*) that have an impact on at least one of the test objectives decisions of the function under test (in order to define the genes of individuals in step 3).

Stubs Since we consider unit testing, stubs' implementation does not care about the original computational content of called functions. They are designed to have the greatest impact on the program data flow after they are called, in order to ease the classification of tests objectives as solved or unfeasible. For that purpose, stubs are implemented in a way that allow them to change the value of any of their *outputs*: global variables that are read in the function under test, memory locations pointed by a pointer taken as input, and, of course, the returned value. Note that in the case we only search for unfeasible test objectives, we can suppose that all of these outputs can take a random value (in a domain defined by their types) at each call of the stub, while when searching for tests cases, it is necessary to keep information of those outputs' values for each different call of the stub, in order to be able to replay the test case afterwards. In practice, in the latter case, stubs contain arrays of values, for each output and each call of the stub. If the number of such values is less than the number of calls at execution (*e.g.* if the function is called in the body of a loop and we could not anticipate the number of calls), then the last values contained in the respective arrays are used as many times as necessary.

MC/DC labels Finally, we generate labels that express MC/DC test objectives. For example, if we have a control statement with a decision of the form A && B, The goal is to show that both conditions A and B have influence on the decision A && B. Since we consider here a conjunction between A and B, we shall generate labels (A true, B true) and (A false, B true) for condition A (and symmetrically for condition B). We take into account Masking MC/DC which allows us to discard inconsistent labels when they appear. Note that before generating labels, we normalize control statement decisions for maximizing the number of conditions of the form of an equality test between a variable and a constant, in order to provide the most efficient fitness function in step 3.

Step 2: Value analysis. In step 2, Value Analysis plug-in is used to identify unfeasible test objectives. We use a "reductio ad absurdum" reasoning. By using

Value Analysis mechanisms, we assert that the variable values necessary to fulfill the test objectives are not possible at their respective code locations. If Value analysis does not complain, that means that the over-approximations of the variables values domains given by Value Analysis do not contain the values targeted by the test objectives. Since the Value Analysis plug-in is sound, it implies that the considered test objectives are unfeasible.

Step 2 is crucial for the overall performance of the process, since it discards a lot of unfeasible test objectives that would substantially slow down the genetic algorithm of step 3, making it waste time trying to solve unsolvable problems.

Step 3: Genetic algorithm. Step 3 uses a genetic algorithm to find test cases for test objectives that have not been determined as unfeasible during step 2.

Individuals' genes are defined as the values of the inputs of the function under test (global variables, actual input parameters of the function under test, and outputs of called functions (stubs)). We consider at each step populations composed of 100 individuals, and the initial population is randomly generated.

In practice, we first launch a global search considering all test objectives at the same time. After that, we launch a second search considering each of the remaining test objectives, one at a time. The **fitness** function evaluates the sum of the distances of the values of variable a to constant K for each condition (a==K) composing the considered test objective (the smaller the better). The fitness function also ranks better individuals that satisfy other conditions (not of the form (a==K)). In the former case, the **fitness** function additionally considers the number of test objectives satisfied by an individual and the number of test objectives code locations that are reached at execution (the bigger the better).

We implement **cross-over** as a complete random combination between two individuals' genes: which genes and how many genes are selected from each parent, are both random. **Mutation** is sometimes completely random: we select a random new value for a random gene of some individual. Other times, we use a local hill climbing algorithm for defining mutations on randomly selected genes, in order to improve convergence of the genetic algorithm (*i.e.* we use mutations that maximize the fitness function locally).

Finally, for **selecting** the 100 individuals that will compose the next generation from individuals, their children obtained by cross-over and the mutated individuals, we use a roulette wheel selection: the probability of selection of an individual for next generation is proportional to the ranking of its score given by the fitness function.

Step 4: CBMC In step 4, we use CBMC to identify unfeasible test objectives and find new test cases, that were not identified/found by previous steps. CBMC is used with a timeout of 15 s for each test objective. As we will see in the results section, CBMC does classify some of the test objectives that could not be handled by the previous steps. CBMC is used before PathCrawler, since it is slightly faster to classify some of the test objectives.

Step 5: PathCrawler In step 5, we use PathCrawler/LTest to identify unfeasible test objectives and find new test cases. We use a global timeout of 120 s for each function under test. As we will see in the results section, PathCrawler is still able to classify some of the test objectives that were not handled by the previous steps.

Step 6: Genetic test suite optimization In step 6, Genetic Algorithms are applied again, not to classify remaining test objectives, but to optimize the already found test cases. In particular we optimize visibility of test cases at end of function under test, *i.e.* the side effects produced by a test case should be visible after the return statement of the function under test. This optimization allows easier handling of generated test cases by human testers who thus can distinguish between two tests cases from their outputs during execution. At this step we also reduce the total number of test cases by finding test cases satisfying several test objectives, in order to reduce burden on human testers that should fill expected test results (*i.e.* oracles) for each test case.

Implementation We have made a lot of effort to optimize performance of our tool. Our code is parallelized at file level, at function level and even sometimes at test objective level (*e.g.* with Genetic Algorithms to classify a specific test objective or with CBMC when several provers are run in parallel). In fact the main issue is not to generate parallelism but to bound parallelism so the machine is not overloaded and remains efficient.

We also designed a simple fingerprint mechanism applied after step 1, to avoid doing any work on functions for which the abstract syntax tree and the called functions signatures do not change from one run of the tool to the next one, particularly optimizing the incremental use of the tool during development.

We finally defined a *lightweight configuration*: steps 1 to 3 only, targeting maximal speed for faster use of the tool during development.

Overall, this architecture allows to build an automatic, fast and practically almost complete test generation tool. The tool is fully automatic and only needs unmodified source code. Speed is brought by steps 2 (Value Analysis) and 3 (Genetic Algorithms) which are quick to respectively identify unfeasible test objectives and find test cases (see Sect. 4). Steps 4 (CBMC) and 5 (PathCrawler) are not that fast, but allow to classify new test objectives that steps 2 and 3 could not handle (this concerns especially unfeasible test objectives in functions with a complex control flow). Despite increasing marginally the global coverage, steps 4 and 5 are still very important since human study of those complex test objectives would be particularly time consuming.

4   Results

Our tool has been implemented in about 40,000 lines of C++ code. We tested it on a real industrial safety-critical project we will call project A, on a test machine running 64 bits Linux Fedora on an Intel I9-9980XE CPU with 18 cores (36 hardware threads), using about 32 GB of RAM.

Project A contains about 82,000 lines of C code with integer data, spread in 230 files and 2100 functions resulting in 23,550 test objectives. Among those

23,550 test objectives, 20,480 are in non-aborted functions, *i.e.* functions without errors (out-of-bound array access, division-by-zero, ...). Table 1 resumes the results of each step of the process on a typical run of the tool on project A. For each step, we detail the number of found test cases, tests objectives determined as unfeasible, remaining test objectives, overall percentage of solved test objectives, and timing information. The vast majority of test objectives is found through Value Analysis and Genetic Algorithms, CBMC and PathCrawler allowing to reach near complete coverage.

Table 1. Results of a typical run on project A

Step	Pre-proc	Value	Gen. Alg.	CBMC	PathCrawler	Gen. Opt.	Total
Found	0	0	18,446	18	14	0	18,478
Unfeasible	0	1709	0	115	56	0	1880
Remaning	20,480	18,771	325	192	122	122	122
Solved	0%	8.34%	98.41%	99.06%	99.40%	99.40%	99.40%
Timing	3:02	2:50		0:41	4:34	17:30	28:37

Those results were confirmed by running our tool on another project of same type and approximately same size: we obtained the same kind of results in terms of speed and coverage for each step of the process.

Besides this very good performance, our tool also has good qualitative results. Firstly, as the test generation process is fully automated no error can be made, contrary to the human-based process in which we found several errors. Secondly, our tool allows quick identification of code lacking protections against run-time errors like out-of-bound array access or division-by-zero. As our tool exercises thoroughly the function under test, it quickly finds missing protections which is of great help for the programmer. Typically on Project A, 10% of functions lack protection, and this can be detected by the lightweight configuration of our tool.

5   Related Work

Each tool we use in the process has already been used for solving test objectives. PathCrawler is precisely designed for that purpose [2,4,5,14]. CBMC has been used by Di Rosa et al. to generate test cases [9], but without identifying unfeasible ones. Genetic Algorithms are well known to be very efficient for generating structural tests [1,12], in particular for MC/DC coverage criterion [13].

The combination of several formal methods has also been done in the past, for example Value Analysis and Deductive Verification (Frama-C/WP) with PathCrawler to extend the detection of unfeasible test objectives by Bardin et al. [3], but without addressing MC/DC coverage criteria.

However, to our knowledge there has been no previous work combining formal methods and genetic algorithms, targeting MC/DC criterion, with such good performance concerning both coverage completeness and generation speed.

6   Conclusion and Future Work

In this paper we have presented a novel automatic structural unit test generation tool combining several formal methods (Abstract Interpretation, Bounded Model Checking and Concolic execution) and Genetic Algorithms to quickly generate ready-to-use test spreadsheets. We tested our tool on a real industrial safety critical project of 82,000 lines of code and demonstrated that it can solve test objectives of MC/DC coverage criterion for 99% of the 20,480 test objectives in about half an hour. We also showed that our tool could solve 98% of the test objectives, in less than 6 min, paving the way to its incorporation inside continuous integration process and development tools. While full unit testing process needs test oracles from the developer, our tool could still be used, without them, to quickly identify unprotected parts of the code, providing to the programmer useful test cases for understanding where problems come from.

For future work, we plan to add floating point computation support in order to handle safety critical software for aerospace and autonomous driving.

References

1. Aggarwal, R., Singh, N.: Search based structural test data generations: a survey/a current state of art. Int. J. Sci. Eng. Res. **8**, 511–520 (2017)
2. Bardin, S., Chebaro, O., Delahaye, M., Kosmatov, N.: An all-in-one toolkit for automated white-box testing. In: Seidl, M., Tillmann, N. (eds.) TAP 2014. LNCS, vol. 8570, pp. 53–60. Springer, Cham (2014). https://doi.org/10.1007/978-3-319-09099-3_4
3. Bardin, S., et al.: Sound and quasi-complete detection of infeasible test requirements. In: International Conference on Software Testing, Verification and Validation (ICST), pp. 1–10. IEEE (2015)
4. Bardin, S., Kosmatov, N., Marre, B., Mentré, D., Williams, N.: Test case generation with PATHCRAWLER/LTEST: how to automate an industrial testing process. In: Margaria, T., Steffen, B. (eds.) ISoLA 2018. LNCS, vol. 11247, pp. 104–120. Springer, Cham (2018). https://doi.org/10.1007/978-3-030-03427-6_12
5. Botella, B., et al.: Automating structural testing of C programs: experience with PathCrawler. In: Proceedings of the 4th International Workshop on the Automation of Software Test, pp. 70–78. IEEE (2009)
6. Canet, G., Cuoq, P., Monate, B.: A value analysis for C programs. In: International Working Conference on Source Code Analysis and Manipulation (2009)
7. Clarke, E., Kroening, D., Lerda, F.: A tool for checking ANSI-C programs. In: Jensen, K., Podelski, A. (eds.) TACAS 2004. LNCS, vol. 2988, pp. 168–176. Springer, Heidelberg (2004). https://doi.org/10.1007/978-3-540-24730-2_15
8. Cousot, P., Cousot, R.: Abstract interpretation: a unified lattice model for static analysis of programs by construction or approximation of fixpoints. In: Symposium on Principles of Programming Languages, pp. 238–252 (1977)
9. Di Rosa, E., Giunchiglia, E., Narizzano, M., Palma, G., Puddu, A.: Automatic generation of high quality test sets via CBMC (2010)
10. Kelly, J.H., Dan, S.V., John, J.C., Leanna, K.R.: A practical tutorial on modified condition/decision coverage. Technical report, NASA Langley (2001)

11. Kirchner, F., Kosmatov, N., Prevosto, V., Signoles, J., Yakobowski, B.: Frama-C: a software analysis perspective. Formal Aspects Comput. **27**(3), 573–609 (2015)
12. McMinn, P.: Search-based software test data generation: a survey. Softw. Test. Verif. Reliab. **14**(2), 105–156 (2004)
13. Minj, J.: Feasible test case generation using search based technique. Int. J. Comput. Appl. **70**(28), 51–54 (2013)
14. Williams, N., Marre, B., Mouy, P., Roger, M.: PathCrawler: automatic generation of path tests by combining static and dynamic analysis. In: Dal Cin, M., Kaâniche, M., Pataricza, A. (eds.) EDCC 2005. LNCS, vol. 3463, pp. 281–292. Springer, Heidelberg (2005). https://doi.org/10.1007/11408901_21

Coverage-Based Testing with Symbolic Transition Systems

Petra van den Bos[1(✉)] and Jan Tretmans[1,2]

[1] Institute for Computing and Information Sciences, Radboud University,
Nijmegen, The Netherlands
{petra,tretmans}@cs.ru.nl
[2] ESI (TNO), Eindhoven, The Netherlands

Abstract. We provide a model-based testing approach for systems comprising both state-transition based control flow, and data elements such as variables and data-dependent transitions. We propose test generation and execution, based on model-coverage: we generate test cases that aim to reach all transitions of the model. To obtain a test case reaching a certain transition, we need to combine reachability in the control flow, and satisfiability of the data elements of the model. Concrete values for data parameters are generated on-the-fly, i.e., during test execution, such that received outputs from the system can be taken into account for the inputs later provided in test execution. Due to undecidability of the satisfiability problem, SMT solvers may return result 'unknown'. Our algorithm deals with this explicitly. We implemented our method in Maude combined with Z3, and use this to demonstrate the applicability of our method on the Bounded Retransmission Protocol benchmark. We measure performance by counting the number of inputs and outputs needed to discover bugs in mutants, i.e., in non-conforming variants of the specification. As a result, we find that we perform 3 times better, according to the geometric mean, than when using random testing as implemented by the tool TorXakis.

1 Introduction

Software testing involves experimentally checking desired properties of a software product by systematically executing that software. The software is stimulated with test inputs, and the actual outputs are compared with expected outputs. Model-Based Testing (MBT) is a form of black-box testing where the software being tested, called System Under Test (SUT), is tested for correctness with respect to a model. The model serves as a formal specification for the SUT, prescribing the behaviour that the SUT shall, and shall not, exhibit. Moreover, the model is the basis for the algorithmic generation of test cases and for the evaluation of actual test outputs.

P. van den Bos and J. Tretmans—Funded by the Netherlands Organisation of Scientific Research (NWO): 13859.

Many of the modelling formalisms used for MBT are based on some kind of state-transition model: states in the model represent an abstraction of the states of the system, and transitions between states represent the actions that the system may perform. Depending on the kind of state-transition model, an action can be the acceptance of an input, the production of an output, an internal step of the system, or the combination of a trigger and the corresponding response.

Plain state-transition formalisms, though a powerful semantic model, are not powerful enough to specify present-day systems. Such systems, in addition to state-transition-modelled control flow, involve complicated data objects, operations on data, inputs and outputs parameterized with data, and conditions on data guarding the enabling of transitions. Consequently, many state-transition formalisms have been extended with the ability to deal with data, variables, parameters, and conditions, often referred to as extended, or symbolic state-transition models.

For a plain state-transition model, test generation corresponds to graph operations on the model, such as selecting a finite path (in case of deterministic models), a tree (in case of nondeterministic models), or a tour through the model. The extension with data, however, complicates the test-generation process. A naive approach of unfolding data, i.e., encoding all possible data values in transitions, and thus mapping the data to a plain state-transition model, leads to the infamous state-space explosion problem. A second disadvantage of unfolding is that all structure and information available in the data definitions and constraints is lost. This information can be very useful in the test selection process. The latter disadvantage also applies to the converse, when mapping all state-transition information to data, i.e., to state variables. Consequently, a more sophisticated way of combining state-transition information with data is necessary where the differences and subtle interplay between the two are taken into account. A common approach is to combine graph-based state-transition system manipulation with the symbolic treatment of data and variables.

In this paper, we present theory, an implementation, and an application of such a model-based testing approach, that combines state-transition-based control flow and symbolic treatment of data and variables. Our models are expressed as *Symbolic Transition Systems* (STS) [8,9], which combine Labelled Transition Systems (LTS) with an explicit notion of data, variables, and data-dependent conditions, founded on first order logic. As the basis for test generation we use the **ioco**-testing theory for LTS [23,24]. The *implementation* or *conformance relation* **ioco** is a formal relation between SUTs and models, that defines precisely when an SUT is correct with respect to its model. The **ioco**-testing theory provides a test generation algorithm that is *sound* and *exhaustive*, i.e., the (possibly infinitely many) test cases generated from an LTS model detect all and only **ioco**-incorrect implementations.

We lift **ioco**-test generation to the symbolic level, analogous to [8]. In addition to [8], we generate test cases that satisfy *switch coverage*, i.e., all symbolic transitions of the STS model are covered in the test cases (as far as nondeterminism allows). Switch coverage is thus a way of test selection, which is sound, but usually not exhaustive.

As an intermediate structure we define a *symbolic execution graph*, which incorporates classical symbolic concepts like path conditions and reachability, and which, in addition, is adapted to nondeterministic STS. We select finite paths, i.e. *test purposes*, from the symbolic execution graph, that guarantee switch coverage. After that, data values are selected in an *on-the-fly* test generation and execution algorithm. This algorithm takes into account previous input and output values, making it more flexible than selecting all input values beforehand.

We define measures for achieved switch coverage, both *a priori*, i.e., during test-purpose generation, and *a posteriori*, i.e., after test execution. Due to unsatisfiable constraints and SUT nondeterminism, full coverage may not always be achieved and a posteriori coverage may be lower than a priori coverage.

To implement the method, we tie together *Maude*, a language and tool set for rewriting systems [5], and *Z3*, an SMT-solver [6]. We encode models in the Maude language, from which test purposes satisfying switch coverage are generated. In this step Maude internally uses Z3 to check constraints. A Python program takes a test purpose and implements the on-the-fly test generation and execution algorithm, where Z3 is used again to generate witnesses serving as input data values satisfying the constraints of the test purpose. Since satisfiability is undecidable, Z3 may produce an 'unknown' result that we explicitly take into account in our algorithm.

The Bounded Retransmission Protocol (BRP), a benchmark in protocol verification and testing [13], is used as a case study. We compare our switch-coverage-driven test generation method with random path, on-the-fly test generation by the MBT tool TorXakis [22,25]. We show that TorXakis in total needs 8 times more inputs and outputs to discover bugs in mutants, i.e., in non-conforming variants of the specification. According to the geometric mean, we find that we perform 3 times better than TorXakis.

Overview. In Sect. 2, we give preliminaries on LTS, **ioco**, data specifications, STS, and the semantics of STS. Symbolic execution graphs are defined in Sect. 3. Section 4 introduces switch coverage, provides the main on-the-fly test-generation and execution algorithm, and proves soundness. The implementation in Maude and Z3 is presented in Sect. 5, and the BRP case study is discussed in Sect. 6. Section 7 concludes, and mentions open issues and future work.

Related work. The technique of symbolic execution was originally applied on programs [18] and applied, among others, for white-box testing [12]. Later on, it has found its way into other fields, such as model-based testing.

Gaston et al. [11] study model-based testing based on Symbolic Transition Systems, as we do. An important difference is that their work restricts output-parameter values to functions over constants and input parameters, i.e., expected output values can always be predicted. This implies that nondeterminism or uncertainty in output parameters cannot be modelled. In the area of Extended

Finite State Machines similar restrictions are made [10,14,20,21]. The test generation in [11] is guided by test purposes, which are finite parts of the symbolic execution of the STS. Originally assumed to be given [17], test purposes in [11] are generated from the model according to two criteria: (i) a maximum length on the sequences of executed switches, which is coarser than our switch coverage, or (ii) exclusion of 'redundant' parts of symbolic execution, e.g., a loop of switches in an STS is only executed once, which is what our switch coverage achieves too, but in general our approach could benefit from this exclusion of redundant behaviours.

The Guarded Labeled Assignment Systems (GLAS) models of [26] are very similar to our STS: the syntactical definition differs, their semantics in terms of symbolic executions are closely related. The paper shows this by analyzing the relation between **ioco** for STS and *i/o-refinement* for GLAS. No test generation method, however, is proposed.

Our work mainly builds on [8,9], except that we do not include internal τ switches. We extend the on-the-fly, random-path test generation of those papers with switch-coverage-driven test selection. In addition, [9] compares a couple of coverage measures: state coverage, location coverage, and symbolic-state (see Sect. 3) coverage. For full, semantic state coverage, all possible combinations of location and variable values have to be covered, which is usually not feasible. For location coverage only all locations have to be covered, independent from variable values; location coverage is implied by our switch coverage. For symbolic-state coverage each symbolic state must be covered, which can usually only be achieved up to some length n of test cases. Full switch coverage can be achieved with symbolic-state coverage if n is chosen high enough, i.e., n should be at least as long as the longest test purpose, which causes it to be more costly than our switch coverage.

2 Preliminaries

2.1 Labeled Transition Systems

In this section, we give a summary of theory on Labeled Transition Systems and the conformance relation **ioco**. Definitions are a bit simpler than in [24], as we restrict to systems without the internal, unobservable τ transitions.

Definition 1. *A* Labeled Transition System *(LTS) with inputs and outputs is a tuple* $(Q, q_0, \Sigma_I, \Sigma_O, T)$ *where:*

- *Q is a set of states, and $q_0 \in Q$ is the initial state,*
- *Σ_I and Σ_O are sets of input and output labels, respectively, with $\Sigma_I \cap \Sigma_O = \emptyset$,*
- *$T \subseteq Q \times \Sigma \times Q$ is the transition relation, where we write $\Sigma = \Sigma_I \cup \Sigma_O$.*

If a state $q \in Q$ has no outgoing transitions with an output label, then we say that q is *quiescent*, denoted $\delta(q)$. This is handled in an explicit way by **ioco**, by adding a self-loop transition with special output label δ.

For an LTS $(Q, q_0, \Sigma_I, \Sigma_O, T)$ with $q \in Q$, $Q' \subseteq Q$, $\mu \in \Sigma \cup \{\delta\}$, $\sigma \in (\Sigma \cup \{\delta\})^*$, and ϵ the empty sequence, we define:

$$\text{init}(Q') = \bigcup_{q \in Q'} \{x \in \Sigma \mid \exists q' \in Q : (q, x, q') \in T\}$$

$$\text{out}(Q') = \{x \in \text{init}(Q') \mid x \in \Sigma_O\} \cup \{\delta \mid \exists q \in Q' : \delta(q)\}$$

$$Q' \text{ after } \epsilon = Q'$$

$$Q' \text{ after } \mu\sigma = \{q' \in Q \mid \exists q'' \in Q' : (q'', \mu, q') \in T \cup \{(q'', \delta, q'') \mid \delta(q'')\}\} \text{ after } \sigma$$

$$\text{traces}(q) = \{\sigma \in (\Sigma \cup \{\delta\})^* \mid \{q\} \text{ after } \sigma \neq \emptyset\}$$

In our notation, we sometimes replace the initial state q_0 of an LTS $\mathcal{L}$ by the LTS itself, e.g. $\text{traces}(\mathcal{L}) = \text{traces}(q_0)$, and $\mathcal{L}$ after $\sigma = \{q_0\}$ after σ. For technical reasons we have to restrict to systems that have no unbounded nondeterminism, i.e., $\mid q$ after $\sigma \mid < \infty$ for all q and σ. This way, the set of reached symbolic states is finite for any trace σ.

The conformance relation **ioco** relates an LTS with an input-enabled LTS. LTS are *input-enabled* if every state has an outgoing transition for every input.

Definition 2. *Let $\mathcal{L}$ be an LTS, and $\mathcal{L}'$ an input-enabled LTS, such that $\mathcal{L}$ and $\mathcal{L}'$ have the same label sets. Then $\mathcal{L}'$ **ioco** $\mathcal{L}$ if for all $\sigma \in \text{traces}(\mathcal{L})$, we have $\text{out}(\mathcal{L}' \text{ after } \sigma) \subseteq \text{out}(\mathcal{L} \text{ after } \sigma)$.*

2.2   Data, Terms, and Constraints

We use basic concepts from the theory of data-type specifications; see e.g., [7]. We use the following notation: B^A is the set of all functions from A to B; $\circ$ is function composition; and $\uplus$ denotes disjoint union. Furthermore, $f : A \rightarrow B$ denotes a function $f \in B^A$. We sometimes use set builder notation as a convenient notation for functions with small domains and codomains, e.g. $\{a \mapsto b\}$ is a function with $\{a \mapsto b\} \in \{b\}^{\{a\}}$, and $\{a \mapsto b\}(a) = b$, for some elements a and b.

Syntax. We assume a data signature $sig = (S, F)$ as given, where S is a non-empty set of *sort names* and F is a non-empty set of *function symbols*. Each function symbol consists of a name f, a list of argument sort names $\langle s_1, \ldots, s_n \rangle \in S^n$, and a result sort name $s \in S$, together written as $f :: s_1, \ldots, s_n \rightarrow s$. If $n = 0$ then f is called a *constant*.

Given a signature, we can construct terms, which may contain variables. Let $\mathcal{X}_s$ be a set of *variables* of sort $s \in S$, and let $\mathcal{X} = \uplus_{s \in S} \mathcal{X}_s$ be the set of all variables. *Terms* of sort s over variables $X \subseteq \mathcal{X}$, denoted $\mathcal{T}_s(X)$, are built from variables $x \in X$ and function symbols $f \in F$, in a sort-safe manner:

- If $x \in X$ is a variable of sort s, then x is a term of sort s;
- if $(f :: s_1, \ldots, s_n \to s) \in F$ is function symbol, and $t_1, \ldots, t_n$ are terms of sorts $s_1, \ldots, s_n$, respectively, then $f(t_1, \ldots, t_n)$ is a term of sort s.

The set of all terms over $X \subseteq \mathfrak{X}$ is $\mathcal{T}(X) = \uplus_{s \in S} \mathcal{T}_s(X)$. The set of variables actually occurring in a term $t \in \mathcal{T}_s(X)$ are called the *free variables* of t, denoted $vars(t)$, with $vars(t) \subseteq X$. A *ground term* is a term in $\mathcal{T}_s(\emptyset)$, i.e., a term without free variables. The function $\mathrm{sort}_t : \mathcal{T}(\mathfrak{X}) \to S$ gives the sort of a term; it is extended to sequences of terms as usual.

We assume that there exists a specific sort $\mathtt{Bool} \in S$, which corresponds to the usual Booleans, with the usual Boolean function symbols in F, such as $True, False :: \to \mathtt{Bool}$, $\neg :: \mathtt{Bool} \to \mathtt{Bool}$, and $\wedge, \vee :: \mathtt{Bool}, \mathtt{Bool} \to \mathtt{Bool}$. Terms of sort $\mathtt{Bool}$ over variables $X \subseteq \mathfrak{X}$ are denoted by $\mathcal{T}_{\mathtt{Bool}}(X)$.

A variable in a term can be substituted by another term. A *term mapping* specifies this substitution; it is a function $m : X \to \mathcal{T}(Y)$, for $X, Y \subseteq \mathfrak{X}$, which is sort-safe: $\mathrm{sort}_t(x) = \mathrm{sort}_t(m(x))$ for any $x \in X$. The set of all term mappings $m : X \to \mathcal{T}(Y)$ is denoted by $\mathcal{T}(Y)^X$. For any $X \subseteq \mathfrak{X}$, $id \in \mathcal{T}(X)^X$ is the *identity term mapping* defined as: $id(x) = x$ for all $x \in X$. Given $m \in \mathcal{T}(Y)^X$ and $t \in \mathcal{T}(Z)$, the simultaneous *substitution* of all $x \in vars(t) \cap X$ by $m(x)$ is denoted $t[m]$. So, substitution is a postfix function on terms: $[m] : \mathcal{T}(Z) \to \mathcal{T}(Z \cup Y)$.

Semantics. The semantics of a data signature $sig = (S, F)$, i.e., the values in its sorts, is constituted by equivalence classes of ground terms. The value of a ground term t denoted $[\![t]\!]$, is defined by $[\![t]\!] = \{t' \mid t' \equiv t\}$. Here, we assume an equivalence on ground terms, $\equiv \subseteq \mathcal{T}(\emptyset) \times \mathcal{T}(\emptyset)$, which is sort-safe: if $t_1 \equiv t_2$ then $\mathrm{sort}_t(t_1) = \mathrm{sort}_t(t_2)$. Such an equivalence $\equiv$ could be specified as a set of equations (equational specification [7]) or as a set of rewrite rules.

The semantics of a data signature $sig = (S, F)$ is then the multi-sorted initial algebra $\mathcal{A} = (\{\mathcal{U}_s \mid s \in S\}, \{f_f \mid f \in F\})$, where $\mathcal{U}_s = \{[\![t]\!] \mid t \in \mathcal{T}_s(\emptyset)\}$ is the set of values of sort s; and for each function symbol $(f :: s_1, \ldots, s_n \to s) \in F$ there is a function $f_f : \mathcal{U}_{s_1} \times \ldots \times \mathcal{U}_{s_n} \to \mathcal{U}_s$ defined by $f_f([\![t_1]\!], \ldots, [\![t_n]\!]) = [\![f(t_1, \ldots, t_n)]\!]$, where $t_1, \ldots, t_n$ are ground terms of sorts $s_1, \ldots, s_n$, respectively. The set of all possible values is $\mathcal{U} = \uplus\{\mathcal{U}_s \mid s \in S\}$. Function $\mathrm{sort}_v : \mathcal{U} \to S$ gives the sort of a value; it is extended to sequences of values as usual.

A *valuation* for $X \subseteq \mathfrak{X}$ is a function assigning values to variables: $\vartheta : X \to \mathcal{U}$, which is sort-safe: $\mathrm{sort}_t(x) = \mathrm{sort}_v(\vartheta(x))$. The set of all valuations for X is denoted $\mathcal{U}^X$. The extension to evaluate terms based on a valuation ϑ is called a *term evaluation* and denoted by $\vartheta_{\mathcal{T}} : \mathcal{T}(X) \to \mathcal{U}$. It is defined as $\vartheta_{\mathcal{T}}(x) = \vartheta(x)$ and $\vartheta_{\mathcal{T}}(f(t_1, \ldots, t_n)) = f_f(\vartheta_{\mathcal{T}}(t_1), \ldots, \vartheta_{\mathcal{T}}(t_n))$. For a sequence of distinct variables $\bar{x} = x_0 \ldots x_n \in X^*$ and a sequence of values $\bar{w} = w_0 \ldots w_n \in \mathcal{U}^*$, we denote with $\bar{x} \mapsto \bar{w}$ the valuation in $\mathcal{U}^{\{x_0, \ldots, x_n\}}$ defined by $(\bar{x} \mapsto \bar{w})(x_i) = w_i$ for all $0 \leq i \leq n$. The semantics of a ground term mapping $m \in \mathcal{T}(\emptyset)^X$ is the valuation $[\![m]\!]$ defined as $[\![m]\!](x) = [\![m(x)]\!]$ for all $x \in X$.

In our test algorithm, we need to represent the values in a valuation $\vartheta \in \mathcal{U}^X$ as terms again. We therefore use any term mapping $tmap(\vartheta) \in \mathcal{T}(\emptyset)^X$ satisfying $(tmap(\vartheta))(x) = t \Rightarrow \vartheta(x) = [\![t]\!]$, for all $x \in X$.

For sort $\texttt{Bool}$ we assume that $[\![\ ]\!]$ interprets ground terms in $\mathcal{T}_{\texttt{Bool}}(\emptyset)$ as usual, e.g., $[\![True]\!] = \texttt{true}$. Boolean terms can be seen as formulas, for which we consider their satisfiability. A Boolean term $t \in \mathcal{T}_{\texttt{Bool}}(X)$ is *satisfiable* if there exists a valuation $\vartheta \in \mathcal{U}^{vars(t)}$ such that $\vartheta_{\mathcal{T}}(t) = \texttt{true}$. Satisfiability, however, is undecidable in general. Hence, a tool solving satisfiability problems in our algorithms may return 'unknown'. Therefore we will distinguish explicitly between semantic satisfiability and a tool $\texttt{solver}$, with $\texttt{solver}(t)$ returning either $\texttt{sat}$, $\texttt{unsat}$, or $\texttt{unknown}$. Moreover, we assume that $\texttt{solver}$ allows to retrieve a valuation that witnesses satisfiability, if $\texttt{solver}(t) = \texttt{sat}$, so that we can use these values as input values for the SUT in our testing algorithm. That is, we assume a function $\texttt{getValues}$ that, given a term $t \in \mathcal{T}_{\texttt{Bool}}(X)$ and a sequence $\bar{p} \in vars(t)^*$, returns values $\bar{w} \in \mathcal{U}^*$, with $\texttt{sort}_v(\bar{w}) = \texttt{sort}_t(\bar{p})$, such that the valuation $\bar{p} \mapsto \bar{w}$ together with a valuation for the remaining variables in $vars(t)$, makes the Boolean term t evaluate to true, i.e., $\texttt{getValues}(t, \bar{p}) = \bar{w}$ implies that $\exists \vartheta \in \mathcal{U}^{vars(t) \setminus \{\bar{p}\}} : (\bar{p} \mapsto \bar{w} \uplus \vartheta)_{\mathcal{T}}(t) = \texttt{true}$.

2.3   Syntax of Symbolic Transition Systems

Definition 3. *A Symbolic Transition System (STS) with inputs and outputs is a tuple $(\mathcal{L}, l_0, \mathcal{V}_l, m_{ini}, \mathcal{V}_p, \Gamma_I, \Gamma_O, \mathcal{R})$ where:*

- $\mathcal{L}$ *is a finite set of* locations,
- $l_0 \in \mathcal{L}$ *is the* initial location,
- $\mathcal{V}_l$ *is a finite set of* location variables,
- $m_{ini} \in \mathcal{T}(\emptyset)^{\mathcal{V}_l}$ *is the* initialization,
- $\mathcal{V}_p$ *is a finite set of* gate parameters *such that $\mathcal{V}_p \cap \mathcal{V}_l = \emptyset$,*
- Γ_I *is a finite set of input* gates,
- Γ_O *is a finite set of output* gates,
- $\mathcal{R} \subseteq \mathcal{L} \times (\Gamma_I \cup \Gamma_O) \times \mathcal{V}_p^* \times \mathcal{T}_{\texttt{Bool}}(\mathcal{V}_l \cup \mathcal{V}_p) \times \mathcal{T}(\mathcal{V}_l \cup \mathcal{V}_p)^{\mathcal{V}_l} \times \mathcal{L}$ *is the* switch *relation with a finite number of elements.*

We require that $\Gamma_I \cap \Gamma_O = \emptyset$, and denote $\Gamma = \Gamma_I \cup \Gamma_O$. The function $\texttt{sort}_g : \Gamma \to S^*$, associates a sequence of sorts to a gate. We refer to the elements of a switch $(l_1, \lambda, p_0 \dots p_k, \phi, \psi, l_2) \in \mathcal{R}$, with source location, gate, parameters, guard, assignment, and destination location, respectively, and we require that:

- $p_0 \dots p_k$ *is a sequence of distinct variables*
- $\texttt{sort}_g(\lambda) = \texttt{sort}_t(p_0 \dots p_k)$
- $\phi \in \mathcal{T}_{\texttt{Bool}}(\mathcal{V}_l \cup \{p_0, \dots, p_k\})$
- $\psi \in \mathcal{T}(\mathcal{V}_l \cup \{p_0, \dots, p_k\})^{\mathcal{V}_l}$

Example 4. Figure 1 shows an example STS in graphical representation. The formal definition of this STS is: $(\{l_0, l_1, l_2\}, l_0, \{x\}, \{x \mapsto 0\}, \{p\}, \{inX?\}, \{outX!, done!\}, \{r_0, r_1, r_2\})$. We have $\mathsf{sort}_g(inX?) = \mathsf{sort}_g(outX!) = \mathtt{Int}$, *and* $\mathsf{sort}_g(done!) = \epsilon$. *We have switches:* $r_0 = (l_0, inX?, p, 1 \leq p \leq 10, \{x \mapsto x + p\}, l_1)$, $r_1 = (l_1, outX!, p, p = x, id, l_0)$, *and* $r_2 = (l_0, done!, \epsilon, x > 15, id, l_2)$. □

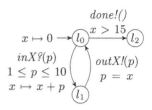

Fig. 1. *Example STS*

2.4 Semantics of Symbolic Transition Systems

We define the semantics of an STS in terms of an LTS. We call this LTS the *interpretation*. We first define the states and labels of this LTS.

Definition 5. *The domain of* semantic states *of $\mathcal{S}$ is SemState $= \mathcal{L} \times \mathcal{U}^{\mathcal{V}_l}$.*

Definition 6. *A* gate value *is an element $(\lambda, \bar{w}) \in \Gamma \times \mathcal{U}^*$ such that* $\mathsf{sort}_g(\lambda) = \mathsf{sort}_v(\bar{w})$. *We denote the set of all gates values with Γ_{val}. We define $\Gamma^O_{val} = \{(\lambda, \bar{w}) \in \Gamma_{val} \mid \lambda \in \Gamma_O\}$, and $\Gamma^I_{val} = \{(\lambda, \bar{w}) \in \Gamma_{val} \mid \lambda \in \Gamma_I\}$.*

For a given semantic state and gate value, there will be a transition in the interpretation LTS, depending on the guard of a switch. If so, we use the assignment from the switch to compute the destination state of this transition.

Definition 7. *Let $q = (l, \vartheta) \in$ SemState be a semantic state, $u = (\lambda_1, \bar{w}) \in \Gamma_{val}$ a gate value, and $r = (l_1, \lambda_2, \bar{p}, \phi, \psi, l_2) \in \mathcal{R}$ a switch. Then r is* enabled *in q for u, denoted enab(q, u, r), if:*

$$l = l_1 \wedge \lambda_1 = \lambda_2 \wedge ((\bar{p} \mapsto \bar{w}) \uplus \vartheta)_T(\phi) = \mathtt{true}$$

If enab(q, u, r), the successor *of q and u for r, denoted succ(q, u, r), is the semantic state:*

$$(l_2, ((\bar{p} \mapsto \bar{w}) \uplus \vartheta)_T \circ \psi)$$

Definition 8. *The* interpretation *of $\mathcal{S}$ is the LTS $[\![\mathcal{S}]\!] = ($SemState$, (l_0, [\![m_{ini}]\!]), \Gamma^I_{val}, \Gamma^O_{val}, T_c)$ with $T_c \subseteq$ SemState $\times \Gamma_{val} \times$ SemState, such that:*

$$T_c = \{(q, u, succ(q, u, r)) \mid q \in SemState \wedge u \in \Gamma_{val} \wedge r \in \mathcal{R} \wedge enab(q, u, r)\}$$

Example 9. Consider the STS of Example 4. Switch r_0 is enabled in initial semantic state $q_0 = (l_0, \{x \mapsto 0\})$ for gate value (inX?,3): $(\{x \mapsto 0\} \uplus \{p \mapsto 3\})_T(1 \leq p \leq 10) = 1 \text{ f}_{\leq} 3 \text{ f}_{\leq} 10 = \mathtt{true}$. Then $succ(q_0, (inX?, 3), r_0) = (l_1, \vartheta)$ with $\vartheta = (\{x \mapsto 0\} \uplus \{p \mapsto 3\})_T \circ \{x \mapsto x + p\} = \{x \mapsto 0 \text{ f}_{+} 3\} = \{x \mapsto 3\}$. Consequently, $((l_0, \{x \mapsto 0\}), (inX?, 3), (l_1, \{x \mapsto 3\}))$ is a transition in the interpretation. Furthermore, switch r_2 is not enabled in q_0 for gate value (done!,ϵ): $(\{x \mapsto 0\} \uplus \emptyset)_T(x > 15) = 0 \text{ f}_{>} 15 = \mathtt{false}$. □

We note that the interpretation of an STS may have an infinite number of states and transitions. Additionally, it hides all information about the structure of an STS, which actually could be used in test generation. We improve on this in the next section, by applying symbolic execution on STS.

3   Symbolic Execution Graphs

This section covers the symbolic execution elements of an STS, resulting in a symbolic execution graph, which is an LTS, having symbolic states, and switches as transitions. Analogous to semantic states, *symbolic states* keep track of the location, and a mapping of location variables to *symbolic values*. The symbolic values of location variables are (syntactic) terms over the parameters, encountered on the switches, instead of (semantical) values from $\mathcal{U}$. The third element of a symbolic state is the *path condition*: a term of sort `Bool`, constraining the possible values of the encountered parameters from the traversed switches, and constructed as a conjunction over the encountered guards of switches.

Since switches with the same gate will use the same gate parameters, and since a single switch can be traversed multiple times, the same parameter may be encountered several times, but it can be bound to different values at each of these points. For our symbolic states to be well-defined, we need to distinguish them. Therefore, we will identify distinct occurrences of parameters by a syntactical mechanism: adding prime (′) symbols to parameter names, each time a switch is taken. This is achieved by simultaneously substituting all variables v by v', so also when v already has some primes. We use the notation $\mathcal{V}'$ to denote the set consisting of variables $\mathcal{V}$ and any of their (multiply) primed variants.

Definition 10. *Let $\mathcal{V}_1, \mathcal{V}_2$ be sets of variables, let $t \in \mathcal{T}(\mathcal{V}_1')$ be a term, and $m \in \mathcal{T}(\mathcal{V}_1')^{\mathcal{V}_2}$ a term mapping. Then we define:*

$$t' = t[\{v \mapsto v' \mid v \in \mathcal{V}_1'\}]$$
$$m' = \{v \mapsto (m(v))' \mid v \in \mathcal{V}_2\}$$

Definition 11. *The domain of symbolic states of $\mathcal{S}$ is denoted SymState, where $SymState = \mathcal{L} \times \mathcal{T}(\mathcal{V}_p')^{\mathcal{V}_l} \times \mathcal{T}_{\texttt{Bool}}(\mathcal{V}_p')$.*

A symbolic state has a transition for a switch, if `solver` returns `sat` or `unknown` for the conjunction of the guard of the switch and the path condition of the symbolic state. We use the term mapping of the state to substitute the location variables of the guard with terms over parameters, and use priming to prevent variables of the guard to become indistinguishable from the parameters of the previously taken switches. To obtain a successor state for an enabled switch, we use the assignment of the switch to update the term mapping, and conjunct the checked guard to the path condition of the current state.

Definition 12. *Let $s = (l, m, \eta) \in SymState$, and $r = (l_1, \lambda, \bar{p}, \phi, \psi, l_2) \in \mathcal{R}$. Then r is* enabled *in s, denoted enab(s, r), if:*

$$l = l_1 \wedge \texttt{solver}(\phi[m'] \wedge \eta') \in \{\texttt{sat}, \texttt{unknown}\}$$

If enab(s, r), the successor *of s for r, denoted succ(s, r), is the symbolic state:*

$$(l_2, [m'] \circ \psi, \phi[m'] \wedge \eta')$$

Example 13. Consider the STS of Example 4. Suppose we check which switches are enabled in symbolic state $q_0 = (l_0, x \mapsto 0, True)$. As $l_1 \neq l_0$, r_1 is not enabled in q_0. Switches r_0 and r_2 do have source location l_0, so we check satisfiability. For r_0 we obtain: $(1 \leq p \leq 10[(x \mapsto 0)']) \wedge (True)' = 1 \leq p \leq 10 \wedge True$, which is clearly satisfiable. Then we obtain the successor: $(l_1, [\{x \mapsto 0\}'] \circ \{x \mapsto x+p\}, 1 \leq p \leq 10[\{x \mapsto 0\}'] \wedge (True)') = (l_1, \{x \mapsto 0 + p\}, 1 \leq p \leq 10 \wedge True)$. Switch r_2 is not enabled in q_0: $x > 15[(x \mapsto 0)'] \wedge (True)' = 0 > 15 \wedge True$. $\square$

We now define a *symbolic execution graph* as an LTS with symbolic states, and transitions labeled by switches. A trace in the graph means that values could be chosen for the parameters, for the switches to be enabled subsequently, or that the trace received the benefit of the doubt, because `solver` returned `unknown`.

Definition 14. *The* symbolic execution graph *(SEG) of S is an LTS $seg(S) = (SymState, (l_0, m_{ini}, True), \Sigma_I, \Sigma_O, T_s)$ with $\Sigma_I = \{(l_1, \lambda, \bar{p}, \phi, \psi, l_2) \in \mathcal{R} \mid \lambda \in \Gamma_I\}$, $\Sigma_O = \{(l_1, \lambda, \bar{p}, \phi, \psi, l_2) \in \mathcal{R} \mid \lambda \in \Gamma_O\}$, $T_s \subseteq SymState \times \mathcal{R} \times SymState$, where:*

$$T_s = \{(s, r, succ(s, r)) \mid s \in SymState \wedge r \in \mathcal{R} \wedge enab(s, r)\}$$

Example 15. In Fig. 2 we compute a part of the SEG for the STS of Example 4. We note that states with an unsatisfiable path condition may actually appear in the SEG, if the chosen `solver` cannot detect its unsatisfiability. $\square$

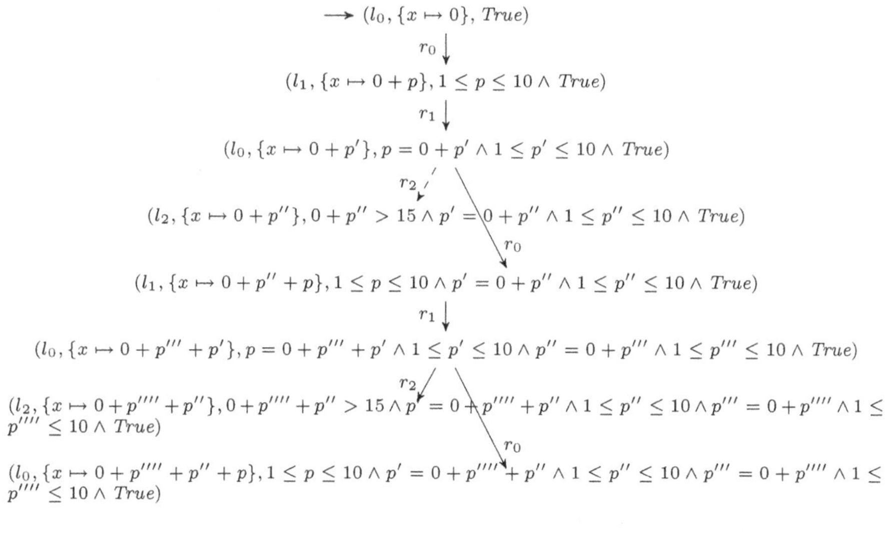

$\longrightarrow (l_0, \{x \mapsto 0\}, True)$

$r_0 \downarrow$

$(l_1, \{x \mapsto 0 + p\}, 1 \leq p \leq 10 \wedge True)$

$r_1 \downarrow$

$(l_0, \{x \mapsto 0 + p'\}, p = 0 + p' \wedge 1 \leq p' \leq 10 \wedge True)$

$r_2 \nearrow'$ $\searrow$

$(l_2, \{x \mapsto 0 + p''\}, 0 + p'' > 15 \wedge p' = 0 + p'' \wedge 1 \leq p'' \leq 10 \wedge True)$

$\searrow r_0$

$(l_1, \{x \mapsto 0 + p'' + p\}, 1 \leq p \leq 10 \wedge p' = 0 + p'' \wedge 1 \leq p'' \leq 10 \wedge True)$

$r_1 \downarrow$

$(l_0, \{x \mapsto 0 + p''' + p'\}, p = 0 + p''' + p' \wedge 1 \leq p' \leq 10 \wedge p'' = 0 + p''' \wedge 1 \leq p''' \leq 10 \wedge True)$

$r_2 \swarrow$

$(l_2, \{x \mapsto 0 + p'''' + p''\}, 0 + p'''' + p'' > 15 \wedge p' = 0 + p'''' + p'' \wedge 1 \leq p'' \leq 10 \wedge p''' = 0 + p'''' \wedge 1 \leq p'''' \leq 10 \wedge True)$

$\searrow r_0$

$(l_0, \{x \mapsto 0 + p'''' + p'' + p\}, 1 \leq p \leq 10 \wedge p' = 0 + p'''' + p'' \wedge 1 \leq p'' \leq 10 \wedge p''' = 0 + p'''' \wedge 1 \leq p'''' \leq 10 \wedge True)$

Fig. 2. A part of the symbolic execution graph for the STS of Example 4. For the path condition of the state reached by the dashed edge, `solver` returned `unknown`.

4   Test Purposes with Switch Coverage

We use traces of the SEG as test purposes for test execution. The path condition of the state reached by the trace describes possible values of parameters, while the trace itself contains all the gates to be encountered.

Definition 16. *An element* $(r_0 \ldots r_n, \eta) \in \text{traces}(seg(\mathcal{S})) \times \mathcal{T}_{\text{Bool}}(\mathcal{V}_p')$ *is a test purpose for* $\mathcal{S}$ *if:*

$$\exists l \in \mathcal{L}, \exists m \in \mathcal{T}(\mathcal{V}_p')^{\mathcal{V}_l} : (l_0, m_{ini}, True) \text{ after } r_0 \ldots r_n = \{(l, m, \eta)\}$$

For a set of test purposes TP we define:

$$cov(TP) = |\bigcup\{\{r_0, \ldots, r_n\} \mid (r_0 \ldots r_n, \eta) \in TP\}|/|\mathcal{R}|$$

Given a set TP for $\mathcal{S}$, *we call* $cov(TP)$ *the a priori switch coverage of TP.*

Example 17. From the SEG of Example 15 we obtain the following test purpose with 100% a priori switch coverage: $(r_0 r_1 r_0 r_1 r_2, 0 + p'''' + p'' > 15 \wedge p' = 0 + p'''' + p'' \wedge 1 \leq p'' \leq 10 \wedge p''' = 0 + p'''' \wedge 1 \leq p'''' \leq 10 \wedge True)$. The test purpose for path $r_0 r_1 r_2$ also gives 100% a priori switch coverage, but in Example 18 we show it is not executable, and therefore has 0% a posteriori switch coverage. □

For a test purpose $(r_0 \ldots r_n, \eta)$ we call $r_0 \ldots r_n$ the *path*, and η the *path condition*. If all switches occur in some finite trace of the SEG, a set of purposes with 100% a priori coverage can be found through breadth first search. In Algorithm 1, we give pseudo code for the test execution of a test purpose, including on-the-fly data generation for parameters. We explain the intuition of it below.

Execution of a test purpose may result in either of three verdicts *Pass*, *Inconclusive*, or *Fail*. Verdict *Fail* means that a non-conformance (with respect to **ioco**) to the given STS specification was found. Verdict *Pass* means that execution was completed, without encountering any non-conformance. Verdict *Inconclusive* means that execution of the test purpose could not be completed, but no non-conformance was detected either.

A test purpose is executed by executing its switches of the path in the given order. A gate value is provided to the SUT, or received from the SUT, if the switch being executed has an input gate, or output gate, respectively. Every time a new gate value is obtained, we update the path condition, by substituting the values from the gate value for the parameters of the switch. If the path condition becomes unsatisfiable by this substitution, we then can immediately return *Inconclusive*, as there is no way the test purpose can be executed completely. Also, we use this path condition to obtain suitable values for parameters of a switch with an input gate. The substitution ensures that all previously observed gate values are taken into account. If solver returns unknown, we resort to using only the guard of the current switch to find values.

The path condition of a test purpose contains (multiply) primed variables, while the parameters of switches are not primed, so for obtaining the parameters of the path condition (e.g., line 8 of Algorithm 1), we use a notation for adding primes to parameters. We denote adding k primes to a parameter p with $(p)^{\prime \cdot k}$, so, e.g., $(p)^{\prime \cdot 0} = p$, and $(p)^{\prime \cdot 3} = p'''$. We extend this notation to sequences.

During execution of the test purpose, we keep track of state (l, ϑ), which is the current semantic state for the observed gate values. We use valuation ϑ to obtain parameter values for the guard of the current switch, if solver returns unknown for the path condition in line 12 of Algorithm 1.

Additionally, we use (l, ϑ) to check whether it enables the output gate value, to check whether we are still on track for reaching the test purpose (line 28). If this is not the case, we need to check if the specification allows a different sequence of switches for the observed gate values (line 36) to see whether the SUT only deviated from the path of the test purpose, or that it is really non-conforming. We therefore keep track of all semantic states that can be obtained for the observed gate values in C. To do this as efficiently as possible, we use the information available in the SEG. As the graph can be infinite, we assume that, if Algorithm 1 is given a test purpose $(r_0, \ldots, r_n, \eta)$ to be executed, it is given a partially computed SEG which contains all traces of length $n + 1$. This is no strong requirement, as to find the test purpose via breadth first search, we already computed (almost) all of these traces. Moreover, computing all traces can be done *before* test execution of the test purposes, and will compensate for computation time needed *during* test execution.

Specifically, the algorithm keeps track of a set C containing pairs $(q, s) \in$ *SemState* $\times$ *SymState*, representing the current semantic state with the corresponding symbolic state, for a sequence of switches, consistent with the gate values observed so far. The set of switches enabled in q is at most init(s), as s describes a set of semantic states, of which q is one. We then use q to select the switches from init(s) actually enabled in q, and compute its successor with the last obtained gate value. The successor of s for these switches can be obtained from the SEG without any computation. If an output gate value, not enabled in (l, ϑ), is received from the SUT, we can check, as described above, whether this gate value is enabled (line 36). If so, the SUT is conforming but deviated from the test purpose, and otherwise it is non-conforming.

For communication with the SUT the algorithm uses two procedures: sendInput provides an input to the SUT, and receiveOutput obtains an enabled output from the SUT.

Example 18. We execute the first test purpose of Example 17 according to Algorithm 1. Hence, we set $(l, \vartheta) := (l_0, \{x \mapsto 0\})$, and $C := \{((l_0, \{x \mapsto 0\}), (l_0, \{x \mapsto 0\}, True))\}$. We discuss the first 2 of 5 iterations of the for-loop:

Iteration 0: As r_0 has input gate inX?, we execute lines 6–22 of the algorithm. Suppose that solver(η) = sat, and that we obtain value 6 for parameter $p^{\prime \cdot (4-0)} = p''''$ on line 7. Then we send (inX?,6) to the SUT. We substitute 6 for p'''' in the path condition: $\eta := 0 + 6 + p'' > 15 \wedge p' = 0 + 6 + p'' \wedge 1 \le p'' \le 10 \wedge p''' = 0 + 6 \wedge 1 \le 6 \le 10$. We obtain $(l, \vartheta) := (l_1, \{x \mapsto 6\})$, and $C := \{(l, \vartheta), (l_1, \{x \mapsto 0 + p\}, 1 \le p \le 10 \wedge True)\}$.

Input: A specification STS $\mathcal{S}$
Input: A test purpose $((r_0 \ldots r_n), \eta)$
Input: A symbolic execution graph $seg(\mathcal{S})$
Input: An SUT with procedures `sendInput` and `receiveOutput`
Output: One of the verdicts: *Pass, Fail, Inconclusive*

```
 1  (l, ϑ) := (l₀, ⟦m_ini⟧);
 2  C := {((l₀, ⟦m_ini⟧), (l₀, m_ini, True))};
 3  for 0 ≤ i ≤ n do
 4      Let (l₁, λ, p̄, φ, ψ, l₂) = rᵢ;
 5      if λ ∈ Γ_I then
 6          if solver(η) = sat then
 7              w̄ := getValues(η, (p̄)'·(n−i));
 8              η := η[tmap((p̄)'·(n−i) ↦ w̄)];
 9              sendInput(λ, w̄);
10              (l, ϑ) := succ((l, ϑ), (λ, w̄), rᵢ);
11              C := {(succ(q, (λ, w̄), r), succ(s, r)) |
                        (q, s) ∈ C, r ∈ init(s), enab(q, (λ, w̄), r)};
12          else if solver(η) = unknown ∧ solver(φ[tmap(ϑ)]) = sat then
13              w̄ := getValues(φ[tmap(ϑ)], p̄);
14              η := η[tmap((p̄)'·(n−i) ↦ w̄)];
15              if solver(η) = unsat then
16                  return Inconclusive;
17              else
18                  sendInput(λ, w̄);
19                  (l, ϑ) := succ((l, ϑ), (λ, w̄), rᵢ);
20                  C := {(succ(q, (λ, w̄), r), succ(s, r)) |
                            (q, s) ∈ C, r ∈ init(s), enab(q, (λ, w̄), r)};
21          else
22              return Inconclusive;
23      else
24          (λ_sut, w̄) = receiveOutput();
25          if (λ_sut, w̄) ∉ Γ^O_val then
26              return Fail;
27          else
28              if enab((l, ϑ), (λ_sut, w̄), rᵢ) then
29                  η := η[tmap((p̄)'·(n−i) ↦ w̄)];
30                  if solver(η) = unsat then
31                      return Inconclusive;
32                  else
33                      (l, ϑ) := succ((l, ϑ), (λ_sut, w̄), rᵢ);
34                      C := {(succ(q, (λ, w̄), r), succ(s, r)) |
                                (q, s) ∈ C, r ∈ init(s), enab(q, (λ, w̄), r)};
35              else
36                  if ∃(q, s) ∈ C, ∃r ∈ init(s) : enab(q, (λ_sut, w̄), r) then
37                      return Inconclusive;
38                  else
39                      return Fail;
40  return Pass;
```

Algorithm 1. Test generation and execution algorithm for test purposes

Iteration 1: Switch r_1 has output gate outX!, so we execute lines 24–39 of the algorithm. We then receive some output from the SUT. We discuss two cases:

1. Suppose that we receive (outX!,6). We then observe that $(\text{outX!}, 6) \in \Gamma^O_{val}$. We see that $enab((l_1, \{x \mapsto 6\}), (\text{outX!}, 6), r_1)$ holds. We substitute 6 for $p'^{\cdot(4-1)} = p''' : \eta := 0 + 6 + p'' > 15 \wedge p' = 0 + 6 + p'' \wedge 1 \le p'' \le 10 \wedge 6 = 0 + 6 \wedge 1 \le 6 \le 10$. Now η is satisfiable (choose valuation $\{p'' \mapsto 10, p' \mapsto 10\}$). We obtain $(l, \vartheta) := (l_0, \{x \mapsto 6\})$, and $C = \{((l, \vartheta), (l_0, \{x \mapsto 0 + p'\}, p = 0 + p' \wedge 1 \le p' \le 10 \wedge True))\}$, and go to the next iteration.

2. Now suppose that we receive (outX!,7). We observe that $(\text{outX!}, 7) \in \Gamma^O_{val}$. As $6 \ne 7$, $enab((l_1, \{x \mapsto 6\}), (\text{outX!}, 7), r_1)$ does not hold. Since no other switch than r_1 is enabled in $(l_1, \{x \mapsto 0 + p\}, 1 \le p \le 10 \wedge True)$, according to the SEG, we find that the condition of line 36 is false, so we return *Fail*. □

For the second test purpose of Example 17 we assumed that `solver` could not detect that the path condition is not satisfiable, so $\text{solver}(\eta) = \text{unknown}$. This leads us to line 12 in Algorithm 1. The second condition in line 12 can be solved, e.g., with $p = 8$, so then according to line 14, $\eta := 0 + 8 > 15 \wedge p' = 0 + 8 \wedge 1 \le 8 \le 10 \wedge True$. Most likely, now any `solver` will detect that this is not satisfiable, $\text{solver}(\eta) = \text{unsat}$, so the algorithm ends in line 16 with verdict *Inconclusive*. The a posteriori coverage is 0%, decreasing from 100% a priori coverage.

Theorem 19 proves soundness of Algorithm 1. For the proofs we refer to [2].

Theorem 19. *Let $t = ((r_0 \ldots r_n), \eta)$ be a test purpose for $\mathcal{S}$, and let $\mathcal{I}$ be an input-enabled LTS, such that $\mathcal{I}$ ioco $[\![\mathcal{S}]\!]$. Then Algorithm 1 does not return Fail for $\mathcal{S}$, t, and $seg(\mathcal{S})$, when using $\mathcal{I}$ as SUT, and some tool* `solver`.

The *a posteriori switch coverage* can be determined after all test purposes have been executed. We define it as $cov(TP')$, where TP' is the set of test purposes for which Algorithm 1 returned verdict *Pass*, with $|C| = 1$ at that point (line 40). This is a conservative approach: a test purpose $(\bar{r}, \eta)$ only counts if we are sure that its execution ends in $(l_0, m_{ini}, True)$ after $\bar{r}$. A more liberal approach would count any test purpose with verdict *Pass*, without requiring $|C| = 1$, meaning that nondeterministically another final state than $(l_0, m_{ini}, True)$ after $\bar{r}$ might have been reached.

5   Implementation of the Test Approach in Maude and Z3

We implemented our testing method with Maude: a language and tool set for rewriting systems. We encode each switch of an STS as a conditional rewriting rule. Such a rule rewrites a symbolic state to its successor state. A rewrite rule is conditional: it can only be applied if the guard, of the switch it encodes, holds. Maude queries SMT-solver Z3 to check $\text{solver}(\phi[m'] \wedge \eta') \in \{\text{sat}, \text{unknown}\}$, as in Definition 12. To do this, we encoded the used Maude data types in the SMT-LIB language, which is an input language for Z3. The 'meta-level' feature of Maude supports this translation, by enabling syntactic inspection of terms.

As our case study only involved integers and booleans, we only constructed translation bindings for these data types. The Maude language, however, can be used to define any data type, so one could make these bindings for any data type that Z3 (or any other SMT solver) supports.

We used Maude's search query to search in the state space of the states, which can be obtained by applying rewriting rules. We use this to find sequences of switches ending on a certain switch. This way, Maude searches in the symbolic execution graph for test purposes contributing to a priori switch coverage.

We wrote a Python program to execute the test purposes, following Algorithm 1. The program queries Z3 again, to find suitable values for input parameters, as outlined in the algorithm.

6   Case Study: The Bounded Retransmission Protocol

To evaluate our approach, we used the Bounded Retransmission Protocol [13] benchmark from the Automata Wiki [1]. This is a repository containing automata in various automata formalisms, which are suitable for benchmarking. For the Bounded Retransmission Protocol the Wiki provides a specification automaton, and 6 mutants. See Fig. 3 for the specification, and the Wiki for all the mutants. Each mutant differs on one aspect from the specification, e.g. a different guard, an extra switch, or an extra assignment.

The Bounded Retransmission Protocol is a variation on the alternating bit protocol. After sending a message, the sender waits for an acknowledgment from the receiving party. If an acknowledgment fails to appear, the sender times out, and sends the message again. This retransmission is executed at most max_rn times, for some number max_rn.

Table 1. Number of inputs and outputs needed for detecting the BRP mutants

	Switch coverage	TorXakis
Mutant 1	44	12
Mutant 2	16	234
Mutant 3	8	12
Mutant 4	6	18
Mutant 5	18	1620
Mutant 6	164	76
Sum	256	1972
Geom. mean	21.5	64.9

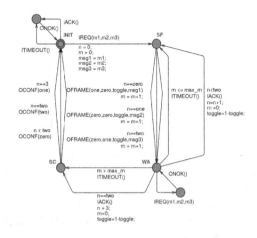

Fig. 3. Specification of BRP

We generated a set of test purposes with 100% switch coverage from the specification, and applied it on the mutants. We then measured the number of inputs and outputs needed until obtaining a *Fail* verdict. To obtain *Fail* for mutant 6, just executing all the switch coverage test purposes was not sufficient. This was caused by the SMT-solver we used (Z3): it always returns the same solution for the same query, and the particular solution did not result in obtaining a *Fail*. Retrieving random solutions from an SMT-solver is out of scope of this paper, but it has been investigated in e.g. [15,16,19], and some techniques are implemented in the tool TorXakis [25]. We chose to solve the problem by randomly generating values for input switch parameters, and then checking the satisfiability of the constraint for these values. As none of the parameters of input switches of the BRP specification were constrained by any of the test purposes, this worked well enough for this case study. We averaged the number of inputs and outputs over 100 executions.

The test purposes were executed in the order of their number of inputs and outputs (longest test purpose first). We applied this heuristic with the idea that the longest test purpose is likely to be better at discovering more difficult faults, which are hidden further away, and at the same time covers a lot of the switches of the specification.

We compared our results with random testing (on gate actions and data values) of STS as implemented in the tool TorXakis [22,25].

Again, we measured the number of inputs and outputs until encountering a *Fail*. We report on the average number over 100 executions for each mutant.

Our test generation produced 6 test purposes to obtain 100% a priori switch coverage. They in total consist of 47 inputs and outputs. As the guards of the nondeterministic switches, i.e. switches having the same gate and source location, are disjunct, we could determine the exact a posteriori switch coverage, which was 100% as well. Table 1 shows the results for testing with our test purposes, and random testing with TorXakis.

The faults in mutants 2, 3, 4, and 5 are detected by the test purpose with the longest path of 18 inputs and outputs. Note that the difference in number of inputs and outputs for mutant 5 is especially big. The fault of mutant 1 is detected by one shorter test purpose, in just 4 inputs and outputs. In total we needed more inputs and outputs because of our heuristic to do the longest test purpose first. Mutant 6 was detected by the longest and the third longest test purpose, if the right values are chosen for the gate parameters. All test purposes are executed before these two test purposes are tried again with (possibly) different values. This causes TorXakis to be faster in detecting the fault than us.

Overall, our approach is better than testing with TorXakis: the total number of inputs and outputs needed to detect the faults of all mutants is 8 times more for TorXakis than for our approach. One can see however, that random testing can be quite effective for faults detectable with few inputs and outputs (mutant 1), and that the thoroughness of covering all switches can sometimes be a bit less effective than random testing (mutant 6). Our approach is significantly better in reaching a switch which is not so likely to be reached by using random test generation (mutant 5), and the number of inputs and outputs to obtain a *Fail* is much more stable than for random testing. Despite the varying results for each mutant, the geometric mean shows that our approach is overall 3 times better than TorXakis.

7 Conclusions and Future Work

We proposed a test generation and execution method for Symbolic Transition Systems. We extend on the work in [8,9], and provide sound test selection based on switch coverage. We select data values as late as possible during test execution, to provide optimal flexibility with respect to received outputs from the SUT. Furthermore, our test generation and execution explicitly deals with solvers returning 'unknown'. The BRP case study shows applicability of our approach.

There are ample opportunities to extend upon this paper in future work:

- The most important extension is adding quiescence, which is a key concept in the **ioco** theory, but which we did not take into account yet. Actually, our test algorithm tests for a weaker form of **ioco** where quiescence is not considered, i.e., removing quiescence from **ioco** in Definition 2 and only requiring inclusion of outputs. Since this weaker form of **ioco** is implied by the original **ioco** of Definition 2, soundness in Theorem 19 is not affected. But it may occur that our algorithm deadlocks when the SUT is quiescent and the test purpose expects an output (line 24). The reason that we did not add quiescence yet, is that it leads to quantified guards in switches: a state is quiescent if there does not exist an output parameter value that makes the guard of an output switch true. It is not yet clear how and where to add these quantified guards. Quiescence can be added as just another output label in the STS. Another option is to add quiescence when constructing the symbolic execution graph, so that quiescence can also be part of test purposes. Yet another option is to take quiescence only into account in the testing algorithm. Whatever option, it will introduce quantified guards, which complicates the formalism and the satisfiability checking.
- By executing test purposes simultaneously, instead of one by one, test execution can proceed until all test purposes received a verdict. This could improve test efficiency. Also, test purposes returning *Inconclusive* could be re-executed, to obtain better a posteriori switch coverage.
- The test algorithm is written down as if we assume *input-eager* interaction with the SUT: the SUT always accepts an input, even though it could have produced an output. This could be relaxed to *input-fair* interaction [3,4].
- The symbolic states of the symbolic execution graph are defined as syntactic objects. When adding semantics, an equivalence could be defined e.g. as in Maude [5], so that the size of the symbolic execution graph could be reduced.
- We have existential quantification for both inputs and outputs in path conditions, whereas universal quantification might be more natural for outputs. This may, however, lead to more unsatisfiable path conditions and moreover, current solvers usually perform worse on formulas with alternating quantification.

- Our switch coverage approach could be combined with traditional data coverage techniques e.g. equivalence partitioning, boundary value analysis, or the techniques for random value selection used in TorXakis. Witnesses of solvers usually do not produce much data coverage, as mutant 6 of the BRP benchmark showed.
- To check scalability, our switch coverage testing approach should be evaluated more extensively, by performing experiments on additional case studies.

Acknowledgments. This work was largely performed while the first author was visiting INRIA/the University of Lille. We would like to thank Vlad Rusu for making this visit possible, and for his feedback and support with using Maude.

References

1. Automata Wiki. automata.cs.ru.nl
2. Homepage Petra van den Bos. petravdbos.nl
3. van den Bos, P., Janssen, R., Moerman, J.: n-Complete test suites for IOCO. Softw. Qual. J. **27**(2), 563–588 (2019)
4. van den Bos, P., Stoelinga, M.: Tester versus bug: a generic framework for model-based testing via games. In: Orlandini, A., Zimmermann, M. (eds.) Proceedings Ninth International Symposium on Games, Automata, Logics, and Formal Verification. Electronic Proceedings in Theoretical Computer Science, 26–28th September 2018, Saarbrücken, Germany, vol. 277, pp. 118–132. Open Publishing Association (2018)
5. Clavel, M., et al.: Maude: specification and programming in rewriting logic. Theoret. Comput. Sci. **285**(2), 187–243 (2002). Rewriting Logic and its Applications
6. de Moura, L., Bjørner, N.: Z3: an efficient SMT solver. In: Ramakrishnan, C.R., Rehof, J. (eds.) TACAS 2008. LNCS, vol. 4963, pp. 337–340. Springer, Heidelberg (2008). https://doi.org/10.1007/978-3-540-78800-3_24
7. Ehrig, H., Mahr, B.: Fundamentals of Algebraic Specification I – Equations and Initial Semantics. EATCS Monographs on Theoretical Computer Science. Springer, Heidelberg (1985). https://doi.org/10.1007/978-3-642-69962-7
8. Frantzen, L., Tretmans, J., Willemse, T.A.C.: Test generation based on symbolic specifications. In: Grabowski, J., Nielsen, B. (eds.) FATES 2004. LNCS, vol. 3395, pp. 1–15. Springer, Heidelberg (2005). https://doi.org/10.1007/978-3-540-31848-4_1
9. Frantzen, L., Tretmans, J., Willemse, T.A.C.: A symbolic framework for model-based testing. In: Havelund, K., Núñez, M., Roşu, G., Wolff, B. (eds.) FATES/RV -2006. LNCS, vol. 4262, pp. 40–54. Springer, Heidelberg (2006). https://doi.org/10.1007/11940197_3
10. Friedman, G., Hartman, A., Nagin, K., Shiran, T.: Projected state machine coverage for software testing. In: Proceedings of the 2002 ACM SIGSOFT International Symposium on Software Testing and Analysis, ISSTA 2002, pp. 134–143. ACM, New York (2002)
11. Gaston, C., Le Gall, P., Rapin, N., Touil, A.: Symbolic execution techniques for test purpose definition. In: Uyar, M.Ü., Duale, A.Y., Fecko, M.A. (eds.) TestCom 2006. LNCS, vol. 3964, pp. 1–18. Springer, Heidelberg (2006). https://doi.org/10.1007/11754008_1

12. Godefroid, P., Levin, M.Y., Molnar, D.A.: SAGE: whitebox fuzzing for security testing. Commun. ACM **55**(3), 40–44 (2012)
13. Helmink, L., Sellink, M.P.A., Vaandrager, F.W.: Proof-checking a data link protocol. In: Barendregt, H., Nipkow, T. (eds.) TYPES 1993. LNCS, vol. 806, pp. 127–165. Springer, Heidelberg (1994). https://doi.org/10.1007/3-540-58085-9_75
14. Huang, W., Peleska, J.: Complete model-based equivalence class testing for nondeterministic systems. Formal Aspects Comput. **29**(2), 335–364 (2017)
15. Huijben, M.: Efficient constrained random sampling for use in a model based testing tool. Master's thesis, Institute for Computing and Information Sciences, Radboud University, Nijmegen, The Netherlands (2019)
16. Iyer, M.A.: Race: a word-level ATPG-based constraints solver system for smart random simulation, p. 299. Citeseer (2003)
17. Jeannet, B., Jéron, T., Rusu, V., Zinovieva, E.: Symbolic test selection based on approximate analysis. In: Halbwachs, N., Zuck, L.D. (eds.) TACAS 2005. LNCS, vol. 3440, pp. 349–364. Springer, Heidelberg (2005). https://doi.org/10.1007/978-3-540-31980-1_23
18. King, J.C.: Symbolic execution and program testing. Commun. ACM **19**(7), 385–394 (1976)
19. Kitchen, N.: Markov Chain Monte Carlo stimulus generation for constrained random simulation. Ph.D. thesis, UC Berkeley (2010)
20. Li, J.J., Wong, W.E.: Automatic test generation from communicating extended finite state machine (CEFSM)-based models. In: Proceedings Fifth IEEE International Symposium on Object-Oriented Real-Time Distributed Computing, ISIRC 2002, pp. 181–185, April 2002
21. Petrenko, A.: Checking experiments for symbolic input/output finite state machines. In: 2016 IEEE Ninth International Conference on Software Testing, Verification and Validation Workshops (ICSTW), pp. 229–237, April 2016
22. TorXakis. https://github.com/torxakis
23. Tretmans, J.: Test generation with inputs, outputs and repetitive quiescence. Softw.—Concepts Tools **17**(3), 103–120 (1996)
24. Tretmans, J.: Model based testing with labelled transition systems. In: Hierons, R.M., Bowen, J.P., Harman, M. (eds.) Formal Methods and Testing. LNCS, vol. 4949, pp. 1–38. Springer, Heidelberg (2008). https://doi.org/10.1007/978-3-540-78917-8_1
25. Tretmans, J.: On the existence of practical testers. In: Katoen, J.-P., Langerak, R., Rensink, A. (eds.) ModelEd, TestEd, TrustEd. LNCS, vol. 10500, pp. 87–106. Springer, Cham (2017). https://doi.org/10.1007/978-3-319-68270-9_5
26. Veanes, M., Bjørner, N.: Alternating simulation and IOCO. In: Petrenko, A., Simão, A., Maldonado, J.C. (eds.) ICTSS 2010. LNCS, vol. 6435, pp. 47–62. Springer, Heidelberg (2010). https://doi.org/10.1007/978-3-642-16573-3_5

BTestBox: A Tool for Testing B Translators and Coverage of B Models

Diego de Azevedo Oliveira[1]($\boxtimes$), Valério Medeiros Jr.[2]($\boxtimes$),
David Déharbe[3]($\boxtimes$), and Martin A. Musicante[4]($\boxtimes$)

[1] Université de Sherbrooke, Sherbrooke, Canada
diegodeazevedooliveira@gmail.com
[2] Instituto Federal de Educação, Ciência e Tecnologia do Rio Grande do Norte,
Natal, Brazil
valerio.medeiros@ifrn.edu.br
[3] Clearsy System Engineering, Aix-en-Provence, France
david.deharbe@clearsy.com
[4] Universidade Federal do Rio Grande do Norte, Natal, Brazil
mam@dimap.ufrn.br

Abstract. The argument of correctness in refinement-based formal software design often disregards source code analysis and code generation. To mitigate the risk of errors in these phases, certifications issued by regulation entities demand or recommend testing the generated software using a code coverage criteria. We propose improvements for the *BTestBox*, a tool for automatic generation of tests for software components developed with the B method. *BTestBox* supports several code coverage criteria and code generators for different languages. The tool uses a constraint solver to produce tests, thus being able to identify dead code and tautological branching conditions. It also generates reports with different metrics and may be used as an extension to the Atelier B. Our tool performs a double task: first, it acts on the B model, by checking the code coverage. Second, the tool performs the translation of lower level B specifications into programming language code, runs tests and compares their results with the expected output of the test cases. The present version of *BTestBox* uses parallelisation techniques that significantly improve its performance. The results presented here are encouraging, showing performance numbers that are one order of magnitude better than the ones obtained in the tool's previous version.

Keywords: B method · Model-based testing · Code coverage

1 Introduction

The B method of software development [1] produces source code by successive refinement from an abstract model. Since compilers are, in general, not dependable, errors in their code may silently introduce bugs during translation [11]. *BTestBox* tests the translated code and assures dependability of the translation.

© Springer Nature Switzerland AG 2019
D. Beyer and C. Keller (Eds.): TAP 2019, LNCS 11823, pp. 83–92, 2019.
https://doi.org/10.1007/978-3-030-31157-5_6

Additionally, *BTestBox* may help the verification process to find counterexamples. Model-based testing (MBT) provides an approach for the automatic generation of test cases from models [6]. Formal methods such as B have been used to assure the behaviour of a specification in many contexts over the years, mostly in the development of critical systems [15,17]. B is based on the Dijkstra's concepts [8]; it uses the generalised substitution theory [10] and a specific notation. A fully developed B module consists of several B components that can be: an abstract machine (the module specification); some possible refinements (of its specification) or an implementation (final refinement). The B components have operations, and each operation represents a function defined in a programming language. The goal is to have a proven implementation. The B code is then translated to a lower level code (machine code or source code). This process is not guaranteed by proof and requires more attention. Code generators from B target computer languages such as C, Ada, and LLVM [5,9].

Testing techniques may supplement formal methods during the verification and validation process. They are used as a lower-cost complement of formal proofs, for an in-depth verification of the system. Software testing can quickly identify failures and expose defects introduced during the code generation and code maintenance [16]. Also, some certificates such as DO-178B, required by the Federal Aviation Administration (FAA), demand the use of software testing and measuring coverage over the code.

BTestBox may be used as an Atelier-B (an IDE used to develop software for critical safety systems) extension to automatically test B specifications. Our tool receives as inputs a B implementation, the target translator, a compiler, a coverage criterion, the folder project, and the logic expression solver (ProB [12]) directory. Then, *BTestBox* generates test cases to cover the criterion for the implementation. The test cases are written in B so that the models are translated and executed in any target language. Next, the results are compared with the expected values, thus producing a report.

BTestBox has undergone a great deal of improvement since the previous version, used in [7,16]. The main differences between the previous and new versions are: *(i)* inclusion of several code coverage criteria, the previous version supported only Statement Coverage; *(ii)* new HTML interface, including reports generated for each coverage criterion; and *(iii)* better support to new case studies both academic and industrial. This support is based on the use of parallelization techniques, in order to improve scalability.

In its current state, *BTestBox* is fully automatic and capable of testing translations from B implementations to C, checking for translation errors and reporting coverage rates for several criteria. The two main contributions of *BTestBox* are: *(i)* a fully automatic model-based process for generation of executable test cases satisfying a given criterion for B implementations, thus avoiding the manual construction of test cases; and *(ii)* verifying the correctness of the B compiler while testing the translated code developed with the B formal method process using the supported criteria test cases consequently, thus helping to find dead code and unnecessary conditions.

This article is organised as follows: Sect. 2 explains the *BTestBox* methodology, the background needed to understand the *BTestBox* process, how the tool works, and how it is associated with the B method. Section 3 shows the results, metrics, threats, and limitations of our tool. Section 4 describes related work. Section 5 presents conclusions and future work.

2 Methodology

This section presents the methodology and the background needed to understand the process. *BTestBox* generates test cases for the code generated from the B implementation according to a given criterion. The tool receives a B implementation, the target translator, a compiler, a coverage criterion, the folder project, and the logic expression solver (ProB [12]) directory. To create the test cases, *BTestBox* generates a control flow graph and uses Hoare logic to generate a predicate characterizing the possible values for the execution paths, according to the chosen criterion. Then, the predicates are solved and the values of the input and output parameters are stored for each valid solution. Our tool prepares components capable of executing and checking the execution of the test cases after the translation. Finally, the test components are translated and executed, and the metrics are reported. The B process with the *BTestBox* is demonstrated in Fig. 1a.

2.1 Path Generation

This section describes how *BTestBox* identifies the paths from a given B implementation. The process uses directed graphs and takes advantage of the B method's properties. Since B operations have only one entry and only one exit, the control flow graphs have one start node and one end node. Different coverage criteria correspond to different sets of paths from the initial to the final node in the graph. For each coverage criterion supported by *BTestBox*, the tool can identify these paths. *BTestBox* supports the following criteria [3]: *Statement Coverage* (ST); *Branch Coverage* (BC); *Path Coverage* (PC); *Clause Coverage* (CC); *Combinatorial Coverage* (CoC). [4] Also *BTextBox* identifies dead code.

Given the B implementation of the "RussMult" operation[1] (Fig. 1b), *BTestBox* builds the graph shown in Fig. 1c.

Since the operation has a loop, the graph is cyclic, and contains potentially infinite paths (even though only finite paths are allowed, due to the fact that each loop must terminate in B and has been proved as such). Instead of repeating the instructions inside the loop and generating different paths for each execution of the loop, *BTestBox* computes the paths inside the loop

---

[1] This operation implements the Russian Multiplication technique, that iteratively doubles one of the factors while halving the other one. The variant and invariant clauses are standard B elements, which are necessary to prove the correctness of the operation, including its termination.

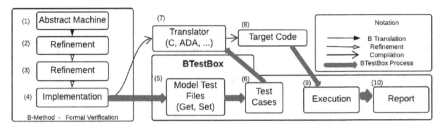

(a) Overview of the B process with the *BTestBox*.

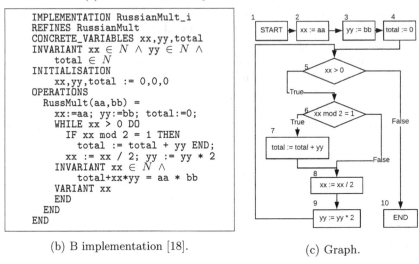

(b) B implementation [18].   (c) Graph.

Fig. 1. Overview, implementation and Russia Multiplication Graph.

once and uses them to represent all the paths created with the loop's repetition. We assume this because of the B method termination property - a loop always has to end. For our example, *BTestbox* generates the following paths: *path 1 = 1, 2, 3, 4, 5, 6, 7, 8, 9, 5, 10*; *path 2 = 1, 2, 3, 4, 5, 6, 8, 9, 5, 10* and *path 3 = 1, 2, 3, 4, 5, 10*. These paths correspond to the control flow of the operation inside the graph. The numbers represent nodes of the graph.

2.2   Generating Predicates

This section presents how *BTestBox* uses Hoare logic to create test conditions. Our tool relies on Hoare triples to compute how a command changes the state. We use the notation: $\{P\}C\{Q\}$, where P represents the precondition for the execution of the command C, and Q is the post-condition established after the command. P and Q are states described by first-order logic formulæ. The precondition may be computed from the command and post-condition.

To obtain a precondition, *BTestBox* applies Hoare logic rules backwards, which is possible due to the termination property being ensured by the B method.

More precisely, the termination is subject of a proof obligation. This proof obligation is produced automatically from the VARIANT clause found in the WHILE construction of the B method language, see Fig. 1(b). We assume that all the proof obligations have been discharged. The predicates for each path generated by *BTestBox* are used to create test cases. These predicates are obtained through a backward traversal of the paths defined by the criterion. For example, using the PC criterion on the model shown in Fig. 1b, it is necessary to test the three paths defined for the example. Other criteria may have different requirements. For instance, if the ST criterion is required, only *path 1* needs to be checked. For the BC criterion, a minimum of two paths would be executed. In accordance with the test criterion, *BTestBox* takes the longest path to obtain the first predicate that will be checked. Given that *path 1* is chosen, the tool begins with node 10 and will reversely sweep the path. Assuming the *true* post-condition for node 10, we have that the triple $\{true\}$ END $\{true\}$ holds for this node. To obtain the precondition for node 5, we note that it represents a guard, where the expression yields to false. This is represented by $[\neg(xx > 0)]$. In this case, we obtain the Hoare triple $\{xx \leq 0\}$ $[\neg(xx > 0)]$ $\{true\}$. After reaching node 5, since it is the guard of a loop, our tool divides the predicate into two: one for the body of the loop and the other for the code preceding the loop. For the BC Criterion, we should make sure that every branch of the graph is visited. This way, commands other than the ones containing guards will not affect the generated conditions. Therefore, the tool will take the backward walk through *path 1*, going from node 9 to node 6. Supposing that the post-condition of node 9 is *true*, we infer that the post-condition of node 6 is also *true*. Node 6 is a guard, which, in this case, is evaluated to *true*. This way we obtain the Hoare triple $\{xx \bmod 2 = 1\}$ $[xx \bmod 2 = 1]$ $\{true\}$ for node 6.

The tool proceeds by continuing to apply the same reasoning which, in the case of *path 1*, yields to the following precondition of the "RussMult" operation:

$$\exists(xx, yy, total).(xx > 0 \land xx \bmod 2 = 1 \land xx \in \mathbb{N} \land total + xx * yy = aa * bb)$$
$$\land \exists(xx, yy, total).(xx \leq 0 \land xx \in \mathbb{N} \land total + xx * yy = aa * bb)$$
$$\land xx : \mathbb{N} \land yy : \mathbb{N} \land total : \mathbb{N} \land aa : \mathbb{N} \land bb : \mathbb{N}$$

In the next step, it is necessary to find if the predicate is verified by at least one solution. Our tool uses the *ProB* constraint solver for find a suitable variable interpretation (if it exists). In our example, *ProB* returned that a possible solution is $aa = 1$, $bb = 0$, $xx = 0$, $yy = 0$, $total = 0$. These values may define the input of a test case.

The expected outputs for the test case are obtained by executing the path. In this case, the values obtained are $aa = 1$, $bb = 0$, $xx = 0$, $yy = 0$, $total = 0$. *BTestBox* continues the process for all the paths required by the criterion.

In this example, it will lead to the following test cases (for the BC Criterion):

	Test 1		Test 2	
Variables	Input	Output	Input	Output
aa	1	1	2	2
bb	0	0	0	0
xx	0	0	0	0
yy	0	0	0	0
total	0	0	0	0

2.3   Creating Test Case Files

Our tool is capable of generating the test cases, inserting operations to manipulate the variables of an implementation under test, executing the translation, comparing the results and reporting them to the user. To do all of this, *BTestBox* creates copies of the user's files and adds "get" and "set" operations. Also, it writes B components using the results of the evaluation of the predicates as the test case files.

The evaluation occurs after the translation is performed using a B compiler. With a compiler provided by the user and supported by our tool, *BTestBox* can compile and execute the translated code. Finally, a HTML report file is generated and presented to the user, displaying the coverage metrics, showing which coverage objectives were not reached and offering a shortcut for all the files used by the test.

3   Results

BTestBox was tested for a variety of different B syntactic features, with the goal of assuring the correctness of the process and the functionality of the tool. Our tool ran more than 120 proved implementations. Additionally, one real B project granted by the *ClearSy* enterprise was put under test. The groups of diverse components executed by our tool are presented below. The groups were divided considering the language structure exercised with the B component.

- The "Clauses" group, with 14 examples, exercises the sees, extends, constants, constraints, imports, promotes, sets, variables and operations. These elements are tested both in groups and separately. The tests observe the changes that each element can perform in the predicate.
- The "Operation Call" group, with 26 examples in different contexts exercises operation calls.
- The "Depth blocks" group, with 89 examples, is sensitive to the if-else, case, skip, while, and assignment instructions. They are grouped and nested to the maximum depth of three.
- The "Industrial project" group, with one big example, is responsible for different contributions to the *BTestBox*, with non-previously tested B syntactic structures. Unfortunately, the tests generated for this case are very time-consuming due to the necessity of set expansions.

All the presented implementations, excluding the "Industrial project", were performed with all the coverage criteria supported by the *BTestBox*. Although contributing to the development of our tool, the industrial project was not able to be fully tested under the *BTestBox* approach because some implementations contain unsupported elements. The current data structures and the elements supported are: *arithmetic operators*; *logical operators*; *sets operators* and *vectors*.

One goal for the development of our tool is to check the scalability of our proposal. To do this, large B files were analysed and metrics were registered. A variety of lexical elements of the B language were created with nested instructions. They were designed to test the scalability of a B translator to LLVM [16]. Those files may be classified by the number of nesting in the body of the operations. The results are shown in Table 1. We initially used a computer with the Windows 10 64 bits operating system, with an Intel Core i56300HQ 2.300 GHz processor with four cores and 8 GB of RAM for the scalability tests. To improve the results, we implemented threads inside the tool. This way, *BTestBox* can run parallelize several steps of it process, and run various operations of one implementation at the same time. This severally reduces the time needed for solving the predicate. In Table 1, it is possible to observe the results of tests performed using a computer with two Intel Xeon Sixteen-Core E5-2698v3 2.300 GHz CPUs allocating with a maximum of 20 cores and 80 GB of RAM. The processing time was reduced approximately by ten times. All of the examples shown in Table 1 can be easily executed in a leased cloud computer (one compute-optimised virtual machines with 20 dedicated vCPUs for one hour) costing less than one US dollar with similar results. Our experiments have shown that processing time is reduced approximately proportionally when we use a computer with more processing cores.

Table 1. Implementations for scalability

Component	Quantity of operations	Execution time with 4 cores	Execution time with 20 cores	Reduced time for evaluation
COMP_1seq1	39	587 s	38 s	93%
COMP_2seq1	199	3102 s	176 s	94%
COMP_3seq1	999	18214 s	2286 s	87%

4   Related Work

Generating test cases from models is a subject that has been studied by research groups for several years. The work [19] contains an interesting systematic review about testing a software system by using a test model of its behaviour, and was useful to our work. Another important work is [13]. Its authors showed a new overview of the current state of the art for model-based testing tools that use requirement-based specification languages. They quote two tools compatible with the B method: ProTest [17] and BZ-TT [2].

BZ-TT contains an environment for boundary-value test generation from Z and B specifications. This tool relies on constraint solving, and its goal is to test every operation of the system in every reachable boundary state. A boundary state is a system state in which at least one of the state variables has a maximum or minimum boundary value. It is not open source, and its last public news was in the year of 2003.

ProB is a tool with support to generate tests from B models. It has an automatic test environment for B specifications and a component called ProTest. Its component uses model-checking techniques to find test sequences that satisfy its test generation parameters. The user has to define the requirements to be satisfied by the test cases. These requirements are operations that must be covered and predicates that must hold true at the end of each test case. The tool only generates abstract test cases that have to be implemented before they can be executed. *BTestBox* is capable of generating executable test scripts. That is an advantage.

BETA [14] generates test code using input space partitioning and logical coverage criteria. It also automates the generation of tests and supports several coverage criteria. The generated tests are based on abstract B models, and some important information about the model are ignored. Information ignored by *BETA* may generate inaccurate tests related to the B concrete model. Differently, *BTestBox* generates test cases directly from a B concrete model, yielding to a closer representation of the software. Another relevant difference is that *BETA* is focused on unit testing, while *BTestBox* performs both unit and module tests. Furthermore, initial experiments of *BTestBox* [7,16] show that the tool may have good scalability properties. This was supported by generating some massive, random tests that were successfully handled by an initial version of the tool.

5   Conclusions and Future Work

Currently, *BTestBox* is a free and open-source tool under Berkeley-licensed software. This tool was born from an international collaboration between academia and software industry. The collaboration resulted in an initial version of the tool. Now, the goal is to increase *BTestBox*'s maturity to deal with industrial applications. The software is in continuous development. We believe that the tool offers an important contribution to the community.

Several components were created with different B syntactic structures to test *BTestBox*'s functionality and correctness. More than 120 concrete B models were created to test the B language translator, and one model, simulating a real used B program, was provided by *ClearSy*. *BTestBox* is already capable of generating tests that verify MC/DC. Our tool is capable of generating tests to verify the Combinatorial Coverage [4]. Since it demands the test of all possible combinations of guards, achieving CoC implies in being successful at MC/DC.

The *BTestBox* current implementation assumes that the program being tested always terminates. We are currently studying alternative approaches to deal with non-terminating programs. These alternatives include the use of time-outs and the treatment of execution logs. Since *BTestBox* uses B translators, if the translator has any limitation with respect to B language then it is also applied to our tool. However, there are several B translators available, and the *BTestBox*'s approach is compatible with all of them. Because the generated tests are also represented in B then there is only one version of our tool for all translators.

Significant improvements were developed in the tool, thus offering excellent results. The parallelisation techniques applied reduced the process time and extended the power to generate tests for larger samples. We also configured the tool to run it on a remote computer with more processor cores. This improvement required changes that made our tool compatible with the most common operating systems (Windows, OS X and Linux). All recent advances presented here are encouraging, showing performance numbers that are one order of magnitude better than for the previous version of the tool.

Acknowledgement. The work is partly supported by the IFRN, the UFRN, the ClearSy and High Performance Computing Center at UFRN (NPAD/UFRN). This study was financed in part by the Coordenação de Aperfeiçoamento de Pessoal de Nível Superior - Brasil (CAPES) - Finance Code 001.

References

1. Abrial, J.: The B-Book - Assigning Programs to Meanings. Cambridge University Press, Cambridge (2005)
2. Ambert, F., et al.: BZ-TT: a tool-set for test generation from Z and B using constraint logic programming. In: Proceedings of FATES 2002, pp. 105–120 (2002)
3. Ammann, P., Offutt, J.: Introduction to Software Testing. Cambridge University Press, Cambridge (2008)
4. Ammann, P., Offutt, J., Huang, H.: Coverage criteria for logical expressions. In: 14th International Symposium on Software Reliability Engineering, ISSRE 2003, pp. 99–107. IEEE (2003)
5. Bonichon, R., Déharbe, D., Lecomte, T., Medeiros Jr., V.: LLVM-based code generation for B. In: Braga, C., Martí-Oliet, N. (eds.) SBMF 2014. LNCS, vol. 8941, pp. 1–16. Springer, Cham (2015). https://doi.org/10.1007/978-3-319-15075-8_1
6. Dalal, S.R., et al.: Model-based testing in practice. In: Proceedings of the 21st International Conference on Software Engineering, pp. 285–294. ACM (1999)
7. Déharbe, D., Azevedo, D., Matos, E.C.B., de Medeiros Jr., V.: BtestBox: an automatic test generator for B method. In: VII Congresso Brasileiro de Software: Teoria e Prática (CBSOFT 2016) - Sessão de ferramentas, pp. 81–88 (2016)
8. Dijkstra, E.W.: A Discipline of Programming, vol. 1. Prentice-Hall, Englewood Cliffs (1976)
9. Clearsy System Engineering: Atelier B User Manual. Aix-en-Provence (1996)
10. Hoare, C.A.R.: Proof of correctness of data representations. In: Broy, M., Denert, E. (eds.) Software Pioneers, pp. 385–396. Springer, Heidelberg (2002). https://doi.org/10.1007/978-3-642-59412-0_24
11. Leroy, X.: Formal verification of a realistic compiler. Commun. ACM **52**(7), 107–115 (2009)

12. Leuschel, M.: User manual - prob documentation (2017). https://www3.hhu.de/stups/prob/index.php/User_Manual
13. Marinescu, R., Seceleanu, C., Le Guen, H., Pettersson, P.: A research overview of tool-supported model-based testing of requirements-based designs. In: Advances in Computers, vol. 98, pp. 89–140. Elsevier (2015)
14. de Matos, E.C.B., Moreira, A.M.: BETA: a B based testing approach. In: Gheyi, R., Naumann, D. (eds.) SBMF 2012. LNCS, vol. 7498, pp. 51–66. Springer, Heidelberg (2012). https://doi.org/10.1007/978-3-642-33296-8_6
15. Medeiros Jr., V.: Método B e a síntese verificada para código de montagem. Ph.D. thesis, UFRN, Federal University of Rio Grande do Norte, Natal (2016)
16. Moreira, A.M., Hentz, C., Déharbe, D., de Matos, E.C.B., Neto, J.B.S., de Medeiros, V.: Verifying code generation tools for the B-method using tests: a case study. In: Blanchette, J.C., Kosmatov, N. (eds.) TAP 2015. LNCS, vol. 9154, pp. 76–91. Springer, Cham (2015). https://doi.org/10.1007/978-3-319-21215-9_5
17. Satpathy, M., Leuschel, M., Butler, M.: ProTest: an automatic test environment for B specifications. ENTCS **111**, 113–136 (2005)
18. Schneider, S.: The B-Method: An Introduction. Palgrave, Basingstoke (2001)
19. Shafique, M.: Systematic review of state based model based testing tools. Ph.D. thesis, Carleton University Ottawa (2010)

Predicting and Testing Latencies with Deep Learning: An IoT Case Study

Bernhard K. Aichernig[1], Franz Pernkopf[2], Richard Schumi[1(✉)], and Andreas Wurm[2]

[1] Institute of Software Technology, Graz University of Technology, Graz, Austria
{aichernig,rschumi}@ist.tugraz.at
[2] Signal Processing and Speech Communication Lab, Graz University of Technology, Graz, Austria
pernkopf@tugraz.at, awurm@student.tugraz.at

Abstract. The Internet of things (IoT) is spreading into the everyday life of millions of people. However, the quality of the underlying communication technologies is still questionable. In this work, we are analysing the performance of an implementation of MQTT, which is a major communication protocol of the IoT. We perform model-based test-case generation to generate log data for training a neural network. This neural network is applied to predict latencies depending on different features, like the number of active clients. The predictions are integrated into our initial functional model, and we exploit the resulting timed model for statistical model checking. This allows us to answer questions about the expected performance for various usage scenarios. The benefit of our approach is that it enables a convenient extension of a functional model with timing aspects using deep learning. A comparison to our previous work with linear regression shows that deep learning needs less manual effort in data preprocessing and provides significantly better predictions.

Keywords: Statistical model checking · Model-based testing · Neural networks · Performance · Latency · Internet of things · MQTT · EMQ

1 Introduction

In recent years, the Internet of things (IoT) is becoming increasingly popular, especially since smart homes are now a major topic for end-users. However, some of the key technologies of the IoT, like its underlying protocols, are still often implemented with a questionable reliability or performance, and should be tested more thoroughly. For example, one major machine-to-machine messaging protocol of the IoT, called message queuing telemetry transport (MQTT) has been implemented several times, but it is an open question, which implementation performs best in a given setting.

MQTT follows a publish-subscribe pattern and allows clients, e.g., sensors in a smart home, to distribute messages by sending them to a central server, called

ⓒ Springer Nature Switzerland AG 2019
D. Beyer and C. Keller (Eds.): TAP 2019, LNCS 11823, pp. 93–111, 2019.
https://doi.org/10.1007/978-3-030-31157-5_7

the *broker* [11]. In recent work [7], we learned latency distributions via linear regression, in order to perform a model-based performance analysis of MQTT broker implementations.

In contrast to previous performance studies [19,29,34,46], we present a statistical model checking (SMC) approach that exploits a neural network for determining the expected latencies for various usage scenarios.

SMC [1] is a simulation-based method that can answer both, quantitative and qualitative questions. These questions are expressed as properties of a stochastic model which are checked by analysing simulations of this model.

Our method is realised with a property-based testing (PBT) tool that (1) generates log data including latencies of simultaneous MQTT messages for training our neural network, (2) simulates our timed models, and (3) supports the evaluation of our simulation results by directly testing a broker. PBT [18] is a random testing technique that tries to falsify a given property. Properties describe the expected behaviour of a system-under-test (SUT) and may be algebraic or model-based. A PBT tool generates inputs and checks if the property holds.

Previously, we had integrated SMC into a PBT tool [6] to check stochastic models as well as implementations. With this technique, we evaluated the expected response time of an industrial web application [2,44], and we also analysed the latencies of MQTT brokers [7]. Now, we build upon this work and enhance our performance analysis approach with a deep learning method that supports a higher degree of automation, because it allows us to omit preprocessing steps.

Figure 1 illustrates our method: (1) we automatically test a broker with multiple clients and record its latencies in log files. For every client, we run a model-based testing process concurrently and generate test cases from a functional model. (2) We train a neural network with the log data to learn the latencies depending on various log features, like the number of active message exchanges. The resulting neural network enables the prediction of latencies for the selected features. It can also be represented as a function that takes the feature values as input and returns an estimator for the latency. We integrate it into our functional model to build a stochastic timed automata (STA) [10] model. (3) For simulating the behaviour of real MQTT clients, we add usage profiles, containing probabilities and waiting times related to messages. (4) We perform SMC on the resulting stochastic model to answer the question: "What is the probability that the message latency is under a certain threshold?". This process can be accelerated by using a virtual time scale, i.e., a fraction of real time. (5) Additionally, we check if our predictions are close to the real probabilities of the broker implementations. For this evaluation, we again apply SMC, but this time we only check fewer samples, since executing a real system is costly.

Related Work. In contrast to our work, classical load testing methods analyse the performance directly on the SUT. Models are mostly used for test-case generation [9] and for modelling user populations [21,41]. Others focus solely on simulation on the model-level [12,14,16,37]. In our work, we exploit the models for both, testing a system as well as simulating the performance on the model.

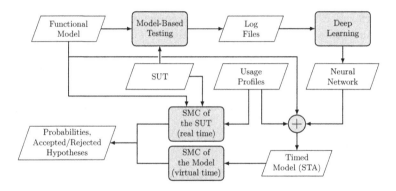

Fig. 1. Overview of the data flow of our method.

The most related tool is UPPAAL SMC [15], because it supports SMC and test-case generation. However, our use of PBT facilitates the definition of specialized generators for complex test-data, which is important for load testing. Furthermore, modelling in a programming language may be more acceptable to programmers and testers.

There are related approaches [25, 42, 47] that are also concerned with learning timed models. In contrast to them, we learn timings and add them to existing functional models, and we perform deep learning instead of automata learning.

The performance of MQTT implementations has been tested in the past [19, 34, 46], but without constructing a performance model for simulating MQTT under different usage scenarios. The most similar work to ours [29] modelled MQTT with probabilistic timed automata and checked performance with SMC. However, they did not validate their model against real implementations, and hence, it did not include real timing behaviour.

To the best of our knowledge our work is novel: we are the first who apply SMC to the performance analysis of MQTT brokers with latencies that were learned by training a neural network.

Note, we reused contents from the theses from Schumi [43] and Wurm [49].

Contributions. This research extends our previous work [7], where we demonstrated our latency evaluation method for MQTT implementations. In particular, we present the following novel contributions: (1) we introduce a deep learning method in order to predict latencies from log data. The advantage of this method is that it supports a higher degree of automation compared to the linear regression that we previously applied. This also leads to more accurate performance predictions of our SMC methodology. (2) We evaluate our method in a more realistic environment. Previously, we ran the broker on the same machine as the clients, i.e., on a server with sufficient hardware resources. For this work, we ran the broker in a virtual machine with limited CPU power, because we wanted to be close to realistic smart home setups, where the broker is often running on a low budget computer, like a Raspberry Pi. (3) We present a comparison of our deep learning method to linear regression, and show how the resulting timed models perform. Finally, we evaluate the accuracy of both prediction methods with measurements of the real implementation.

Structure. First, Sect. 2 introduces the background of SMC, PBT, STA, and deep learning based on our previous work [6,7,43,49] Next, in Sect. 3 we give an example and demonstrate our method. Then, Sect. 4 presents an evaluation with an open-source MQTT implementation. Finally, we conclude in Sect. 5.

2   Background

2.1   Statistical Model Checking (SMC)

SMC is a verification method for checking qualitative and quantitative properties of a stochastic model or system. These properties are usually defined with (temporal) logics. In order to answer questions like "What is the probability that the model satisfies a property?" or "Is the probability that the model satisfies a property above or below a certain threshold?", a statistical model checker produces samples, i.e., random walks on the stochastic model and checks whether the property holds for these samples. Various SMC algorithms are applied in order to compute the total number of samples needed to find an answer for a specific question, or to compute a stopping criterion. This criterion determines when we can stop sampling, because we have found an answer with a required certainty. In this work, we focus on the following algorithm, because it enables a probability estimation with a certain accuracy [35,36].

Monte Carlo simulation with Chernoff-Hoeffding bound. The algorithm computes the required number of simulations n in order to estimate the probability γ that a stochastic model satisfies a Boolean property. The procedure is based on the Chernoff-Hoeffding bound [28] that provides a lower limit for the probability that the estimation error is below a value ϵ. Assuming a confidence $1 - \delta$ the required number of simulations is $n \geq 1/(2\epsilon^2) \ln(2/\delta)$.

The n simulations represent Bernoulli random variables $X_1, \ldots, X_n$ with outcome $x_i = 1$ if the property holds for the i-th simulation run and $x_i = 0$ otherwise. Let the estimated probability be $\bar{\gamma}_n = (\sum_{i=1}^{n} x_i)/n$, then the probability that the estimation error is below ϵ is greater than our required confidence. Formally we have: $Pr(|\bar{\gamma}_n - \gamma| \leq \epsilon) \geq 1 - \delta$. After the calculation of the number of required samples n, a standard Monte Carlo simulation is performed [36].

2.2   Property-Based Testing (PBT)

PBT is a random-testing technique that aims to check the correctness of properties. A property is a high-level specification of the expected behaviour of a function- or system-under-test that should always hold. With PBT, inputs can be generated automatically by applying data generators, e.g., a random list generator. The inputs are fed to the function or system-under-test and the property is evaluated. If it holds, then this indicates that the function or system works as expected, otherwise a counterexample is produced.

One of the key features of PBT is its support for model-based testing. Models encoded as extended finite state machines (EFSMs) [31] can serve as sources for state-machine properties. An EFSM is a 6-tuple (S, s_0, V, I, O, T). S is a finite set of states, $s_0 \in S$ is the initial state, V is a finite set of variables, I is a finite set of inputs, O is a finite set of outputs, T is a finite set of transitions. A transition $t \in T$ can be described as a 6-tuple (s_s, i, g, op, o, s_t), s_s is the source state, i is an input, g is a guard, op is a sequence of assignment operations, o is an output, s_t is the target state [31].

In order to create a state-machine property for an EFSM, we have to write a specification comprising the initial state, commands, and a generator for the next transition given the current state of the model. Commands encapsulate (1) preconditions that define the permitted transition sequences, (2) postconditions that specify the expected behaviour, and (3) execution semantics of transitions for the model and the SUT. A state-machine property states that for all permitted transition sequences, the postcondition must hold after the execution of each command [30,39]. Simplified, such properties can be defined as follows:

$$cmd.runModel, cmd.runActual : S \times I \rightarrow S \times O$$
$$cmd.pre : I \times S \rightarrow Boolean, cmd.post : (S \times O) \times (S \times O) \rightarrow Boolean$$
$$\forall s \in S, i \in I, cmd \in Cmds :$$
$$cmd.pre(i, s) \implies cmd.post(cmd.runModel(i, s), cmd.runActual(i, s))$$

We have two functions to execute a command on the model and on the SUT: $cmd.runModel$ and $cmd.runActual$. The precondition $cmd.pre$ defines the valid inputs for a command. The postcondition $cmd.post$ compares the outputs and states of the model and the SUT after the execution of a command.

PBT is a powerful testing technique that allows a flexible definition of generators and properties via inheritance or composition. The first implementation of PBT was QuickCheck for Haskell [18]. Numerous reimplementations followed for other programming languages. We use FsCheck[1] for C#.

2.3   Integration of SMC into PBT

Recently, we have demonstrated that SMC can be integrated into a PBT tool in order to perform SMC of PBT properties [6]. With this approach, we can verify stochastic models, like in classical SMC, as well as stochastic implementations. For the integration, we introduced our own new SMC properties that take a PBT property, configurations for the PBT execution, and parameters for the specific SMC algorithm as input. Then, our properties perform an SMC

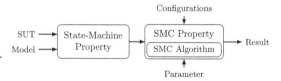

Fig. 2. Data flow diagram of an SMC property.

---

[1] https://fscheck.github.io/FsCheck

Algorithm 1 Pseudo code of the ChernoffProperty.

Input: *prop*: PBT property, *config*: PBT configuration, ϵ: required error bound, δ: confidence parameter

1: **function** QUICKCHECK
2:   $n \leftarrow \left\lceil \frac{1}{2\epsilon^2} \log \frac{2}{\delta} \right\rceil$ ▷ Calculate the required number of samples
3:   $passCnt \leftarrow 0$ ▷ Counter for the passed property checks
4:   **for** $i \leftarrow 1$ to n **do**
5:     **if** $prop.Check(config)$ **then**
6:       $passCnt \leftarrow passCnt + 1$ ▷ Increase pass counter
7:   **return** $passCnt/n$

---

algorithm by utilizing the PBT tool as simulation environment, and they return either a quantitative or qualitative result, depending on the algorithm. Figure 2 illustrates how we evaluate a PBT state-machine property within an SMC property. The state-machine property requires a model and an SUT in order to perform PBT as explained above. The SMC property then uses this PBT state-machine property to produce samples according to the PBT configuration. The samples and also parameters are needed for the specific SMC algorithm, which produces the quantitative or qualitative result.

Algorithm 1 shows the pseudo code of a *ChernoffProperty*, which performs a Monte Carlo simulation with Chernoff-Hoeffding bound as described in Sect. 2.1. The inputs of this algorithm are a PBT property *prop*, configurations for PBT *config*, an error bound ϵ and a parameter for the confidence δ. First, the algorithm computes the required number of samples with a specified accuracy given by ϵ and δ. Then, we initialise a counter for the number of passing samples *passCnt*. Next, we run a for-loop that creates samples with the specified number of samples. The actual evaluation is done with the *Check* method of the PBT property, which takes the *config* object as input and generates a sample. The method returns true, if the property was fulfilled and false otherwise. In the case that it was true, we increase the counter for the passed samples. Finally, after the desired number of samples was evaluated, the result is the value of this counter divided by the total number of samples.

2.4   Stochastic Timed Automata

Several probabilistic extensions of timed automata [8] have been proposed. Here, we follow the definition of stochastic timed automata (STA) by Ballarini et al. [10]: an STA is a tuple $(L, l_0, A, C, I, E, F, W)$ comprising a classical timed automaton (L, l_0, A, C, I, E), probability density functions (PDFs) $F = (f_l)_{l \in L}$ for the sojourn time, and natural weights $W = (w_e)_{e \in E}$ for the edges. L is a finite set of locations, $l_0 \in L$ is the initial location, A is a finite set of actions, C is a finite set of clocks with valuations $u(c) \in \mathbb{R}_{>0}$, $I : L \mapsto \mathcal{B}(C)$ is a finite set of invariants for the locations and $E \subseteq L \times A \times \mathcal{B}(C) \times 2^C \times L$ is a finite set of edges between locations, with an action, a guard and a set of clock resets.

The transition relation can be described as follows. For a state given by the pair (l, u), where l is a location and u a clock valuation $u \in C \rightarrow \mathbb{R}_{\geq 0}$, the PDF f_l is used to choose the sojourn time d, which changes the state to

$(l, u + d)$, where we lift the plus operator to the clock valuation as follows: $u + d =_{def} \{c \mapsto u(c) + d \mid c \in C\}$. After this change, an edge e is selected out of the set of enabled edges $E(l, u + d)$ with the probability $w_e / \sum_{h \in E(l, u+d)} w_h$. Then, a transition to the target location l' of e and $u' = u + d$ is performed. For our models the underlying stochastic process is a semi-Markov process, since the clocks are reset at every transition, but we do not assume exponential waiting times, and therefore, the process is not a standard continuous-time Markov chain.

2.5 Deep Learning

Deep neural networks (DNNs) consist of artificial neurons arranged in multiple layers and each layer is connected to its preceding layer. DNNs are inspired by biology and capable of processing complex dependencies in data [13, 20, 24, 33]. An artificial neuron is based on one or more inputs x_i and a corresponding weight w_i, a bias b and an *activation function* (or transfer function). It can be mathematically described as $a = b + \sum_i^m x_i w_i = \boldsymbol{w}^T \boldsymbol{x}$ for m features using w_0 forf b. After applying the activation function $f(\cdot)$, we obtain the output (or activation) z of the neuron, which is $z = f(a) = f(\boldsymbol{w}^T \boldsymbol{x})$. Note that lowercase bold symbols such as $\boldsymbol{w}$ denote vectors and the transpose is denoted by a superscript T. Bold uppercase symbols such as $\boldsymbol{X}$ are used for matrices.

The layers are structured in one input layer, multiple hidden layers, and one output layer. The input layer is the first layer of the network and processes the input $\boldsymbol{X}$, a $n \times m$ matrix consisting of n samples, where each sample is represented by m features. The output layer is the last layer and produces the results for the dependent variable (or target variable) $\boldsymbol{y}$. For regression analysis, this layer only consists of one neuron with linear activation function.

Activation functions are monotonic functions and have to be derivable so they can be used in backpropagation for training the neural network. In this work, we used the rectified linear unit (ReLU) activation function. It is defined as $f(a) = \max(0, a)$ and ranges from 0 to infinity. The ReLU function usually leads to better results than other activation functions [23].

Backpropagation. Training, also referred to as (deep) learning, with backpropagation is split into a forward and a backward step. The forward step is identical to a prediction and processes the input through the network and calculates the output. The backward step calculates the error by comparing the output of the network y_i to the target value t_i, propagates it back and updates the parameters of the network. The loss function J we are using is the mean squared error (MSE) function multiplied by the factor $\frac{1}{2}$ (to simplify the derivation), i.e., $J_{MSE} = \frac{1}{2n} \sum_i^n (y_i - t_i)^2 = \frac{1}{2n} \sum_i^n e_i^2$. The derivative of the squared error function J, with respect to w_{jk} being the weight between the neurons j and k, is $\frac{\partial J}{\partial w_{jk}} = \frac{\partial J}{\partial z_k} \frac{\partial z_k}{\partial a_k} \frac{\partial a_k}{\partial w_{jk}} = \delta_k z_j$, where $\delta_k = \frac{\partial f_k(a_k)}{\partial a_k} e_k$ if k is an output neuron and $\delta_k = \frac{\partial f_k(a_k)}{\partial a_k} \sum_l \delta_l w_{kl}$ with $l \in L$ (all subsequent neurons of k), if k is a hidden neuron. Gradient descent is applied to update the weight w_{jk}. With the learning rate η, the change of the weight is defined as $\Delta w_{jk} = -\eta \delta_k z_j$. The standard gradient descent update step can be extended with other parameters as in the *ADAM* (Adaptive Moment Estimation) optimizer [32].

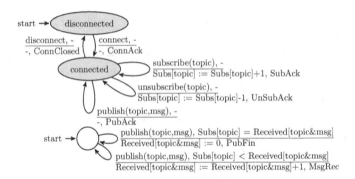

Fig. 3. Functional model for an MQTT client.

Model Evaluation. To evaluate and compare results of different models we use the MSE or R^2 value [38]. R^2 is a measure for the goodness of a fit. A value of 1 denotes a perfect fit, while a value of 0 indicates a bad fit and occurs when the model estimates the mean of the dependent variable. Using the residual sum of squares (RSS) and the total sum of squares (TSS), it is computed as $R^2 = 1 - \frac{\text{RSS}}{\text{TSS}} = 1 - \frac{\sum_i^n (y_i - t_i)^2}{\sum_i^n (t_i - \bar{t})^2}$, with the mean value of the target variable $\bar{t}$.

3   Method

In this section, we show how we derive timed models from logs and how we can apply these models to simulate stochastic usage profiles.

Model-Based Testing. Our SUT is an MQTT broker that allows clients to connect/disconnect, subscribe/unsubscribe to topics and publish messages for such topics. Each of these actions can be performed with a corresponding control message, which is defined by the MQTT standard [11]. We treat the broker as a black box and test it from a client's perspective.

The upper state machine in Fig. 3 represents the messages that we test. This state machine was constructed manually and is inspired by a previous work [45], where we applied active automata learning for Mealy machines of MQTT implementations. We run multiple of these state machines concurrently to produce log data that includes latencies for simultaneous messages of several clients. Each transition of the state machine is labelled with an input i, an optional guard g / optional assignment operations op, and an output o. Some transition inputs are parametrised with generated data, e.g., a topic for *subscribe*. We apply PBT generators to produce inputs and their required data. Previously, we have demonstrated the data generation for such functional models and also model-based testing [4,5]. To keep it simple, we assume that a client can only subscribe to topics to which it did not subscribe before (the same for unsubscribe).

For managing the subscriptions, we have a global map *Subs* that stores the subscription numbers per topic. This map is needed when publishing, because we check if the number of received messages corresponds to the number of subscribed

Table 1. Example log data excerpt of the Erlang MQTT broker EMQ.

Msg	#ActiveMsgs	#TotalSubs	TopicSize	MsgSize	#Subs	#Receivers	Latency [ms]
connect	69	144	-	-	-	-	1347.88
subscribe	70	184	14	-	-	-	1015.58
subscribe	71	199	14	-	-	-	814.01
publish	71	205	14	52	1	1	319.88

clients. In order to perform this check, we have a second state machine (Fig. 3 bottom) that represents the message receivers. This machine stores the number of received messages in a map *Received* that takes the topic concatenated with the message as key. The map is updated for each message receiver, and when all messages were delivered, then a *PubFin* output is produced. For simplicity, we omit some assignment operations, e.g., for a subscriptions set.

Based on this functional model, we perform model-based testing with a PBT tool, which generates random test cases that are executed on an MQTT broker. During this testing phase, we capture the latencies of messages in a log file. Note that the latency is the duration that a client must wait until it receives a response to a sent message from the broker or until the message is delivered to all receivers in case of a *publish*.

Example log data from the MQTT broker EMQ is presented in Table 1. It shows that we record the message type (*Msg*), the number of active clients or open message exchanges (*#ActiveMsgs*), the total number of subscriptions (*#TotalSubs*), the size of a topic (*TopicSize*) and message string (*MsgSize*), the number of subscribers for a topic when a *publish* occurs (*#Subs*), the number of receivers of a published message (*#Receivers*), and the latency.

Initially, we had a larger set of 21 features, because the optimal set of features for predicting the latency was not obvious. Hence, we recorded various attributes which potentially affect the latency, such as the time when a message was sent, the message ID, the number of open message exchanges at the moment a message was sent and when a response was observed. Furthermore, some features represented the memory usage of the broker and exception messages. However, most of these features did not show sufficient influence on the latency, i.e., they only had a minor or no correlation. Therefore, we focus on the most relevant features shown in Table 1.

For this initial logging phase, the available transitions in the current state of the functional model are chosen with a uniform distribution. In the *disconnected* state, the only choice is a *connect* message and in the *connected* state all other messages are selected with equal frequency. We do not apply any sojourn times between sending messages in this phase, since we want to capture latencies in situations with a high number of concurrent messages. We collected log data by running 100 test cases with a random number of clients (3–100) and a length of 50 messages. This produced log files with about 300,000 entries and required about one hour.

We also performed more extensive test runs with more test cases and clients. However, this larger test data did not show a significant difference and a larger number of clients led to an increased number of timeouts. Although predicting the probability of timeouts might also be interesting, it is not the focus of this work. Our aim is to maximise the satisfaction of the clients or users. Hence, we are primarily interested in the latencies under normal operating conditions.

Training the Neural Network. In previous work [7], we showed that multiple linear regression can be applied to learn latency distributions of MQTT brokers. To achieve an accurate model, we had to perform extensive feature analysis and preprocessing. First, we checked if we can find any bias in our logs. Then, we removed log entries with disproportionately long latencies (the top 5% per message type). Next, we only selected features that have a significant influence on the target variable, using the Pearson correlation coefficient [40]. Additionally, we checked if certain features only affect specific message types, which can, e.g., be resolved by setting these features to zero for this message.

Now, we learn the latencies using deep neural networks (DNNs). The neural network has the advantage, that we only need to perform a minimum of preprocessing. Deep learning produces a regression model that describes the relationship of the log variables (or features) with the target variable, i.e., the latency.

Before we train a neural network, the minimum amount of preprocessing is performed to increase the quality of the data. First, we remove unsuccessful events, which failed because of timeouts or exceptions. Then, we use the *1-of-K scheme* (also one-hot encoding) [13] to convert the categorical variable *Msg* into binary indicator variables. Afterwards, the input features are scaled using a Min-Max scaler, which transforms the features to values between 0 and 1, i.e.,

$$x_{i,\text{scaled}} = \frac{x_i - \min_{j=1,\ldots,n}(x_{ij})}{\max_{j=1,\ldots,n}(x_{ij}) - \min_{j=1,\ldots,n}(x_{ji})}$$

Next, the dataset is shuffled and split into a training and validation set, using 10-fold cross-validation, in order to prevent overfitting [26]. As input features for the final model we select *Msg*, *#ActiveMsgs* and *#Subs*. The features *TopicSize* and *MsgSize* are omitted, because they are kept constant in our experiments. We also remove *#Receivers* as it is redundant with *#Subs*. Furthermore, *#TotalSubs* is the accumulated sum of all subscriptions on the brokers and not relevant in the conducted experiments. To train the neural network, we use MSE as loss function and the ADAM optimizer with default parameters provided in [32].

Our DNN architectures consist of up to 10 densely connected layers (with $6 - 512$ neurons each), ReLU activation functions and linear activations in the output layer. The weights are initialised using the Glorot uniform initialiser [22]. We also used long short-term memory networks [27] and gated recurrent units [17], but they do show advantages in terms of R^2 and the execution time is worse. The best results were achieved using DNNs with three hidden layers, with 265, 128 and 64 neurons. The trained model is then exported and used in SMC as a function *latency* that takes *Msg*, *#ActiveMsgs* and *#Subs* as arguments and returns the predicted latency:

$$latency : Msg \times \mathbb{N}_{>0} \times \mathbb{N}_{\geq 0} \to \mathbb{R}.$$

```
MinTimeBetwMsg:  0,  MaxTimeBetwMsg:  500,
MsgWeights:{connect:  1,  disconnect:  1,  publish:  5,  subscribe:  3,  unsubscribe:  2}
```

Listing 1.1. Usage profile with time bounds and weights for messages.

Statistical Model Checking. In order to apply SMC for a realistic usage scenario, we introduce usage profiles that describe the behaviour of a client, i.e., how long it should wait between sending messages, and with what probabilities it should send certain messages. An example usage profile is shown in Listing 1.1. The time between messages is selected uniformly inside the bounds [MinTimeBetwMsg, MaxTimeBetwMsg] and we have weights that define the message frequency. This usage profile is added to the functional model and also the neural network that we trained with our log data is integrated via its function representation. This gives us a combined timed model in the form of a stochastic timed automaton, as explained in Sect. 2.4 and illustrated in Fig. 4.

In this model, the *connected* and *disconnected* locations have a uniform distribution given by an upper and lower bound $[a, b]$. These bounds come from our usage profile. All other locations also have such intervals, but with the difference that they have the same upper and lower bound z. The reason is that these locations should apply a concrete delay that was produced by our neural network within the *latency* function. In contrast to the functional model, these additional locations simulate the timing behaviour of a message by applying the learned latencies. These locations have one incoming edge that represents sending a message and an outgoing edge for the response.

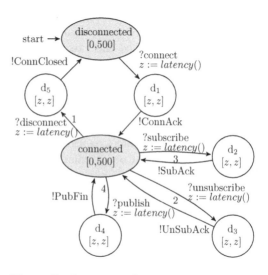

Fig. 4. Stochastic timed automaton for the timing behaviour of an MQTT client.

Moreover, the weights w_e from our usage profile are added to the transitions for sending messages. Note that we have omitted the parameters of the *latency* function and also assignments for these parameters for brevity.

With such a stochastic timed automata model, we can evaluate the performance dependent on a usage profile, and we can simulate a complete MQTT setup by running multiple models concurrently. A run of the model can be defined as: $(l_0, u_0) \xrightarrow{d_1, a_1} (l_1, u_1) \xrightarrow{d_2, a_2} \ldots$ and it produces a test case (d_1, a_1), $(d_2, a_2), \ldots$, where d_i is a delay and $a_i \in A$. An example test case of length 2 looks like this: *(83, ?connect), (493, !ConAck), (212, ?subscribe)(309, !SubAck).*

While we execute the model, we can check properties to answer questions, like "What is the probability that the latency of each interaction of a client within a given MQTT setup is under a certain threshold?". In order to estimate this probability, we perform a Monte Carlo simulation with Chernoff-Hoeffding bound. Running this evaluation with a high accuracy requires many samples, which becomes quickly infeasible on a slow SUT. Hence, we conduct this simulation on our model, because we can accelerate its execution by applying a virtual time that is a fraction of real time. For example, predicting the probability that the message latency for a client within an MQTT setup with 70 clients is under a threshold of 1.4 s with parameters $\epsilon = 0.05$ and $\delta = 0.01$, requires 1060 samples and returns a probability of 0.63, when a test-case length of two is considered.

Previously [7], we have demonstrated how such predictions can be efficiently evaluated with the sequential probability ratio test [48], a form of hypotheses testing that we applied to directly evaluate the SUT. Such an evaluation is usually more efficient than a Monte Carlo simulation of the SUT, because we need fewer samples, since we can stop when there is sufficient evidence.

However, since this algorithm only gives us a yes or no answer and we are interested in a more detailed comparison, we perform a Monte Carlo simulation directly on the SUT in order to evaluate our prediction. This simulation is done with fewer samples since the execution of the SUT is costly and cannot be accelerated like the execution of the model. We perform this simulation with 100 samples, which is about 1/10 of the samples we used for the analysis of our model. When we evaluate the same question as before with the same number of clients and threshold, we obtain a probability of 0.56. This is close to our predicted probability of 0.63, i.e., it is within the error bound of the second simulation, which is about $\epsilon = 0.16$ when the same confidence is considered as before. This means that our prediction was quite accurate.

Implementation. Our method was implemented in a similar way, as described in our previous work [2,44], where we illustrated how timed models can be executed with PBT. Previously, we introduced custom generators for the simulation of response times, which work similarly for latencies. Moreover, we demonstrated the application of user profiles that work in the same way as our usage profiles, and we presented a test-case generation algorithm for PBT that can perform the initial model-based testing phase as well as the execution of our timed model. For brevity, we omit the details of the implementation.

4   Evaluation

We evaluated our method by applying it to an open-source MQTT implementations: EMQ 2.3.5, running with the default configurations and quality of service level one. We analyse our deep learning method by comparing it to our previously used linear regression, we assess the accuracy of both methods, and show how well the resulting timed models perform for our prediction with SMC.

Setting. The evaluation was performed on a Windows server (version 2008 R2) with a 2.1 GHz Intel Xeon E5-2620 v4 CPU with 8 Cores and 32 GB RAM. This machine was running the clients and the broker was running in a (VirtualBox) virtual machine on this server in order to avoid an influence of the network.

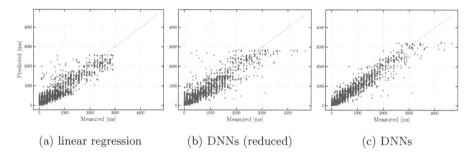

| (a) linear regression | (b) DNNs (reduced) | (c) DNNs |

Fig. 5. Comparison of measured and predicted latencies for linear regression and DNNs using the entire dataset with 7 features (see Table 1) and a reduced version with only 3 features.

This virtual machine was configured with 4 GB of RAM and with one CPU core that was scaled down to 5% of the CPU power in order to simulate a broker with a limited hardware, like a Raspberry Pi. Note that, a possible influence of the client processes on the broker might cause a threat to validity of our evaluation. To face this issue, we measured the CPU load, to make sure that it is no bottleneck. During the evaluation, the CPU load was below 60% most of the time, and there were only some rare peaks, where the CPU was over 90%. The RAM usage of the broker and of our test clients was insignificant.

We applied Visual Studio 2012 with .NET framework 4.5, NUnit 2.64, and FsCheck 2.92 in order to run the tests and for SMC. The library M2Mqtt[2] served as a client interface to facilitate the interaction with the brokers.

Evaluation of our DNNs. Compared to our previous approach, the multiple linear regression, deep learning performed significantly better in terms of R^2-value and at the same time required almost no effort in preprocessing. With deep learning we achieved an R^2-value of 0.9145 using all features of Table 1. When reducing the dataset to a smaller number of features (i.e., *Msg*, *#ActiveMsgs* and *#Subs*) we achieved a value of 0.8585. This was done because the resulting neural network was simple and robust. With the multiple linear regression we could only achieve a value of 0.6943, for the same three features, which we could improve to 0.8567 after extensive preprocessing. Table 2 gives a summary of our obtained R^2-values.

Figure 5 shows the predicted compared to the measured latency values of the multiple linear regression and deep learning with and without the feature set reduction. The diagonal dashed line represents a complete match between predicted and true values. It can be seen that for deep learning the data points are much closer to the diagonal line. Note that the values in Fig. 5a do not include all latency values, because of the removed outliers.

Fitting the multiple linear regression requires 285.1357 ms and a prediction needs 0.0176 ms on average, while the neural network requires 862609.8151 ms (14 min) to train and 0.8468 ms on average to predict. These experiments were

---

[2] https://m2mqtt.wordpress.com

Table 2. R^2-values for different feature sets and learning methods.

Method	Features	R^2-value
linear regression without preprocessing	*Msg, #ActiveMsgs, #Subs*	0.6943
linear regression with preprocessing	*Msg, #ActiveMsgs, #Subs*	0.8567
DNNs with 3 features	*Msg, #ActiveMsgs, #Subs*	0.8585
DNNs with 8 features	*Msg, #ActiveMsgs, #TotalSubs, TopicSize, MsgSize, publish, #Subs, #Receivers*	0.9145

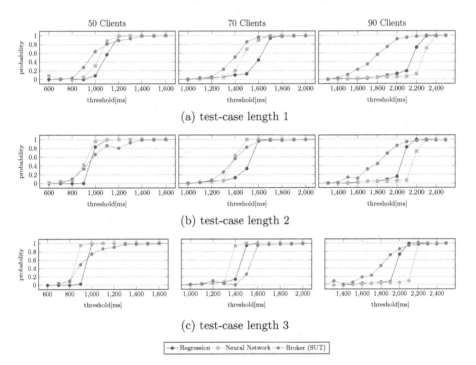

(a) test-case length 1

(b) test-case length 2

(c) test-case length 3

Fig. 6. Simulation results with 50, 70 & 90 clients for predictions with a regression, a neural network and the real prob. of the SUT for test-case length 1–3.

performed on a MacBook Pro with an Intel Core i5-6360U 2 GHz dual core CPU and 8 GB of RAM running macOS 10.14.1.

Evaluation of our timed model. Another important factor in addition to the quality of our neural network is how well the resulting timed model performs for our predictions with SMC. In order to analyse the accuracy of our model, we compare our predictions to the actual observations at the broker, and we show the difference to our previously applied linear regression method.

We perform this evaluation as explained in Sect. 3, in order to answer the question: "What is the probability that the latency of each interaction of a client within a given MQTT setup is under a certain threshold?". Hence, we check the probability that all messages within a sequence (of a given length) of a client within a certain MQTT setup have a latency under this threshold.

We checked various thresholds and different numbers of clients by following the steps of Sect. 3 and by using the same usage profile and timed model. Additionally, we tested another timed model with the difference that it included latency distributions that were learned via linear regression as explained in our previous work [7]. Both learning methods were applied to the same log data, which was produced with model-based testing as explained before.

As shown in Sect. 3, we apply a Monte Carlo simulation with Chernoff-Hoeffding bound with 1060 samples, to evaluate both timed models. Moreover, we apply a Monte Carlo simulation with 100 samples at the broker to analyse the accuracy of our predictions. The results are displayed in Fig. 6. It shows the probabilities for our given question for different numbers of clients (in the columns), different test-case lengths (in the rows), and various thresholds. For example, in the first graph (50 clients, test-case length 1), we can see that the probability of the broker starts to increase at 0.9 s and reaches probability one at about 1.4 s. The curves for the regression and neural network show a similar behaviour, but the points of the neural network are significantly closer to that of the broker. For instance, if we take a look at 1.1 s the probability of the broker is 0.8, the prediction with the neural network is 0.88, and with regression it was only 0.56. Hence, with deep learning we are close and well within the error bound as explained in Sect. 3 and the regression was not as accurate.

A decrease in the probability of our given question can also be observed in all other graphs, when the test-case length or the number of clients increases. It can be seen that the prediction with the neural network is closer to the observed probability than the regression in most cases with smaller client numbers. For 90 clients, we see that the regression is better. We believe the reason for this is that we did not have many log entries with high numbers of clients and the regression can make a better extrapolation based on the existing data. Moreover, we see that our prediction becomes worse, when the test-case length increases. This might be due to the variance of the latency, which becomes more decisive for longer test cases. Unfortunately, we did not include variance estimates of the latency in our deep learning method due to computational complexity limits. This will be discussed below.

Note that an advantage of the simulation on the model-level is that it runs much faster than on the SUT. With a virtual time of 1/10 of the actual time, we can perform simulations that would take days on the SUT within hours. The computation time for both our prediction is 3–8 min per data point depending on the number of client and test-case length. For the evaluation of the SUT, it is about 4–10 min. These times are similar, because we ran about 1/10 of the samples on the SUT and our models run 10 times faster.

In summary, it can be said that our deep learning method performed better in almost all cases with a small number of clients ($\leq$ 70), only for a higher number of clients the prediction with regression showed better results.

Discussion. The evaluation showed that our deep learning-based method allows us to predict the probability that a client can send a sequence of messages without having to wait longer than a certain threshold for a reply or for the delivery of the message. Moreover, we checked if the predicted probability is close to the real probability of the SUT. Although our results are promising, there are still limitations and threats to the validity that we want to discuss.

A threat to the validity of our prediction method could be that there are other deep learning approaches that might allow a more accurate prediction, because they can consider the variance of the latency and not only the mean. However, for our simulation-based method the complexity of the neural network was also an issue, because our aim was to perform a fast simulation. Hence, we select a standard neural network, because its prediction time was small enough for a fast simulation.

One could argue that our model-based method does not make sense, because we could just directly run our evaluations on a real system. We believe that our method is valuable, because it enables a fast model simulation with a virtual time, i.e., a fraction of real time. This allows us to evaluate much more scenarios than on a real system, when we consider the same time frame. The benefit becomes especially prominent, when a system with a costly test execution should be evaluated or when usage profiles with long delays are considered.

A limitation of our learning method is that the creation of our prediction models takes a long time, because we need costly steps, like the generation of log data and the training of the neural network. However, we believe that the model creation effort pays off, because once we have our timed model we can reuse it for the evaluation of different usage scenarios. We can evaluate various usage profiles or populations, and we could even exploit the model for other application areas, like for deployment testing, which we recently demonstrated [3].

5   Conclusion

We applied deep learning to extend existing functional models for a performance prediction with SMC. This method can answer questions about the expected latency for various usage scenarios.

First, we collected log data by running model-based testing with a functional model. Then, we applied this data to train a neural network that we integrated into our model together with a usage profile. The resulting model is a stochastic timed automaton that was simulated with SMC, i.e., with a Monte Carlo method.

An advantage of our method is that we can automatically enhance an existing functional model with timing aspects, which allows us to predict the performance for various usage scenarios with a fast model simulation. The prediction can be accelerated with a virtual time that is a fraction of real time.

Another benefit is that we can do both, SMC and testing of models and systems, inside a PBT tool. This enables an easy verification of predictions, and it facilitates the model and property definition in a high-level programming language, which makes our method accessible to testers from industry.

We have evaluated our method by applying it to an open-source MQTT implementation and by a comparison with a different learning method. The results are promising. We showed that our prediction is more accurate for several evaluation settings, and we were able to reduce the manual preprocessing with our deep learning method.

In principle, our method can also be applied to other performance indicators than latencies, e.g., to energy consumption. The evaluation of such indicators would be an interesting and highly relevant topic for future work.

References

1. Agha, G., Palmskog, K.: A survey of statistical model checking. ACM Trans. Model. Comput. Simul. (TOMACS) **28**(1), 6:1–6:39 (2018)
2. Aichernig, B.K., et al.: Learning and statistical model checking of system response times. Softw. Qual. J. **27**, 757–795 (2019)
3. Aichernig, B.K., Kann, S., Schumi, R.: Statistical model checking of response times for different system deployments. In: Feng, X., Müller-Olm, M., Yang, Z. (eds.) SETTA 2018. LNCS, vol. 10998, pp. 153–169. Springer, Cham (2018). https://doi.org/10.1007/978-3-319-99933-3_11
4. Aichernig, B.K., Schumi, R.: Property-based testing with FsCheck by deriving properties from business rule models. In: ICSTW, pp. 219–228. IEEE (2016)
5. Aichernig, B.K., Schumi, R.: Property-based testing of web services by deriving properties from business-rule models. Softw. Syst. Model. **18**, 889–911 (2019)
6. Aichernig, B.K., Schumi, R.: Statistical model checking meets property-based testing. In: ICST, pp. 390–400. IEEE (2017)
7. Aichernig, B.K., Schumi, R.: How fast is MQTT? In: McIver, A., Horvath, A. (eds.) QEST 2018. LNCS, vol. 11024, pp. 36–52. Springer, Cham (2018). https://doi.org/10.1007/978-3-319-99154-2_3
8. Alur, R., Dill, D.L.: A theory of timed automata. Theor. Comput. Sci. **126**(2), 183–235 (1994)
9. Arts, T.: On shrinking randomly generated load tests. In: Erlang 2014, pp. 25–31. ACM (2014)
10. Ballarini, P., Bertrand, N., Horváth, A., Paolieri, M., Vicario, E.: Transient analysis of networks of stochastic timed automata using stochastic state classes. In: Joshi, K., Siegle, M., Stoelinga, M., D'Argenio, P.R. (eds.) QEST 2013. LNCS, vol. 8054, pp. 355–371. Springer, Heidelberg (2013). https://doi.org/10.1007/978-3-642-40196-1_30
11. Banks, A., Gupta, R.: MQTT version 3.1.1. OASIS Standard, December 2014
12. Becker, S., Koziolek, H., Reussner, R.H.: The Palladio component model for model-driven performance prediction. J. Syst. Softw. **82**(1), 3–22 (2009)
13. Bishop, C.M.: Pattern Recognition and Machine Learning. Information Science and Statistics. Springer, New York (2006)
14. Book, M., Gruhn, V., Hülder, M., Köhler, A., Kriegel, A.: Cost and response time simulation for web-based applications on mobile channels. In: QSIC, pp. 83–90. IEEE (2005)

15. Bulychev, P.E., et al.: UPPAAL-SMC: statistical model checking for priced timed automata. In: QAPL. EPTCS, vol. 85, pp. 1–16. Open Publishing Association (2012)
16. Chen, X., Mohapatra, P., Chen, H.: An admission control scheme for predictable server response time for web accesses. In: WWW, pp. 545–554. ACM (2001)
17. Cho, K., et al.: Learning phrase representations using RNN encoder-decoder for statistical machine translation. arXiv preprint arXiv:1406.1078 (2014)
18. Claessen, K., Hughes, J.: QuickCheck: a lightweight tool for random testing of Haskell programs. In: ICFP, pp. 268–279. ACM (2000)
19. Collina, M., Corazza, G.E., Vanelli-Coralli, A.: Introducing the QEST broker: scaling the IoT by bridging MQTT and REST. In: PIMRC, pp. 36–41. IEEE (2012)
20. Deng, L., Yu, D.: Deep learning: methods and applications. Found. Trends Sig. Process. **7**(3–4), 197–387 (2014)
21. Draheim, D., Grundy, J.C., Hosking, J.G., Lutteroth, C., Weber, G.: Realistic load testing of web applications. In: CSMR, pp. 57–70. IEEE (2006)
22. Glorot, X., Bengio, Y.: Understanding the difficulty of training deep feedforward neural networks. In: AISTATS. JMLR Proceedings, vol. 9, pp. 249–256. JMLR.org (2010)
23. Glorot, X., Bordes, A., Bengio, Y.: Deep sparse rectifier neural networks. In: AISTATS. JMLR Proceedings, vol. 15, pp. 315–323. JMLR.org (2011)
24. Goodfellow, I., Bengio, Y., Courville, A.: Deep Learning. MIT Press, Cambridge (2016)
25. Grinchtein, O.: Learning of Timed Systems. Ph.D. thesis, Uppsala University (2008)
26. Hawkins, D.M.: The problem of overfitting. J. Chem. Inf. Model. **44**(1), 1–12 (2004)
27. Hochreiter, S., Schmidhuber, J.: Long short-term memory. Neural Comput. **9**(8), 1735–1780 (1997)
28. Hoeffding, W.: Probability inequalities for sums of bounded random variables. J. Am. Stat. Assoc. **58**(301), 13–30 (1963)
29. Houimli, M., Kahloul, L., Benaoun, S.: Formal specification, verification and evaluation of the MQTT protocol in the Internet of Things. In: ICMIT, pp. 214–221. IEEE, December 2017
30. Hughes, J.: QuickCheck testing for fun and profit. In: Hanus, M. (ed.) PADL 2007. LNCS, vol. 4354, pp. 1–32. Springer, Heidelberg (2006). https://doi.org/10.1007/978-3-540-69611-7_1
31. Kalaji, A.S., Hierons, R.M., Swift, S.: Generating feasible transition paths for testing from an extended finite state machine. In: ICST, pp. 230–239. IEEE (2009)
32. Kingma, D.P., Ba, J.: Adam: a method for stochastic optimization. arXiv preprint arXiv:1412.6980 (2014)
33. LeCun, Y., Bengio, Y., Hinton, G.: Deep learning. Nature **521**(7553), 436–444 (2015)
34. Lee, S., Kim, H., Hong, D., Ju, H.: Correlation analysis of MQTT loss and delay according to QoS level. In: ICOIN, pp. 714–717. IEEE (2013)
35. Legay, A., Delahaye, B., Bensalem, S.: Statistical model checking: an overview. In: Barringer, H., et al. (eds.) RV 2010. LNCS, vol. 6418, pp. 122–135. Springer, Heidelberg (2010). https://doi.org/10.1007/978-3-642-16612-9_11
36. Legay, A., Sedwards, S.: On statistical model checking with PLASMA. In: TASE, pp. 139–145. IEEE (2014)
37. Lu, Y., Nolte, T., Bate, I., Cucu-Grosjean, L.: A statistical response-time analysis of real-time embedded systems. In: RTSS, pp. 351–362. IEEE (2012)

38. Nagelkerke, N.J.: A note on a general definition of the coefficient of determination. Biometrika **78**(3), 691–692 (1991)
39. Papadakis, M., Sagonas, K.: A PropEr integration of types and function specifications with property-based testing. In: Erlang 2011, pp. 39–50. ACM (2011)
40. Pearson, K.: Note on regression and inheritance in the case of two parents. Proc. R. Soc. London **58**, 240–242 (1895)
41. Tyagi, R.S.: A comparative study of performance testing tools. Int. J. Adv. Res. Comput. Sci. Softw. Eng. IJARCSSE **3**(5), 1300–1307 (2013)
42. Schmidt, J., Ghorbani, A., Hapfelmeier, A., Kramer, S.: Learning probabilistic real-time automata from multi-attribute event logs. Intell. Data Anal. **17**(1), 93–123 (2013)
43. Schumi, R.: Predicting and testing system response-times with statistical model checking and property-based testing. Ph.D. thesis, Graz University of Technology (2018)
44. Schumi, R., Lang, P., Aichernig, B.K., Krenn, W., Schlick, R.: Checking response-time properties of web-service applications under stochastic user profiles. In: Yevtushenko, N., Cavalli, A.R., Yenigün, H. (eds.) ICTSS 2017. LNCS, vol. 10533, pp. 293–310. Springer, Cham (2017). https://doi.org/10.1007/978-3-319-67549-7_18
45. Tappler, M., Aichernig, B.K., Bloem, R.: Model-based testing IoT communication via active automata learning. In: ICST, pp. 276–287. IEEE (2017)
46. Thangavel, D., Ma, X., Valera, A.C., Tan, H., Tan, C.K.: Performance evaluation of MQTT and CoAP via a common middleware. In: ISSNIP, pp. 1–6. IEEE (2014)
47. Verwer, S., de Weerdt, M., Witteveen, C.: A likelihood-ratio test for identifying probabilistic deterministic real-time automata from positive data. In: Sempere, J.M., García, P. (eds.) ICGI 2010. LNCS (LNAI), vol. 6339, pp. 203–216. Springer, Heidelberg (2010). https://doi.org/10.1007/978-3-642-15488-1_17
48. Wald, A.: Sequential Analysis. Courier Corporation, North Chelmsford (1973)
49. Wurm, A.: Predicting the latency of MQTT brokers using deep learning. Master's thesis, Graz University of Technology (2018)

Learning Communicating State Machines

Alexandre Petrenko$^{(\boxtimes)}$ and Florent Avellaneda

CRIM, Montreal, Canada
{Alexandre.Petrenko,Florent.Avellaneda}@crim.ca

Abstract. We consider the problems of learning and conformance testing of components in a modular system. We assume that each component can be modelled as a Finite State Machine (FSM), the topology of the system is known, but some (or all) component FSMs are unknown and have to be learned by testing the whole system, as it cannot be disassembled. Thus the classical problem of active inference of an automaton in isolation is now further lifted to a system of communicating FSMs of an arbitrary topology. As opposed to the existing work on automata learning, the proposed approach neither needs a Minimally Adequate Teacher, also called the Oracle, nor uses it a conformance tester to approximate equivalence queries. The approach further enhances a SAT solving method suggested by the authors and allows to adaptively test conformance of a system with unknown components assuming that internal communications are observable. The resulting tests are much smaller than the classical universal conformance tests derived from the composite machine of the system.

Keywords: Component-based systems · Communicating FSMs ·
Active inference · FSM learning · Conformance testing · Adaptive testing ·
Testing in context · SAT solving

1 Introduction

Software industry often uses a component-based development approach to create software intense systems by selecting appropriate off-the-shelf components and assembling them with a well-defined architecture [13]. While practitioners are typically using ad hoc development techniques, model-based software engineering is investigating formal approaches which can offer automation to various phases of modular system development. In most cases, however, the components do not come with formal models, just with executable or in some cases source code. Models are nevertheless highly desired since they document the design, support test generation and model checking various properties and facilitate refactoring of a system. This explains a growing interest in automata inference. This important topic is addressed in many works, see, e.g., [2, 3, 5, 6, 8, 14], which treat a system as one black box unit, even if it contains components with known models and only some need to be learned. Most of the existing methods for query learning of an automaton model in isolation involve a Minimally Adequate Teacher, also called the Oracle, and use conformance or random tests to approximate equivalence queries [2, 3, 16, 17, 25]. Grey box inference, i.e., learning modular systems has only recently started to be investigated [1, 20]. In our previous work [20], we considered a system of two communicating FSMs, one

© Springer Nature Switzerland AG 2019
D. Beyer and C. Keller (Eds.): TAP 2019, LNCS 11823, pp. 112–128, 2019.
https://doi.org/10.1007/978-3-030-31157-5_8

modelling an embedded component and another - its known context and proposed a SAT solving approach to test and infer the embedded component. In fact, testing and model inference are closely related problems [4, 19], which could be solved by the SAT solving approach. In this paper, we further advance this approach to apply to a system of communicating FSMs with an arbitrary number of components and arbitrary topology.

The difference between black and grey box inference is as follows. When a given system is treated as a black box, a correctly learnt conjecture must be equivalent to a black box FSM. If however, the system is treated as a grey box, conjectures for components of a grey box are not necessarily equivalent to their respective FSMs, they are only required to compose an FSM that is equivalent to the composed FSM of the grey box. This fact has been successfully used in the area of logical design to optimize a given sequential circuit containing several components. Redesigned components must preserve the external behavior of the original circuit [25].

The interest towards modelling systems by communicating FSMs can be traced back to the eighties since an important work of Zafiropulo et al. [26]. Luo et al. [15] suggested a method for conformance testing of interacting FSMs based on determining a composite FSM that presents the external observable behavior of component FSMs. Such a machine exists assuming that the system has a single message in transit and does not fall into livelock. Thus, the system is treated as a black box, even if its topology is known.

Systems of communicating FSMs with unknown components are also considered in previous work [9, 10, 21]. The goal is to verify a given system by detecting intermittent errors. The proposed approach combines techniques for machine inference, testing and reachability analysis. Inferring a composite FSM of the system, an approximated model in the form of a Σ-quotient is obtained; the precision of the model is defined by the inference parameter Σ. Components models can then be obtained from the Σ-quotient by projections. Differently from that work, the proposed approach infers exact models and does not need to disassemble the system for unit testing.

Another body of related work addresses the so-called unknown component problem, where a basic task is to synthesize an unknown component that when combined with the known part of the system (the context) satisfies a given overall specification. This problem arises in various applications ranging from sequential synthesis to the design of discrete controllers [25]. The monograph [24] details the approach for reducing this problem to solving equations over languages and FSMs. This problem statement is in fact similar to conformance testing and learning of unknown components considered in this paper since both problem statements require a specification composite FSMs. The approach based on solving FSM equations targets the largest solution from which a minimal one can then be chosen for the unknown component, while the SAT solving approach directly determines an FSM of a minimal size. For systems with several unknown components and unknown composite FSMs, only the SAT solving approach elaborated in this paper is applicable.

The paper is organized as follows. Section 2 provides definitions related to state machines and automata. Composition, topology and composite FSM for communicating FSMs are formally defined in Sect. 3. A SAT solving method for simultaneous inference of communicating machines from their observed traces is presented in

Sect. 4. Section 5 details a method for checking conformance of a system with unknown components and Sect. 6 describes the method for learning component FSMs in an arbitrary grey box. Section 7 concludes.

2 Definitions

A *Finite State Machine* or simple machine M is a 5-tuple (S, s_0, I, O, T), where S is a finite set of states with an initial state s_0; I and O are finite non-empty disjoint sets of inputs and outputs, respectively; T is a transition relation $T \subseteq S \times I \times O \times S$, $(s, a, o, s') \in T$ is a transition. When we need to refer to the machine being in state $s \in S$, we write M/s.

M is *complete* (completely specified) if for each tuple $(s, a) \in S \times I$ there exists transition $(s, a, o, s') \in T$, otherwise it is *partial*. M is a *trivial* FSM, denoted Φ, if $T = \varnothing$. It is *deterministic* if for each $(s, a) \in S \times I$ there exists at most one transition $(s, a, o, s') \in T$, otherwise it is *nondeterministic*. FSM M is a *submachine* of $M' = (S', s_0, I, O, T')$ if $S \subseteq S'$ and $T \subseteq T'$.

An *execution* of M/s is a finite sequence of transitions forming a path from s in the state transition diagram of M. The machine M is *initially* connected, if for any state $s \in S$ there exists an execution from s_0 to s. Henceforth, we consider only deterministic initially connected machines.

A *trace* of M/s is a string in $(IO)^*$ which labels an execution from s. Let $Tr(s)$ denote the set of all traces of M/s and Tr_M denote the set of traces of M. For trace $\omega \in Tr(s)$, we use s-after-ω to denote the state M reached after the execution of ω from s; for an empty trace ε, s-after-$\varepsilon = s$. When s is the initial state we write M-after-ω instead of s_0-after-ω.

Given a string $\omega \in (IO)^*$, the *I-restriction* of ω is a string obtained by deleting from ω all symbols that are not in I, denoted $\omega_{\downarrow I}$.

The *I*-restriction of a trace $\omega \in Tr(s)$ is said to be a *transfer* sequence from state s to state s-after-ω. The length of ω, denoted $|\omega|$, is defined as the length of its *I*-restriction. A *prefix* of trace $\omega \in Tr(s)$ is a trace $\omega' \in Tr(s)$ such that the *I*-restriction of the latter is a prefix of the former.

Given an input sequence α and state s, we let $out(s, \alpha)$ denote the O-restriction of the trace that has α as its *I*-restriction. States $s, s' \in S$ are *equivalent w.r.t.* α, denoted $s \cong_\alpha s'$, if $out(s, \alpha) = out(s', \alpha)$; they are *distinguishable* by α, denoted $s \not\cong_\alpha s'$ or simply $s \not\cong s'$, if $out(s, \alpha) \neq out(s', \alpha)$. States s and s' are *equivalent* if they are equivalent w.r.t. all input sequences, i.e., $Tr(s) = Tr(s')$, denoted $s \cong s'$. The equivalence and distinguishability relations between FSMs are similarly defined, e.g., FSMs are equivalent if their initial states are equivalent.

Given two FSMs $M = (S, s_0, I, O, T)$ and $M' = (S', s_0', I, O, T')$, their *product* $M \times M'$ is the FSM (P, p_0, I, O, H), where $p_0 = (s_0, s_0')$ such that P and H are the smallest sets satisfying the following rule: If $(s, s') \in P$, $(s, x, o, t) \in T$, $(s', x, o, t') \in T$, then $(t, t') \in P$ and $((s, s'), x, o, (t, t')) \in H$. It is known that if M and M' are complete machines then they are equivalent if and only if the product $M \times M'$ is complete.

We also use the classical automaton model. A *Finite Automaton A* is a 5-tuple (P, p_0, X, T, F), where P is a finite set of states with the initial state p_0; X is a finite alphabet; T is a transition relation $T \subseteq S \times X \cup \{\varepsilon\} \times S$, where ε represents an internal action, and F is a set of *final* or *accepting* states, defining the language of A, denoted $L(A)$. We shall use several operations over automata, namely, expansion, restriction, and intersection, following [24].

Given an automaton $A = (P, p_0, X, T, F)$, and a finite alphabet U, the *U-expansion* of automaton A is the automaton, denoted $A_{\uparrow U}$, obtained by adding at each state a self-loop transition labeled with each action in $U \backslash X$.

For an automaton A and an alphabet U, the *U-restriction* of automaton A is the automaton, denoted $A_{\downarrow U}$, obtained by replacing each transition with the symbol in $X \backslash U$ by an ε-transition between the same states.

Given automata $A = (P, p_0, X, T, F_A)$ and $B = (R, r_0, Y, Z, F_B)$, such that $X \cap Y \neq \varnothing$, the *intersection* $A \cap B$ is the largest initially connected submachine of the automaton $(P \times R, (p_0, r_0), X \cap Y, Q, F_A \times F_B)$, where for each symbol $a \in X \cap Y$ and each state $(p, r) \in P \times R$, $((p, r), a, (p', r')) \in Q$, if $(p, a, p') \in T$ and $(r, a, r') \in Z$. The intersection operation is associative, hence it applies to more than two automata.

We also define an automaton corresponding to a given FSM M. The automaton, denoted by $A(M)$, is obtained by splitting each transition of M labeled by input/output into two transitions labeled by input and output, respectively, and connecting them with an auxiliary non-final state. The original states of M are only final states of $A(M)$, hence the language of $A(M)$ coincides with the set of traces of M.

3   FSM Composition

We consider a system of communicating FSMs defined as follows. Let $M_1, ..., M_k$ be a set of component FSMs in the system, where $M_i = (S_i, s_{i0}, X_i \cup V_i, O_i \cup U_i, T_i)$, is a complete deterministic machine. The input alphabets are partitioned into external X_i and internal V_i inputs. The output alphabets are also partitioned into external O_i and internal U_i outputs. The sets of states, inputs and outputs are assumed to be pairwise disjoint, except for pairs of sets of inputs V_i and outputs $U_j, j \neq i$. These sets define the topology of the given system, namely, if $V_i \cap U_j \neq \varnothing$, then the output of M_j is connected to the input of M_i.

Formally, the *topology* of the given system is the set $\{(V_i, U_j) \mid V_i \cap U_j \neq \varnothing, i, j \in \{1, ..., k\}\}$, denoted $T(M_1, ..., M_k)$. We define a well-defined topology by excluding insufficiently connected machines.

Then the topology of the given communicating FSMs is *well-defined*, if for each $i = 1, ..., k$, $V_i = \varnothing$ implies $U_i \neq \varnothing$, $U_i = \varnothing$ implies $V_i \neq \varnothing$, and $\cup_i^k V_i = \cup_i^k U_i$. Intuitively, a component without internal inputs (outputs) must have internal outputs (inputs), and all internal inputs as well as outputs must be corresponding outputs and inputs, respectively. Since simple removal of isolated machines could make topologies of the resulting systems well-defined, we assume henceforth well-definedness for granted. In this paper, we also assume that all communications between machines are unicast, so multicast is not used. Formally, this constrains the topology of a given system by requiring that all the sets of internal inputs are pairwise disjoint.

In the following, we shall use $X = \cup_{i=1}^{k} X_i$ for the set of external inputs, $O = \cup_{i=1}^{k} O_i$ for the set of external outputs and $I = \cup_{i=1}^{k} V_i = \cup_{i=1}^{k} U_i$ for the set of internal actions.

The behavior of a system of communicating FSMs is controlled by its environment which submits external inputs and receives external outputs. If the environment is allowed to submit inputs before it receives an external output, the system may need to buffer actions using queues. Then their size is defined by the number of consecutive inputs preceding the output caused by the first input. It is usual in testing to consider a so-called slow environment that ensures that there is only a single message in transit [15]. A *slow* environment can be modelled as a "chaos" automaton $Env = (\{p_0, p_1\}, p_0, X \cup O, T, \{p_0\})$, where $T = \{(p_0, x, p_1) \mid x \in X\} \cup \{(p_1, o, p_0) \mid o \in O\}$. After issuing an external input to the system it enters the non-initial state p_1 and returns to the final state when an external output is produced by the system where it issues a next input. Its language is the set $(XO)^*$.

In a system that has only a single message in transit, an internal output of one machine is immediately consumed only by one machine as its input, the communications are thus performed in fact by rendezvous. This allows to define an FSM composition operator using the intersection of their corresponding automata which has all the possible executions of the system with the slow environment.

Given $M_1, \ldots, M_k$, where $M_i = (S_i, s_{i0}, X_i \cup V_i, O_i \cup U_i, T_i)$, let $A(M_1), \ldots, A(M_k)$ be automata corresponding to the given FSMs. The *composite automaton*, denoted $A(M_1, \ldots, M_k)$, is the intersection $\cap_{i=1}^{k} A(M_i)_{\uparrow I} \cap Env_{\uparrow I}$. The language of $A(M_1, \ldots, M_k)$ is the set of all accepted words labelling all the executions of the closed system of communicating FSMs with the slow environment. The external behavior of the system is expressed in terms of external inputs X and outputs O, so it is the set of $(X \cup O)$-restrictions of accepted words of $A(M_1, \ldots, M_k)$, i.e., the set of external traces of the system. They are traces of an FSM that could be obtained by removing ε-transitions in $A(M_1, \ldots, M_k)_{\downarrow X \cup O}$ and pairing each input with a subsequent output, if it exists, to an FSM transition's label. Final states of $A(M_1, \ldots, M_k)$ become states of the FSM. If some external input is not followed by an external output it is deleted from the corresponding final state of $A(M_1, \ldots, M_k)_{\downarrow X \cup O}$, making the FSM partial. Thus, a complete FSM can be obtained only if the automaton $A(C)$ has no livelocks, i.e., cycles labelled by internal actions in I [24]. We let $C(M_1, \ldots, M_k)$ denote the resulting complete machine, called the *composite FSM* of the system.

Example. Consider two communicating FSMs M_1 and M_2 shown in Fig. 1(a) and (b), respectively [20]. The composite FSM $C(M_1, M_2)$ is in Fig. 1(c). The composite automaton $A(M_1, M_2)$ is shown in Fig. 2.

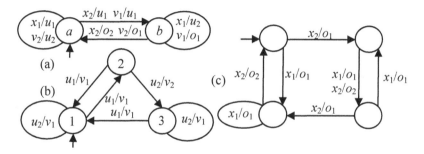

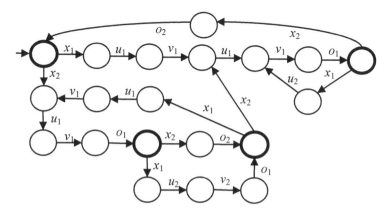

Fig. 1. The FSM M_1 (a), FSM M_2 (b) and composite FSM $C(M_1, M_2)$ (c).

Fig. 2. The composite automaton $A(M_1, M_2)$, final states are in bold.

4   Inference from Traces

In this section, we address the following inference problem. Given a system of k communicating FSMs with a known topology $T(M_1, \ldots, M_k)$, such that some component FSMs are unknown, assume that we are also given a set of traces produced by each component when some sequences of external inputs are applied to the system. We want to infer for each unknown component a conjecture consistent with the observed traces.

Given a string $\omega \in (IO)^*$, let $Pref(\omega)$ be the set of all prefixes of ω. We define a (linear) FSM $W(\omega) = (X, x_0, I, O, D_\omega)$, where D_ω is a transition relation, such that $|X| = |\omega| + 1$, and there exists a bijection $f\colon X \to Pref(\omega)$, such that $f(x_0) = \varepsilon$, $(x_i, a, o, x_{i+1}) \in D_\omega$ if $f(x_i)ao = f(x_{i+1})$ for all $i = 0, \ldots, |\omega| - 1$, in other words, $W(\omega)$ has the set of traces $Pref(\omega)$. We call it the ω-*machine*. Similarly, given a finite prefix-closed set of traces $\Omega \subset (IO)^*$ of some deterministic FSM, let $W(\Omega) = (X, x_0, I, O, D_\Omega)$ be the acyclic deterministic FSM such that Ω is the set of its traces, called an Ω-*machine*. The bijection f relates states of this machine to traces in Ω.

While the set of traces of the Ω-machine is Ω, there are many FSMs which contain the set Ω among their traces. An FSM $C = (S, s_0, I, O, T)$ is called an Ω-*conjecture*, if $\Omega \subseteq Tr_C$.

The states of the Ω-machine $W(\Omega) = (X, x_0, I, O, D_\Omega)$ and an Ω-conjecture $C = (S, s_0, I, O, T)$ are closely related to each other. Formally, there exists a mapping $\mu\colon X \to S$, such that $\mu(x) = s_0$-after-$f(x)$, the state reached by C with the trace $f(x) \in \Omega$. The mapping μ is unique and induces a partition π_C on the set X such that x and x' belong to the same block of the partition π_C, denoted $x = \pi_C\, x'$, if $\mu(x) = \mu(x')$.

Given an Ω-conjecture C with the partition π_C, let D be an Ω'-conjecture with the partition π_D, such that $\Omega' \subseteq \Omega$, we say that the partition π_C is an *expansion* of the partition π_D, if its projection onto states of Ω' coincides with the partition π_D.

We now lift the above notions to a system of communicating FSMs.

Given k FSMs, let $\Omega_1, \ldots, \Omega_k$ be the sets of their observed traces and $W(\Omega_i) = (Z_i, z_{i0}, X_i \cup V_i, O_i \cup U_i, D_{\Omega i})$, $i = 1, \ldots, k$ be the Ω-machines. We want to determine for each $W(\Omega_i)$ a conjecture $N_i = (S_i, s_0, X_i \cup V_i, O_i \cup U_i, T_i)$ with at most n_i states, i.e., $|S_i| \leq n_i$. Each state of the Ω-conjectures is represented by a variable s, that belongs to one of the sets $S_1 = \{1, \ldots, n_1\}$, $S_2 = \{n_1 + 1, \ldots, n_1 + n_2\}, \ldots, S_k = \left\{ \sum_{i=1}^{k-1} n_i + 1, \ldots, \right.$ $\left. \sum_{i=1}^{k} n_i \right\}$. To simplify further formulas, we use m_i to denote $\sum_{j=1}^{i} n_j$ so that $S_i = \{m_{i-1} + 1, \ldots, m_i\}$. Thus we need to find k mappings $\mu_i\colon Z_i \to S_i$, $i = 1, \ldots, k$ satisfying the following constraints:

$$\forall z, z' \in Z_i : \text{if } z \not\cong z' \text{ then } \mu_i(z) \neq \mu_i(z') \text{ and}$$
$$\text{if } \exists a \in X_i \cup V_i \text{ s.t. } out(z, a) = out(z', a) = o, \text{ where } o \in O_i \cup U_i, \text{ then} \qquad (1)$$
$$\mu_i(z) = \mu_i(z') \Rightarrow \mu_i(z)\text{-after-}ao = \mu_i(z')\text{-after-}ao$$

A mapping μ_i satisfying (1) defines a partition on Z_i and each block becomes a state of the Ω_i-conjecture, we use $\pi(N_i)$ to denote the partition. All the mappings, if exist, define a global partition $\pi(N_1, \ldots, N_k)$ on $\cup_{i=1}^{k} Z_i$, the states of all k conjectures.

Inspired by [12], we translate these formulas to SAT using unary coding for integer variables, represented by m_k Boolean variables $v_{z,1}, \ldots, v_{z,mk}$, where $m_k = \sum_{i=1}^{k} n_i$.

For each $z \in Z_i$ and all $i = 1, \ldots, k$ we have the clauses:

$$v_{z,m_{i-1}+1} \vee \ldots \vee v_{z,m_i} \qquad (2)$$

They mean that each state of each Ω-machine must be in at least one block.

For each $z \in Z_i$, all $i = 1, \ldots, k$, and all $p, q \in \{m_{i-1} + 1, \ldots, m_i\}$ such that $p \neq q$, we have the clauses:

$$\neg v_{z,p} \vee \neg v_{z,q} \tag{3}$$

They mean that each state of each Ω-machines must be in at most one block. We use auxiliary variables $e_{z,z'}$. For each $z \in Z_i$ and each $z' \in Z_j$ such that $i \neq j$

$$\neg e_{z,z'} \tag{4}$$

For every $z, z' \in Z_i$ such that $z \not\equiv z'$ and all $i = 1, \ldots, k$, we have

$$\neg e_{z,z'} \tag{5}$$

For every $z, z' \in Z_i$ such that $out(z, a) = out(z', a) = o$ for some $o \in O_i \cup U_i$ and all $i = 1, \ldots, k$, we have

$$e_{z,z'} \Rightarrow e_{z-\text{after}-ao,z'-\text{after}-ao} \tag{6}$$

For every $z, z' \in Z_i$, all $i = 1, \ldots, k$, and all $p \in \{m_{i-1} + 1, \ldots, m_i\}$

$$e_{z,z'} \wedge v_{z,p} \Rightarrow v_{z',p} \tag{7}$$

$$\neg e_{z,z'} \wedge v_{z,p} \Rightarrow \neg v_{z',p} \tag{8}$$

The resulting Boolean formula is the conjunction of clauses (2)–(8). If it is satisfiable then a solution is a set of conjectures for all unknown components. A solution might not necessarily be unique, hence to solve the problems of conformance testing and learning we need to make sure that the found set of conjectures is unique or to determine another set of non-equivalent conjectures.

This is achieved by using the following procedure inferring all conjectures for the unknown components at once. We let Π denote a set of global partitions each of which defines k conjectures already inferred from the previously observed traces. To ensure generation of different conjectures, partitions are used to formulate additional constraints. The procedure generates a set of conjectures, such that the number of states of each conjecture does not exceed a given upper bound, if they exist. The conjectures are verified for livelock by composing them (with the known FSMs, if any) into a composite automaton, as explained in the previous section. If it has a livelock then the procedure tries to find another set of conjectures and uses the global partition induced by the conjectures to avoid repeated regeneration in further iterations. The procedure is formalized in the following algorithm.

Algorithm 1. *Infer_conjectures*$(\{\Omega_1, ..., \Omega_k\}, \{M_1, ..., M_m\}, \{n_1, ..., n_k\}, \Pi)$

Input: Sets of FSM traces $\Omega_1, ..., \Omega_k$, a set of known FSMs $M_1, ..., M_m$, a set of integers $n_1, ..., n_k$, and a set of global partitions Π

Output: A set of k conjectures and an updated set of partitions or False.

1. *formula* = conjunction of the clauses (2) - (8)
2. **loop do**
3.   **for all** $\pi \in \Pi$ **do**
4.   *clause* = False
5.   **for all** z, z' such that $z =_\pi z'$ **do**
6.   *clause* = *clause* $\vee \neg e_{z,z'}$
7.   **end for**
8.   *formula* = *formula* $\wedge$ *clause*
9.   **end for**
10.   **if** *formula* is not satisfiable **then**
11.   **return** False
12.   **end if**
13. $\{N_1, ..., N_k\} := call\text{-}solver(formula)$
14.   **if** $A(N_1, ..., N_k, M_1, ..., M_m)$ has no livelock **then**
15.   **return** $\{N_1, ..., N_k\}$, Π
16.   **end if**
17. $\Pi := \Pi \cup \pi(N_1, ..., N_k)$
18. **end loop**

To check the satisfiability of a formula one can use any of the existing solvers, calling the function *call-solver (formula)*.

5 Checking Conformance with Unknown Components

In this section, we consider the following conformance testing problem. Given a system of communicating FSMs, such that some component FSMs are unknown, assume that we are also given an FSM that describes the expected external behavior of the system, called a specification composite FSM. We assume that the system has no livelocks, so its external behavior can be represented by a complete composite FSM. We need to determine whether the composite FSM of the system conforms (is equivalent) to the specification or find a counterexample, i.e., an external test that distinguishes them, otherwise. Moreover, if the system conforms to the specification then we want to learn all its unknown component FSMs. We assume that all the internal interfaces are observable, but only external inputs are controllable, so the system is a grey box with a single message in transit. The problem reflects a practical situation when in a modular system some components are replaced by their updated versions and one needs to test whether the external behavior is not changed.

The proposed method for checking conformance and learning component FSMs verifies whether the current conjectures obtained from already observed traces when composed together with known component FSMs behave as the given specification FSM. If they do not then the product of the specification and composite FSMs is used to determine a sequence of external inputs that distinguishes them. It is applied to the grey box obeying the property of a slow environment Env, so observed traces are inputs always interleaved with outputs. The observed traces extend the set of traces of unknown components unless the grey box does not produce the output sequence of the specification. In the last case, the external input sequence is returned as a counterexample, the current conjectures are also reported as a diagnostics of the observed non-conformance of the grey box. The process iterates as long as the current conjectures form a conforming system. The method calls Algorithm 1 that builds conjectures, checks whether they are unique and returns them, if it is the case, terminating the process. Algorithm 1 calls in turn a SAT solver constraining it to avoid solutions of already considered conjectures. The solver may not find any solution when the assumed bounds on the state numbers are insufficiently low. In this case, the algorithm needs to be executed with increased bounds. The procedure is implemented in Algorithm 2.

Let GB denote the system of the component FSMs $M_1, \ldots, M_{k'}, \ldots, M_k$, such that the first k', $0 < k' \leq k$ components are unknown, and $n_1, \ldots, n_{k'}$ are the bounds on the number of their states, respectively. We let M denote a complete FSM over the same external inputs and outputs as GB, called the specification FSM.

Algorithm 2. Checking conformance and learning components
Input: A GB with known components $M_{k'+1}, \ldots, M_k$ and a specification FSM M.
Output: Unknown component FSMs or a test that distinguishes the composite FSM of GB from M.

1. $\Omega_i := \varnothing, i = 1, \ldots, k$
2. $\Pi := \varnothing$
3. **while** conjectures $N_1, \ldots, N_{k'}$ and Π are returned by *Infer_conjectures*($\{\Omega_1, \ldots, \Omega_{k'}\}, \{M_{k'+1}, \ldots, M_k\}, \{n_1, \ldots, n_{k'}\}, \Pi$) **do**
4.   **if** $C(M_1, \ldots, M_k) \times C(N_1, \ldots, N_{k'}, \ldots, M_k)$ is complete **then**
5.   **return** $N_1, \ldots, N_{k'}$
6.   **end if**
7.   Let βa be an external input sequence such that β is the shortest transfer sequence to a state with the undefined input a in $C(M_1, \ldots, M_k) \times C(N_1, \ldots, N_{k'}, \ldots, M_k)$
8.   Let σ be the external trace and $\sigma_1, \ldots, \sigma_{k'}$ be unknown components' traces observed when the input sequence βa is applied to GB
9.   **If** σ is not the trace of $C(M_1, \ldots, M_k)$ **then**
10.   **return** "the test βa distinguishes GB from M and the conjectures $N_1, \ldots, N_{k'}$"
11.   **end if**
12. $\Omega_i := \Omega_i \cup \{\sigma_i\}, i = 1, \ldots, k'$
13. **end while**
14. **return** "the bounds $n_1, \ldots, n_{k'}$ are too low"

Note that the Boolean formula used by the SAT solver is built incrementally; a current formula is saved and new clauses are added when any set Ω_i or Π is augmented.

Theorem 1. Algorithm 2 learns unknown components of a conforming grey box or returns a counterexample test, otherwise.

Sketch of Proof. If in line 5, $C(M_1, ..., M_k) \times C(N_1, ..., N_{k'}, M_{k'+1}, ..., M_k)$ is complete, then the grey box is equivalent to the specification and $N_1, ..., N_{k'}$ is a solution for unknown components. If in line 9, σ is not a trace of $C(M_1, ..., M_k)$, then since σ is an external trace, the test βa as its input sequence distinguishes GB from the specification M. At each iteration in the while loop, a trace is added to at least one set Ω_i. Thus, at least one potential solution $N_1, ..., N_{k'}$ is eliminated among the possible solutions. Since the number of states in components is fixed, the number of potential solutions is bounded. Thus, the loop will end when all potential solutions are eliminated. ∎

The algorithm was implemented in C++ with MiniSat solver [7] and we use this prototype for experiments in a VirtualBox with 8 GB of RAM and i5-7500 processor.

Table 1. Testing conformance and learning component FSMs.

Step	External trace	Added variables	Added clauses	Time μs
1	ε	5	6	13
2	$x_1 o_1$	30	63	17
3	$x_2 o_1$	22	42	10
4	$x_1 o_1 x_2 o_2$	14	29	8
5	$x_1 o_1 x_1 o_1$	43	90	15
6	$x_1 o_1 x_1 o_1 x_1 o_1$	53	115	415
7	$x_2 o_1 x_1 o_1 x_2 o_1$	136	300	48
8	$x_1 o_1 x_2 o_2 x_2 o_1 x_1 o_1$	176	391	158
9	$x_1 o_1 x_2 o_2 x_1 o_1 x_1 o_1 x_2 o_2$	314	701	109
10	$x_1 o_1 x_1 o_1 x_2 o_2 x_1 o_1$	272	628	89
11	$x_1 o_1 x_1 o_1 x_2 o_2 x_1 o_1 x_1 o_1 x_2 o_2$	215	479	76
12	$x_1 o_1 x_1 o_1 x_1 o_1 x_1 o_1 x_2 o_2$	235	525	226
13	$x_2 o_1 x_1 o_1 x_1 o_1 x_1 o_1 x_2 o_1$	651	1481	199
14	$x_1 o_1 x_1 o_1 x_2 o_2 x_2 o_1 x_1 o_1 x_2 o_1$	626	1411	173
Total		2792	6261	1156

Example. We consider the communicating FSMs shown in Fig. 1. Assuming that both FSMs are unknown, but their composite FSM shown in Fig. 1(c) is known, we use the prototype tool to learn the component FSMs. Let the bounds on the number of states in the components be two for M_1 and three for M_2.

Algorithm 2 executes 14 cycles in about one millisecond and terminates. As expected, no test distinguishing the system from the specification FSM is found. Figure 3 shows the resulting conjectures N_1 and N_2. The conjecture N_2 is a partial machine, the first two states can be merged to obtain a minimal FSM with two states. Their composite FSM is equivalent to the specification FSM in Fig. 2. One can notice that the learnt conjectures are simpler that the original FSMs; in fact, they have fewer transitions and the minimal form of the second conjecture has not three, but two states. Table 1 provides a summary of execution details for all cycles of Algorithm 2, namely, the number of variables and clauses added in each step and time in microseconds. It is interesting to notice in Table 1 that time required to solve a SAT instance does not grow linearly with the number of variables and clauses. In our incremental approach, newly added clauses often just speed up the process of finding a solution. In the context of automata learning, similar observations were also previously reported [19]. This indicates that the number of variables and clauses cannot be directly used to characterize the complexity of the SAT solving approach to the FSM inference problem. It is intuitively clear that the more component FSMs are unknown the higher the complexity of the learning and testing problems. In the running example, we consider that both component FSMs are unknown, if, however, we assume that only M_2 is unknown then conformance testing and learning a single unknown component FSM requires fewer tests.

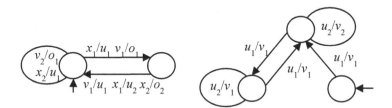

Fig. 3. The resulting conjectures N_1 and N_2.

To demonstrate how Algorithm 2 executes when given a nonconforming grey box, we assume that the second component FSM is like M_2 in Fig. 2(b), except for a transition from state 3 to state 1 that has the label u_1/v_2 instead of u_1/v_1. The first seven executed steps are exactly the steps shown in Table 1. Then three more steps are performed to determine the sequence of external inputs $x_2x_1x_2x_2$ that distinguishes the composed FSM of the mutated system from the specification FSM. The two produce different external traces $x_2o_1x_1o_1x_2o_1x_2o_1$ and $x_2o_1x_1o_1x_2o_1x_2o_2$.

We now compare the cost of checking conformance of the grey box system with observable internal communications to that of the black box system without such observations. As Table 1 indicates, to test conformance of the given grey box 13 tests suffice and overall 60 test actions (47 external inputs and 13 resets) need to be applied to the system. When internal interactions cannot be observed, the whole system becomes a black box. To test communicating FSMs we use universal conformance tests which could be derived from their composite FSM. In our example, the composite FSM is shown in Fig. 1(c). The conformance tests should be constructed assuming that the number of states in the system can reach six, since the bounds for the components' state number are two and three, respectively. Considering the set $\{x_2x_1x_2, x_1x_2\}$ as a characterization set W of the composite FSM, the W-method [23] generates 40 input sequences of the total length of 276. We conclude that the proposed approach for testing conformance of communicating FSMs as a grey box offers an important save in testing efforts. Testing a system as a grey box is adaptive, since test actions are determined based on the observations and compared to the execution of universal conformance tests against the system treated as a black box it could not be less effective. To the best of our knowledge, it is the first method for adaptive conformance testing of communicating FSMs of an arbitrary topology.

6   Learning a Grey Box

In this section, we consider the problem of inferring communicating FSMs. This is a generalization of the classical FSM inference problem [11, 18, 22] to a system of FSMs. As in the previous section, we are given a system of communicating FSMs with a known topology and external input alphabet. It is assumed that all the internal interfaces are observable, but only external inputs are controllable, so the system is a grey box with a single message in transit. We also assume that the grey box has no livelock, so its external behavior can be represented by an FSM.

Differently from the conformance testing problem in Sect. 5, we now know neither specification composite FSM nor any component FSM. We need to learn all component FSMs at once. Yet, as before, we fix the upper bounds on the number of states of each component. As discussed above, the "right" bounds could be determined by iterative execution of our learning method with increasing bounds.

We let GB denote a system of unknown FSMs $M_1, \ldots, M_k$ and $n_1, \ldots, n_k$ be the bounds on the number of their states, respectively. The learning procedure is implemented in Algorithm 3. It is an enhancement of Algorithm 2 replacing the specification FSM M by the composite FSM of the current conjectures.

Algorithm 3. Learning a grey box
Input A grey box GB with a known external alphabet and integers $n_1, \ldots, n_k$
Output Conjectures for all k components
1. $\Omega_i := \emptyset, i = 1, \ldots, k$
2. $\Pi := \emptyset$
3. $N_i = \Phi$ (trivial FSM), $i = 1, \ldots, k$
4.   **while** conjectures $D_1, \ldots, D_k$ and Π are returned by *Infer_conjectures*($\{\Omega_1, \ldots, \Omega_k\}, \{\}, \{n_1, \ldots, n_k\}, \Pi$) **do**
5.   **if** $C(D_1, \ldots, D_k) \times C(N_1, \ldots, N_k)$ is complete **then**
6. $\Pi := \Pi \cup \pi(D_1, \ldots, D_k)$
7.   **else**
8.   Let βa be an input sequence such that β is the shortest transfer sequence to a state with the undefined input a in $C(D_1, \ldots, D_k) \times C(N_1, \ldots, N_k)$
9.   Let σ be the external trace and $\sigma_1, \ldots, \sigma_k$ be components' traces observed when the input sequence βa is applied to GB
10. $\Omega_i := \Omega_i \cup \{\sigma_i\}, i = 1, \ldots, k$
11.   **if** σ is not a trace of $C(N_1, \ldots, N_k)$ **then**
12. $\{N_1, \ldots, N_k\}, \Pi := $ *Infer_conjectures*($\{\Omega_1, \ldots, \Omega_k\}, \{\}, \{n_1, \ldots, n_k\}, \Pi$)
13.   **end if**
14.   **end if**
15. **end while**
16. **return** $N_1, \ldots, N_k$

The algorithm returns the conjectures as a main result, but also it determines sets of observed traces of each component used to infer them. The uniqueness of the conjectures is that they form a composite FSM of the given grey box, as stated in the following.

Theorem 2. Algorithm 3 returns the conjectures N_1, ..., N_k such that $C(N_1, ..., N_k) \cong C(M_1, ..., M_k)$ and for each grey box with components L_1, ..., L_k such that L_i has at most n_i states, $Tr_{Li} \supseteq \Omega_i$ for each L_i and the topology $T(M_1, ..., M_k)$ we have $C(L_1, ..., L_k) \cong C(M_1, ..., M_k)$.

Proof. When Algorithm 3 terminates, the result N_1, ..., N_k is such that $C(N_1, ..., N_k) \cong C(M_1, ..., M_k)$ because N_1, ..., N_k are FSMs consistent with traces $\{\Omega_1, ..., \Omega_k\}$, and all other solutions L_1, ..., L_k are such that $C(L_1, ..., L_k) \cong C(N_1, ..., N_k)$ or have livelock.

Now we prove by contradiction that if there exist L_1, ..., L_k such that for each L_i, $Tr_{Li} \supseteq \Omega_i$ and the number of states does not exceed n_i, then $C(L_1, ..., L_k) \cong C(M_1, ..., M_k)$. Assume that there exist L_1, ..., L_k such that $C(L_1, ..., L_k) \not\cong C(M_1, ..., M_k)$. Because the formula used in *Infer_conjectures* $(\{\Omega_1, ..., \Omega_k\}, \{\}, \{n_1, ..., n_k\}, \Pi)$ is not satisfiable when Algorithm 3 returns N_1, ..., N_k, the global partition induced by L_1, ..., L_k is in Π. This would mean that either $C(L_1, ..., L_k) \cong C(N_1, ..., N_k)$ or there exists σ in Ω such that σ is not a trace of $C(L_1, ..., L_k)$. However, these two cases are not possible. ∎

The algorithm was also implemented in C++ with MiniSat solver and we use this prototype for experiments as in Sect. 5.

Example. We consider our running example of the FSMs shown in Fig. 1. Assume we know only the external alphabet and the bounds on the number of states in the components, two for M_1 and three for M_2.

Algorithm 3 executes 42 cycles in about ten milliseconds and terminates returning the same conjectures as Algorithm 2, see Fig. 3. 24 cycles out of 42 do not add any new traces, they just update the set of global partitions by adding a single clause in line 7 of Algorithm 3. Table 2 provides the details for the remaining 18 steps; the missing numbers belong to 24 omitted steps. The observations made in Sect. 5 about relations between time and the number of variables and clauses in Table 1 are also valid for Table 2.

As Table 2 indicates to learn both components of the given grey box 17 tests suffice and overall 76 test actions (59 external inputs and 17 resets) need to be applied to the system. Comparing this to the scenario of learning components with a given specification composite FSM where 13 tests with 60 test actions are used, we can conclude that the absence of an oracle played by the specification FSM complicates the inference problem. Notice that if in this example, the FSM M_1 is known and only M_2 needs to be learnt then it is sufficient to use only 5 tests with 19 test actions (14 external inputs and 5 resets).

Table 2. Learning the grey box.

Step	External trace	Added variables	Added clauses	Time μs
1	ε	5	6	22
2	$x_1 o_1$	30	63	59
3	$x_2 o_1$	22	42	46
5	$x_1 o_1 x_1 o_1$	39	84	47
6	$x_1 o_1 x_2 o_2$	18	35	36
7	$x_1 o_1 x_1 o_1 x_1 o_1$	53	115	63
8	$x_1 o_1 x_1 o_1 x_1 o_1 x_1 o_1$	63	140	107
9	$x_1 o_1 x_2 o_2 x_1 o_1$	122	284	123
13	$x_1 o_1 x_1 o_1 x_1 o_1 x_2 o_2 x_1 o_1$	188	436	199
18	$x_1 o_1 x_1 o_1 x_2 o_2 x_1 o_1$	228	535	196
22	$x_2 o_1 x_1 o_1$	129	293	206
23	$x_2 o_1 x_1 o_1 x_1 o_1$	228	550	203
24	$x_2 o_1 x_1 o_1 x_2 o_1$	122	263	188
27	$x_2 o_1 x_1 o_1 x_2 o_1 x_1 o_1 x_2 o_2$	231	525	294
28	$x_1 o_1 x_2 o_2 x_2 o_1 x_1 o_1 x_2 o_1$	522	1177	336
30	$x_1 o_1 x_2 o_2 x_1 o_1 x_1 o_1 x_2 o_2$	291	653	318
36	$x_1 o_1 x_1 o_1 x_2 o_2 x_2 o_1 x_1 o_1 x_2 o_1$	642	1450	643
40	$x_2 o_1 x_1 o_1 x_1 o_1 x_1 o_1 x_2 o_1$	504	1150	620
Total		3437	7825	9846

7 Conclusions

We considered the problems of learning components and conformance testing of a modular system. The system is modelled by FSMs communicating by message passing with a single message in transit. Communications between machines defines the topology of the system. The composite FSM represents the external behavior of the system. Formulating the learning problem we assume that some or all component FSMs are unknown and have to be learned by testing the whole system, as it cannot be disassembled. The system is then tested as a grey box, since internal actions are observed when external tests are executed. Thus the classical problem of active inference of an automaton in isolation is now further lifted to a system of communicating FSMs of an arbitrary topology. To the best of our knowledge, no method was proposed to solve this problem yet. Compared to the existing work on automata learning, the proposed approach neither needs a Minimally Adequate Teacher (Oracle), nor uses it a conformance tester to approximate equivalence queries.

The problem of conformance testing of communicating FSMs with unknown components is quite similar to the above problem. Since checking conformance of a given system requires a specification FSM, a composite FSM is used as an oracle for conformance testing. The proposed approach allows to adaptively test conformance of a system with unknown components. The resulting tests are much smaller that the classical universal conformance tests derived from the composite FSM of the system. Moreover, unknown components are also learned once the system is found to be conformant.

It is worth to notice that while we assumed that all the internal interactions can be observed, the approach works even when a given system is partially observable. Any part of a system with fully observable inputs and outputs can be learnt as a single FSM that is a composite FSM of all components of the subsystem.

As a future work it could be interesting to relax some assumptions used in the proposed approach, e.g., determinism and absence of queues and to investigate learning of systems which use communications other than message passing.

Acknowledgements. This work was partially supported by MEI (Ministère de l'Économie et Innovation) of Gouvernement du Québec and NSERC of Canada.

References

1. Abel, A., Reineke, J.: Gray-box learning of serial compositions of mealy machines. In: Rayadurgam, S., Tkachuk, O. (eds.) NFM 2016. LNCS, vol. 9690, pp. 272–287. Springer, Cham (2016). https://doi.org/10.1007/978-3-319-40648-0_21
2. Angluin, D.: Learning regular sets from queries and counterexamples. Inf. Comput. **75**(2), 87–106 (1987)
3. Bennaceur, A., Giannakopoulou, D., Hähnle, R., Meinke, K.: Machine Learning for Dynamic Software Analysis: Potentials and Limits. LNCS, vol. 11026. Springer, Cham (2018). https://doi.org/10.1007/978-3-319-96562-8
4. Berg, T., Grinchtein, O., Jonsson, B., Leucker, M., Raffelt, H., Steffen, B.: On the correspondence between conformance testing and regular inference. In: Cerioli, M. (ed.) FASE 2005. LNCS, vol. 3442, pp. 175–189. Springer, Heidelberg (2005). https://doi.org/10.1007/978-3-540-31984-9_14
5. Biermann, A.W., Feldman, J.A.: On the synthesis of finite-state machines from samples of their behavior. IEEE Trans. Comput. **100**(6), 592–597 (1972)
6. De la Higuera, C.: Grammatical Inference: Learning Automata and Grammars. Cambridge University Press, Cambridge (2010)
7. Eén, N., Sörensson, N.: An extensible SAT-solver. In: Giunchiglia, E., Tacchella, A. (eds.) SAT 2003. LNCS, vol. 2919, pp. 502–518. Springer, Heidelberg (2004). https://doi.org/10.1007/978-3-540-24605-3_37
8. Gold, E.M.: Complexity of automaton identification from given data. Inf. Control **37**(3), 302–320 (1978)
9. Groz, R., Li, K., Petrenko, A., Shahbaz, M.: Modular system verification by inference, testing and reachability analysis. In: Suzuki, K., Higashino, T., Ulrich, A., Hasegawa, T. (eds.) FATES/TestCom -2008. LNCS, vol. 5047, pp. 216–233. Springer, Heidelberg (2008). https://doi.org/10.1007/978-3-540-68524-1_16
10. Groz, R., Li, K., Petrenko, A.: Integration testing of communicating systems with unknown components. Ann. Telecommun. **70**(3–4), 107–125 (2015)
11. Groz, R., Simao, A., Petrenko, A., Oriat, C.: Inferring FSM models of systems without reset. In: Bennaceur, A., Hähnle, R., Meinke, K. (eds.) Machine Learning for Dynamic Software Analysis: Potentials and Limits. LNCS, vol. 11026, pp. 178–201. Springer, Cham (2018). https://doi.org/10.1007/978-3-319-96562-8_7

12. Heule, M.J.H., Verwer, S.: Exact DFA identification using SAT solvers. In: Sempere, J.M., García, P. (eds.) ICGI 2010. LNCS (LNAI), vol. 6339, pp. 66–79. Springer, Heidelberg (2010). https://doi.org/10.1007/978-3-642-15488-1_7

13. Jaffar-ur Rehman, M., Jabeen, F., Bertolino, A., Polini, A.: Testing software components for integration: a survey of issues and techniques. Softw. Test. Verif. Reliab. **17**, 95–133 (2007)

14. Kella, J.: Sequential machine identification. IEEE Trans. Comput. **100**(3), 332–338 (1971)

15. Luo, G., von Bochmann, G., Petrenko, A.: Test selection based on communicating nondeterministic finite-state machines using a generalized Wp-method. IEEE Trans. Softw. Eng. **20**(2), 149–162 (1994)

16. Meinke, K.: CGE: a sequential learning algorithm for mealy automata. In: Sempere, J.M., García, P. (eds.) ICGI 2010. LNCS (LNAI), vol. 6339, pp. 148–162. Springer, Heidelberg (2010). https://doi.org/10.1007/978-3-642-15488-1_13

17. Peled, D., Vardi, M.Y., Yannakakis, M.: Black box checking. J. Automat. Lang. Comb. **7**(2), 225–246 (2001)

18. Petrenko, A., Avellaneda, F., Groz, R., Oriat, C.: From passive to active FSM inference via checking sequence construction. In: Yevtushenko, N., Cavalli, A.R., Yenigün, H. (eds.) ICTSS 2017. LNCS, vol. 10533, pp. 126–141. Springer, Cham (2017). https://doi.org/10.1007/978-3-319-67549-7_8

19. Petrenko, A., Avellaneda, F., Groz, R., Oriat, C.: FSM inference and checking sequence construction are two sides of the same coin. Softw. Qual. J. (2018). https://doi.org/10.1007/s11219-018-9429-3

20. Petrenko, A., Avellaneda, F.: Conformance testing and inference of embedded components. In: Medina-Bulo, I., Merayo, M.G., Hierons, R. (eds.) ICTSS 2018. LNCS, vol. 11146, pp. 119–134. Springer, Cham (2018). https://doi.org/10.1007/978-3-319-99927-2_10

21. Shahbaz, M., Shashidhar, K.C., Eschbach, R.: Iterative refinement of specification for component based embedded systems. In: Proceedings of the 2011 International Symposium on Software Testing and Analysis, pp. 276–286 (2011)

22. Steffen, B., et al.: Active automata learning: from DFAs to interface programs and beyond. In: ICGI, pp. 195–209 (2012)

23. Vasilevski, M.P.: Failure diagnosis of automata. Cybernetics **9**(4), 653–665 (1973)

24. Villa, T., Yevtushenko, N., Brayton, R.K., Mishchenko, A., Petrenko, A., Sangiovanni-Vincentelli, A.L.: The Unknown Component Problem: Theory and Applications. Springer, Heidelberg (2012). https://doi.org/10.1007/978-0-387-68759-9

25. Villa, T., Petrenko, A., Yevtushenko, N., Mishchenko, A., Brayton, R.: Component-based design by solving language equations. Proc. IEEE **103**(11), 2152–2167 (2015)

26. Zafiropulo, P., West, C., Rudin, H., Cowan, D., Brand, D.: Towards analyzing and synthesizing protocols. IEEE Trans. Commun. **28**(4), 651–661 (1980)

Repairing Timed Automata Clock Guards through Abstraction and Testing

Étienne André[1,2,3] ![ORCID], Paolo Arcaini[3] ![ORCID], Angelo Gargantini[4] ![ORCID], and Marco Radavelli[4(✉)] ![ORCID]

[1] Université Paris 13, LIPN, CNRS, UMR 7030, 93430 Villetaneuse, France
[2] JFLI, CNRS, Tokyo, Japan
[3] National Institute of Informatics, Tokyo, Japan
[4] University of Bergamo, Bergamo, Italy
marco.radavelli@unibg.it

Abstract. Timed automata (TAs) are a widely used formalism to specify systems having temporal requirements. However, exactly specifying the system may be difficult, as the user may not know the exact clock constraints triggering state transitions. In this work, we assume the user already specified a TA, and (s)he wants to validate it against an oracle that can be queried for acceptance. Under the assumption that the user only wrote wrong guard transitions (i.e., the structure of the TA is correct), the search space for the correct TA can be represented by a Parametric Timed Automaton (PTA), i.e., a TA in which some constants are parametrized. The paper presents a process that (i) abstracts the initial (faulty) TA ta_{init} in a PTA pta; (ii) generates some test data (i.e., timed traces) from pta; (iii) assesses the correct evaluation of the traces with the oracle; (iv) uses the IMITATOR tool for synthesizing some constraints φ on the parameters of pta; (v) instantiate from φ a TA ta_{rep} as final repaired model. Experiments show that the approach is successfully able to partially repair the initial design of the user.

1 Introduction

Timed automata (TA) [4] represent a widely used formalism for modeling and verifying concurrent timed systems. A common usage is to develop a TA describing the running system and then apply analysis techniques to it (e.g., [15]). However, exactly specifying the system under analysis may be difficult, as the user may not know the exact clock constraints that trigger state transitions, or may perform errors at design time. Therefore, validating the produced TA against the real system is extremely important to be sure that we are analyzing a faithful representation of the system. Different testing techniques have been proposed for timed automata, based on different coverage criteria as, e.g., transition coverage [25] and fault-based coverage [2,3], and they can be used for TA validation.

This work is partially supported by ERATO HASUO Metamathematics for Systems Design Project (No. JPMJER1603), JST and by the ANR national research program PACS (ANR-14-CE28-0002).

D. Beyer and C. Keller (Eds.): TAP 2019, LNCS 11823, pp. 129–146, 2019.
https://doi.org/10.1007/978-3-030-31157-5_9

However, once some failing tests have been identified, it remains the problem of detecting and removing (*repair*) the fault from the TA under validation. How to do this in an automatic way is challenging. One possible solution could be to use mutation-based approaches [2,3] in which mutants are considered as possible repaired versions of the original TA; however, due to the continuous nature of timed automata, the number of possible mutants (i.e., repair actions) is too big also for small TAs and, therefore, such approaches do not appear to be feasible. We here propose to use a *symbolic representation* of the possible repaired TAs and we reduce the problem of repairing to finding an assignment of this symbolic representation.

Contribution. In this work, we address the problem of testing/validating TAs under the assumption that only clock guards may be wrong, that is, we assume that the structure (states and transitions) is correct. Moreover, we assume to have an oracle that we can query for acceptance of timed traces, but whose internal structure is unknown: this oracle can be a Web-service, a medical device, a protocol, etc. In order to symbolically represent the search space of possible repaired TAs, we use the formalism of parametric timed automata (PTAs) [6] as an abstraction to represent all possible behaviors under all possible clock guards.

We propose a framework for automatic repair of TAs that takes as input a TA ta_{init} to repair and an *oracle*. The process works as follows: *(i)* starting from ta_{init}, we build a PTA pta where to look for the repaired TA; *(ii)* we build a symbolic representation of the language accepted by pta in terms of an *extended parametric zone graph* $\mathcal{EPZG}$; *(iii)* we then generate some test data TD from $\mathcal{EPZG}$; *(iv)* we assess the correct evaluation of TD by querying the *oracle*, so building the test suite TS; *(v)* we feed the tests TS to the IMITATOR [10] tool that finds some constraints φ that restrict pta only to those TAs that correctly evaluate all the tests in TS; *(vi)* as the number of TAs that are correct repairs may be infinite, we try to obtain, using a constraint solver based on local search, the TA ta_{rep} closest to the initial TA ta_{init}. Note that trying to modify as less as possible the initial TA is reasonable if we assume the competent programmer hypothesis [22].

To evaluate the feasibility of the approach, we performed some preliminary experiments showing that the approach is able to (partially) repair a faulty TA.

Outline. Section 2 explains the definitions we need in our approach. Then Sect. 3 presents the process we propose that combines model abstraction, test generation, constraint generation, and constraint solving. Section 4 describes experiments we performed to evaluate our process. Finally, Sect. 5 reviews some related work, and Sect. 6 concludes the paper.

2 Definitions

A *timed word* [4] over an alphabet of actions Σ is a possibly infinite sequence of the form $(a_0, d_0)(a_1, d_1) \cdots$ such that, for all integer $i \geq 0$, $a_i \in \Sigma$ and $d_i \leq d_{i+1}$. A timed language is a (possibly infinite) set of timed words.

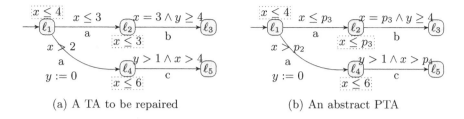

(a) A TA to be repaired   (b) An abstract PTA

Fig. 1. Running example

We assume a set $\mathbb{X} = \{x_1, \ldots, x_H\}$ of *clocks*, i.e., real-valued variables that evolve at the same rate. A clock valuation is $\mu : \mathbb{X} \to \mathbb{R}_{\geq 0}$. We write $\mathbf{0}$ for the clock valuation assigning 0 to all clocks. Given $d \in \mathbb{R}_{\geq 0}$, $\mu + d$ is s.t. $(\mu + d)(x) = \mu(x) + d$, for all $x \in \mathbb{X}$. Given $R \subseteq \mathbb{X}$, we define the *reset* of a valuation μ, denoted by $[\mu]_R$, as follows: $[\mu]_R(x) = 0$ if $x \in R$, and $[\mu]_R(x) = \mu(x)$ otherwise.

We assume a set $\mathbb{P} = \{p_1, \ldots, p_M\}$ of *parameters*. A parameter *valuation* v is $v : \mathbb{P} \to \mathbb{Q}_+$. We assume $\bowtie \in \{<, \leq, =, \geq, >\}$. A *clock guard* g is a constraint over $\mathbb{X} \cup \mathbb{P}$ defined by a conjunction of inequalities of the form $x \bowtie \sum_{1 \leq i \leq M} \alpha_i p_i + d$, with $p_i \in \mathbb{P}$, and $\alpha_i, d \in \mathbb{Z}$. Given g, we write $\mu \models v(g)$ if the expression obtained by replacing each x with $\mu(x)$ and each p with $v(p)$ in g evaluates to true.

2.1   Parametric Timed Automata

Definition 1 (PTA). *A PTA $\mathcal{A}$ is a tuple $\mathcal{A} = (\Sigma, L, \ell_0, F, \mathbb{X}, \mathbb{P}, I, E)$, where: (i) Σ is a finite set of actions, (ii) L is a finite set of locations, (iii) $\ell_0 \in L$ is the initial location, (iv) $F \subseteq L$ is the set of accepting locations, (v) $\mathbb{X}$ is a finite set of clocks, (vi) $\mathbb{P}$ is a finite set of parameters, (vii) I is the invariant, assigning to every $\ell \in L$ a clock guard $I(\ell)$, (viii) E is a finite set of edges $e = (\ell, g, a, R, \ell')$ where $\ell, \ell' \in L$ are the source and target locations, $a \in \Sigma$, $R \subseteq \mathbb{X}$ is a set of clocks to be reset, and g is a clock guard.*

Given $e = (\ell, g, a, R, \ell')$, we define $\mathsf{Act}(e) = a$.

Example 1. Consider the PTA in Fig. 1b, containing two clocks x and y and three parameters p_2, p_3 and p_4. The initial location is ℓ_1.

Given v, we denote by $v(\mathcal{A})$ the non-parametric structure where all occurrences of a parameter p_i have been replaced by $v(p_i)$. We denote as a *timed automaton* any such structure $v(\mathcal{A})$.

The *synchronous product* (using strong broadcast, i.e., synchronization on a given set of actions), or *parallel composition*, of several PTAs gives a PTA (see [8] for a common formal definition).

Definition 2 (Concrete semantics of a TA). *Given a PTA $\mathcal{A} = (\Sigma, L, \ell_0, F, \mathbb{X}, \mathbb{P}, I, E)$, and a parameter valuation v, the semantics of $v(\mathcal{A})$ is given by the timed transition system (TTS) $(S, s_0, \to)$, with*

- $S = \{(\ell, \mu) \in L \times \mathbb{R}_{\geq 0}^H \mid \mu \models v(I(\ell))\}$, $s_0 = (\ell_0, \mathbf{0})$,
- $\rightarrow$ consists of the discrete and (continuous) delay transition relations: (i) discrete transitions: $(\ell, \mu) \xmapsto{e} (\ell', \mu')$, if $(\ell, \mu), (\ell', \mu') \in S$, and there exists $e = (\ell, g, a, R, \ell') \in E$, such that $\mu' = [\mu]_R$, and $\mu \models v(g)$. (ii) delay transitions: $(\ell, \mu) \xmapsto{d} (\ell, \mu + d)$, with $d \in \mathbb{R}_{\geq 0}$, if $\forall d' \in [0, d], (\ell, \mu + d') \in S$.

Moreover we write $(\ell, \mu) \xrightarrow{(e, d)} (\ell', \mu')$ for a combination of a delay and discrete transition if $\exists \mu'' : (\ell, \mu) \xmapsto{d} (\ell, \mu'') \xmapsto{e} (\ell', \mu')$.

Given a TA $v(\mathcal{A})$ with concrete semantics $(S, s_0, \rightarrow)$, we refer to the states of S as the *concrete states* of $v(\mathcal{A})$. A *run* of $v(\mathcal{A})$ is an alternating sequence of concrete states of $v(\mathcal{A})$ and pairs of edges and delays starting from the initial state s_0 of the form $s_0, (e_0, d_0), s_1, \cdots$ with $i = 0, 1, \ldots$, $e_i \in E$, $d_i \in \mathbb{R}_{\geq 0}$ and $s_i \xrightarrow{(e_i, d_i)} s_{i+1}$. The *associated timed word* is $(\mathsf{Act}(e_0), d_0)(\mathsf{Act}(e_1), \sum_{0 \leq i \leq 1} d_i) \cdots$. A run is *maximal* if it is infinite or cannot be extended by any discrete action. The (timed) language of a TA, denoted by $\mathcal{L}(v(\mathcal{A}))$, is the set of timed words associated with maximal runs of $v(\mathcal{A})$. Given $s = (\ell, \mu)$, we say that s is reachable in $v(\mathcal{A})$ if s appears in a run of $v(\mathcal{A})$. By extension, we say that ℓ is reachable in $v(\mathcal{A})$; and by extension again, given a set T of locations, we say that T is reachable if there exists $\ell \in T$ such that ℓ is reachable in $v(\mathcal{A})$.

Example 2. Consider the TA $\mathcal{A}$ in Fig. 1a. Consider the following run ρ of $\mathcal{A}$:

$$\left(\ell_1, \begin{pmatrix} x = 0 \\ y = 0 \end{pmatrix}\right) \xrightarrow{(\mathsf{a}, 2.5)} \left(\ell_4, \begin{pmatrix} x = 2.5 \\ y = 0 \end{pmatrix}\right) \xrightarrow{(\mathsf{c}, 2)} \left(\ell_5, \begin{pmatrix} x = 4.5 \\ y = 2 \end{pmatrix}\right)$$

We write "$x = 2.5$" instead of "μ such that $\mu(x) = 2.5$". The associated timed word is $(\mathsf{a}, 2.5)(\mathsf{c}, 4.5)$.

2.2 Symbolic Semantics

Let us now recall the symbolic semantics of PTAs (see e.g., [9,18,19]).

Constraints. We first need to define operations on constraints. A linear term over $\mathbb{X} \cup \mathbb{P}$ is of the form $\sum_{1 \leq i \leq H} \alpha_i x_i + \sum_{1 \leq j \leq M} \beta_j p_j + d$, with $x_i \in \mathbb{X}$, $p_j \in \mathbb{P}$, and $\alpha_i, \beta_j, d \in \mathbb{Z}$. A *constraint* C (i.e., a convex polyhedron) over $\mathbb{X} \cup \mathbb{P}$ is a conjunction of inequalities of the form $lt \bowtie 0$, where lt is a linear term.

Given a parameter valuation v, $v(C)$ denotes the constraint over $\mathbb{X}$ obtained by replacing each parameter p in C with $v(p)$. Likewise, given a clock valuation μ, $\mu(v(C))$ denotes the expression obtained by replacing each clock x in $v(C)$ with $\mu(x)$. We say that v *satisfies* C, denoted by $v \models C$, if the set of clock valuations satisfying $v(C)$ is nonempty. Given a parameter valuation v and a clock valuation μ, we denote by $\mu|v$ the valuation over $\mathbb{X} \cup \mathbb{P}$ such that for all clocks x, $\mu|v(x) = \mu(x)$ and for all parameters p, $\mu|v(p) = v(p)$. We use the notation $\mu|v \models C$ to indicate that $\mu(v(C))$ evaluates to true. We say that C is *satisfiable* if $\exists \mu, v$ s.t. $\mu|v \models C$.

$$s_1 = (\ell_1, 0 \leq x = y \leq 4 \wedge p_2 \geq 0 \wedge p_3 \geq 0 \wedge p_4 \geq 0 \qquad)$$
$$s_2 = (\ell_2, 0 \leq x = y \leq p_3 \wedge p_2 \geq 0 \wedge p_3 \geq 0 \wedge p_4 \geq 0 \qquad)$$
$$s_3 = (\ell_3, x = y \geq p_3 \wedge p_2 \geq 0 \wedge p_3 \geq 4 \wedge p_4 \geq 0 \qquad)$$
$$s_4 = (\ell_4, p_2 < x \leq 6 \wedge y \geq 0 \wedge p_2 < x - y \leq 4 \wedge 4 > p_2 \geq 0 \wedge p_3 \geq 0 \wedge p_4 \geq 0 \qquad)$$
$$s_5 = (\ell_5, p_2 < x \wedge p_4 < x \wedge y > 1 \wedge p_2 < x - y \leq 4 \wedge 4 > p_2 \geq 0 \wedge p_3 \geq 0 \wedge 6 > p_4 \geq 0)$$

Fig. 2. Parametric zone graph of Fig. 1b

We define the *time elapsing* of C, denoted by $C^{\nearrow}$, as the constraint over $\mathbb{X}$ and $\mathbb{P}$ obtained from C by delaying all clocks by an arbitrary amount of time. That is, $\mu'|v \models C^{\nearrow}$ iff $\exists \mu : \mathbb{X} \to \mathbb{R}_+, \exists d \in \mathbb{R}_+$ s.t. $\mu|v \models C \wedge \mu' = \mu + d$. Given $R \subseteq \mathbb{X}$, we define the *reset* of C, denoted by $[C]_R$, as the constraint obtained from C by resetting the clocks in R, and keeping the other clocks unchanged. We denote by $C{\downarrow}_{\mathbb{P}}$ the projection of C onto $\mathbb{P}$, i.e., obtained by eliminating the variables not in $\mathbb{P}$ (e.g., using Fourier-Motzkin [24]). $\bot$ denotes the constraint over $\mathbb{P}$ representing the empty set of parameter valuations.

Definition 3 (Symbolic semantics). *Given a PTA $\mathcal{A} = (\Sigma, L, \ell_0, F, \mathbb{X}, \mathbb{P}, I, E)$, the symbolic semantics of $\mathcal{A}$ is the labeled transition system called parametric zone graph $\mathcal{PZG} = (E, \mathbf{S}, \mathbf{s}_0, \Rightarrow)$, with*

- $\mathbf{S} = \{(\ell, C) \mid C \subseteq I(\ell)\}$, $\mathbf{s}_0 = \left(\ell_0, (\bigwedge_{1 \leq i \leq H} x_i = 0)^{\nearrow} \wedge I(\ell_0)\right)$, *and*
- $((\ell, C), e, (\ell', C')) \in \Rightarrow$ *if* $e = (\ell, g, a, R, \ell') \in E$ *and* $C' = \left([[C \wedge g)]_R \wedge I(\ell'))^{\nearrow} \wedge I(\ell')\right.$ *with* C' *satisfiable.*

That is, in the parametric zone graph, nodes are symbolic states, and arcs are labeled by *edges* of the original PTA. A symbolic state is a pair (ℓ, C) where $\ell \in L$ is a location, and C its associated constraint. In the successor state computation in Definition 3, the constraint is intersected with the guard, clocks are reset, the resulting constraint is intersected with the target invariant, then time elapsing is applied, and finally intersected again with the target invariant. This graph is (in general) *infinite* and, in contrast to the zone graph of timed automata, no finite abstraction can be built for properties of interest; this can be put in perspective with the fact that most problems are undecidable for PTAs [7].

Example 3. Consider again the PTA $\mathcal{A}$ in Fig. 1b. The parametric zone graph of $\mathcal{A}$ is given in Fig. 2, where e_1 is the edge from ℓ_1 to ℓ_2 in Fig. 1b, e_2 is the edge from ℓ_2 to ℓ_3, e_3 is the edge from ℓ_1 to ℓ_4, and e_4 is the edge from ℓ_4 to ℓ_5. The inequalities of the form $0 \leq x = y \leq 4$ come from the fact that clocks are initially both equal to 0, evolve at the same rate, and are constrained by the invariant.

2.3 Reachability Synthesis

We will use reachability synthesis to solve the problem in Sect. 3. This procedure, called EFsynth, takes as input a PTA $\mathcal{A}$ and a set of target locations T, and attempts to synthesize all parameter valuations v for which T is reachable in $v(\mathcal{A})$. EFsynth$(\mathcal{A}, T)$ was formalized in e.g., [19] and is a procedure that traverses the parametric zone graph of $\mathcal{A}$; EFsynth may not terminate (because of the infinite nature of the graph), but computes an exact result (sound and complete) if it terminates.

Example 4. Consider again the PTA $\mathcal{A}$ in Fig. 1b. EFsynth$(\mathcal{A}, \{\ell_5\})$ returns $0 \leq p_2 < 4 \wedge 0 \leq p_4 \leq 6 \wedge p_3 \geq 0$. Intuitively, this corresponds to all parameter constraints in the parametric zone graph in Fig. 2 associated to symbolic states with location ℓ_5 (there is a single such state).

3   A Repairing Process Using Abstraction and Testing

In this paper, we address the *guard-repair* problem of timed automata. Given a reference TA ta_{init} and an oracle $\mathcal{O}$ knowing an unknown timed language $\mathcal{TL}$, our goal is to modify ("repair") the timing constants in the clock guards of $\mathcal{A}$ such that the repaired automaton matches the timed language $\mathcal{TL}$. The setting assumes that the oracle $\mathcal{O}$ can be queried for acceptance of timed words by $\mathcal{TL}$; that is, $\mathcal{O}$ can decide whether a timed word belongs to $\mathcal{TL}$, but the internal structure of the object leading to $\mathcal{TL}$ (e.g., an unknown timed automaton) is unknown. This setting makes practical sense when testing black-box systems.

> **guard-repair problem:**
> INPUT: an initial TA ta_{init}, an unknown timed language $\mathcal{TL}$
> PROBLEM: Repair the constants in the clock guards of ta_{init} so as to obtain a TA ta_{rep} such that $\mathcal{L}(ta_{rep}) = \mathcal{TL}$

While the ultimate goal is to solve this problem, in practice the best we can hope for is to be *as close as possible* to the unknown oracle TA, notably due to the undecidability of language equivalence of timed automata [4] (e.g., if $\mathcal{TL}$ was generated by another TA).

3.1   Overview of the Method

From now on, we describe the process we propose to automatically repair an initial timed automaton ta_{init}. Figure 3 describes the approach:

Step ① a PTA *pta* is generated starting from the initial TA ta_{init}.

Step ② the extended parametric zone graph $\mathcal{EPZG}$ (an extension of $\mathcal{PZG}$) is built.

Step ③ a test generation algorithm generates relevant test data *TD* from $\mathcal{EPZG}$.

Step ④ *TD* is evaluated using the oracle, therefore building the test suite *TS*.

Step ⑤ some constraints φ are generated, restricting *pta* to the TAs that evaluate correctly the generated tests *TS*.

Step ⑥ one possible TA satisfying the constraints φ is obtained.

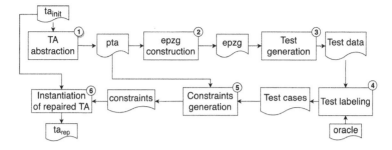

Fig. 3. Automatic repair process

Algorithm 1. Automatic repair process $\mathsf{Repair}(ta_{init}, \mathcal{O})$

---

input   : ta_{init}: initial timed automaton to repair
input   : $\mathcal{O}$: an oracle assessing the correct evaluation of timed words
output : φ: set of valuations repairing ta_{init}
1 $pta \leftarrow \mathsf{AbstractInPta}(ta_{init})$
2 $\mathcal{EPZG} \leftarrow \mathsf{BuildEpzg}(pta)$
3 $TD \leftarrow \mathsf{GenerateTestData}(\mathcal{EPZG})$;   /* Generate test data from $\mathcal{EPZG}$ */
4 $TS \leftarrow \mathsf{LabelTests}(TD, \mathcal{O})$;   /* A test is a pair (trace, assessment) */
5 **return** $\varphi \leftarrow \mathit{GenConstraints}(pta, TS)$

Function GenConstraints(pta, TS)

---

1 $MBA \leftarrow \{w \mid (w, \text{true}) \in TS\}$;   /* Tests that must be accepted */
2 $MBR \leftarrow \{w \mid (w, \text{false}) \in TS\}$;   /* Tests that must be rejected */
3 **return** $\bigwedge_{w \in MBA} \mathit{ReplayTW}(pta, w) \wedge \bigwedge_{w \in MBR} \neg\mathit{ReplayTW}(pta, w)$

Algorithm 1 formalizes steps ①–⑤ for which we can provide some theoretical guarantees (i.e., the non-emptiness of the returned valuation set, and its inclusion of $\mathcal{TL}$). For step ⑥, instead, different approaches could be adopted: in the paper, we discuss a possible one. We emphasize that, with the exception of Step ①, our process is entirely automated. We describe each phase in details in the following sections.

3.2   Step ①: Abstraction

Starting from the initial ta_{init}, through *abstraction*, the user obtains a PTA *pta* that generalizes ta_{init} in all the parts that can be possibly changed in order to repair ta_{init} (line 1 in Algorithm 1). For instance, a clock guard with a constant value can be parametrized. Therefore, *pta* represents the set of all the TAs that can be obtained when repairing ta_{init}. *pta* is built on the base of the domain knowledge of the developer who has a guess of the guards that may be faulty.

Example 5. Consider again the TA in Fig. 1a. A possible abstraction of this TA is the PTA in Fig. 1b, where we chose to abstract some of the timing constants with parameters. Note that not all timing constants must necessarily be substituted with parameters; also note that a same parameter can be used in different places (this is the case of p_3).

Assumption. We define below an important assumption for our method; we will discuss in Sect. 3.9 how to lift it.

Assumption 1. *We here assume that pta is a correct abstraction, i.e., it contains a TA that precisely models the oracle. That is, there exists $v_{\mathcal{O}}$ such that $\mathcal{L}(v_{\mathcal{O}}(pta)) = \mathcal{TL}$.*

Note that this assumption is trivially valid if faults lay in the clock guards (which is the setting of this work), and if all constants used in clock guards are turned to parameters.

3.3   Step ②: Construction of the Extended Parametric Zone Graph

Starting from *pta*, we build a useful representation of its computations in terms of an *extended parametric zone graph* $\mathcal{EPZG}$ (line 2 in Algorithm 1). This original data structure will be used for test generation. In the following, we describe how we build $\mathcal{EPZG}$ from $\mathcal{PZG}$. We extend the parametric zone graph $\mathcal{PZG}$ with the two following pieces of information:

the parameter constraint characterizing each symbolic state: from a state (ℓ, C), the parameter constraint is $C{\downarrow}_{\mathbb{P}}$ and gives the exact set of parameter valuations for which there exists an equivalent concrete run in the automaton. That is, a state (ℓ, C) is reachable in $v(\mathcal{A})$ iff $v \models C$ (see [19] for details).

the minimum and maximum arrival times: that is, we compute the minimum (m_i) and maximum (M_i) over all possible parameter valuations of the possible absolute times reaching this symbolic state.

While the construction of the first information is standard, the second one is original to our work and requires more explanation. We build for each state a (possibly unbounded) interval that encodes the absolute minimum and maximum arrival time. This can be easily obtained from the parametric zone graph by adding an extra clock never reset (that encodes the absolute time), and projecting the obtained constrained on this extra clock, thus giving minimum and maximum times over all possible parameter valuations.

Example 6. Consider again the PTA $\mathcal{A}$ in Fig. 1b and its parametric zone graph in Fig. 2. The parameter constraints associated to each of the symbolic states, and the possible absolute reachable times, are given in Table 1.

Remark 1. If all locations of the original PTA contain an invariant with at least one inequality of the form $x \triangleleft p$ or $x \triangleleft d$, with $\triangleleft \in \{<, \leq\}$, and if the parameters are bounded, then the maximum arrival time in each symbolic state will always be

Table 1. Description of the states of the extended parametric zone graph

Symbolic states	Parameter constraint	Reachable times
s_1	$p_2 \geq 0 \wedge p_3 \geq 0 \wedge p_4 \geq 0$	$x_{abs} = 0$
s_2	$p_2 \geq 0 \wedge p_3 \geq 0 \wedge p_4 \geq 0$	$x_{abs} \in [0,4]$
s_3	$p_2 \geq 0 \wedge p_3 \geq 4 \wedge p_4 \geq 0$	$x_{abs} \in [4,\infty)$
s_4	$4 > p_2 \geq 0 \wedge p_3 \geq 0 \wedge p_4 \geq 0$	$x_{abs} \in (0,4]$
s_5	$4 > p_2 \geq 0 \wedge p_3 \geq 0 \wedge 6 > p_4 \geq 0$	$x_{abs} \in (1,6]$

finite. Note that this condition is not fulfilled in Example 6 because ℓ_2 features an invariant $x \leq p_3$, with p_3 unbounded, thus allowing to remain arbitrarily long in ℓ_2 for an arbitrarily large value of p_3. Therefore, the arrival time in ℓ_3 is $x_{abs} \in [4,\infty)$.

3.4   Step ③: Test Data Generation

Starting from $\mathcal{EPZG}$, we generate some test data (line 3 in Algorithm 1) in terms of timed words.

Constructing Timed Words. We use the minimal and maximum arrival times in the abstract PTA to generate test data. That is, we will notably use the *boundary* information, i.e., runs close to the fastest and slowest runs, to try to discover the actual timing guards of the oracle.

The procedure to generate a timed word from the EPZG is as follows:
1. Pick a run $s_0 e_0 s_1 \cdots s_n$ from $\mathcal{EPZG}$.
2. Construct the timed word $(a_0, d_0)(a_1, d_1) \cdots (a_{n-1}, d_{n-1})$, where $a_i = \mathsf{Act}(e_i)$ and d_i belongs to the interval of reachable times associated with symbolic state s_{i+1}, for $0 \leq i \leq n-1$. Note that, depending on the policy (see below), we sometimes choose on purpose valuations *outside* of the reachable times.

Given an EPZG, we generate, for each finite path of the EPZG up to a given depth K, one timed word. In order to chose a timed word from a (symbolic) path of the EPZG, we identified different policies.

Policies. For each $k < K$, we instantiate $(a_0, d_0)(a_1, d_1) \cdots (a_k, d_k)$ by selecting particular values for each d_i using different policies:
- $\mathsf{P}_{\pm 1}$: $d_j \in I_{\pm 1}$, where $I_{\pm 1} = \{m_i - 1, m_i, m_i + 1, M_i - 1, M_i, M_i + 1\}$ and m_i and M_i are the minimum and maximum arrival times of the symbolic state.
- $\mathsf{P}_{\mathsf{minMax2}}$: $d_j \in I_{minMax2}$ with $I_{minMax2} = I_{\pm 1} \cup \{(m_i + M_i)/2\}$.
- $\mathsf{P}_{\mathsf{minMax4}}$: $d_j \in I_{minMax4}$ with $I_{minMax4} = I_{minMax2} \cup \{m_i + (M_i - m_i)/4, m_i + ((M_i - m_i)/4) * 3\}$.
- $\mathsf{P}_{\mathsf{rnd}}$: d_j being a random value such that $m_i \leq d_j \leq M_i$.

Example 7. Consider again the PTA $\mathcal{A}$ in Fig. 1b and its parametric zone graph in Fig. 2 together with reachable times in Table 1. Pick the run $s_1 e_3 s_4 e_4 s_5$. First note that $\mathsf{Act}(e_3) = a$ and $\mathsf{Act}(e_4) = c$. According to Table 1, the reachable times associated with s_4 are $(0, 4]$ while those associated with s_5 are $(1, 6]$. Therefore, a possible timed word generated with $\mathsf{P}_{\pm 1}$ is $(a, 1)(c, 5)$. Note that this timed word does not belong to the TA to be repaired (Fig. 1a) because of the guard $x > 2$; however, it does belong to an instance TA of Fig. 1b for a sufficiently small value of p_2 (namely $v(p_2) < 1$). We will see later that such tests are tagged as failing.

3.5   Step ④: Test Labeling

Then, every test sequence in *TD* is checked against the oracle in order to label it as accepted or not (line 4 in Algorithm 1), therefore the test suite *TS*; a test case in *TS* is a pair $(w, \mathcal{O}(w))$, being w a timed word, and $\mathcal{O}(w)$ the evaluation of the oracle, i.e., $\mathcal{O}(w)$ is defined as a Boolean the value of which is $w \in \mathcal{TL}$.[1] A test case *fails* if $ta_{init}(w) \neq \mathcal{O}(w)$, i.e., the initial TA and the oracle timed language disagree. Note that, if is no test case fails, ta_{init} is considered correct[2] and the process terminates.

In different settings, different oracles can be used. In this work, we assume that the oracle is the real system of which we want to build a faithful representation; the system is black-box, and it can only be queried for acceptance of timed words. In another setting, the oracle could be the user who can easily assess which words should be accepted, and wants to validate their initial design. Of course, the type of oracle also determines how many test data we can provide for assessment: while a real implementation can be queried a lot (modulo the time budget and the execution time of a single query), a human oracle usually can evaluate only few tests.

3.6   Step ⑤: Generating Constraints from Timed Words

Given the test suite *TS*, our approach generates constraints φ that restrict *pta* to only those TAs that correctly evaluate the tests (line 5 in Algorithm 1).

In this section, we explain how to "replay a timed word", i.e., given a PTA $\mathcal{A}$, how to synthesize the exact set of parameter valuations v for which a finite timed word belongs to the timed language of $v(\mathcal{A})$. Computing the set of parameter valuations for which a given *finite* timed word belongs to the timed language can be done easily by exploring a small part of the symbolic state space. Replaying a timed word is also very close to the ReplayTrace procedure in [12] where we synthesized valuations corresponding to a trace, i.e., a timed word without the time information—which is decidable.

---

[1] To limit the number of tests, we only keep the maximal accepted traces (i.e., we remove accepted traces included in longer accepted traces), and the minimal rejected traces (i.e., we remove rejected traces having as prefix another rejected trace).

[2] This does not necessarily mean that both TAs have the same language, but that the tests did not exhibit any discrepancy.

From timed words to timed automata. First, we convert the timed word into a (non-parametric) timed automaton. This straightforward procedure was introduced in [11], and simply consists in converting a timed word of the form $(a_1, d_1), \cdots, (a_n, d_n)$ into a sequence of transitions labeled with a_i and guarded with $x_{abs} = d_i$ (where x_{abs} measures the absolute time, i.e., is an extra clock never reset). Let TW2PTA denote this procedure.[3]

Example 8. Consider again the timed word w mentioned in Example 7: $(a, 0.5)(c, 5)$. The result of TW2PTA(w) is given in Fig. 4.

Fig. 4. Translation of timed word $(a, 0.5)(c, 5)$

Synchronized product and synthesis. The second part of step ⑤ consists in performing the synchronized product of TW2PTA(w) and $\mathcal{A}$, and calling EFsynth on the resulting PTA with the last location of the timed word as the target of EFsynth. Let ReplayTW(pta, w) denote the entire procedure of synthesizing the valuations associated that make a timed word possible.

Example 9. Consider again the PTA $\mathcal{A}$ in Fig. 1b and the timed word $(a, 0.5)(c, 5)$ translated to a (P)TA in Fig. 4. The result of EFsynth applied to the synchronized product of these two PTAs with $\{\ell_2^{TW}\}$ as target location set is $0 \leq p_1 < 5 \wedge 0 \leq p_2 < \frac{1}{2} \wedge p_3 \geq 0$. This set indeed represents all possible valuations for which $(a, 0.5)(c, 5)$ is a run of the automaton. Note that the result can be non-convex. If we now consider the simpler timed word $(a, 3)$, then the result of ReplayTW($\mathcal{A}, w$) becomes $p_3 \geq 3 \wedge p_2 \geq 0 \wedge p_4 \geq 0 \vee p_2 < 3 \wedge p_3 \geq 0 \wedge p_4 \geq 0$ This comes from the fact that the action a can correspond to either e_1 (from ℓ_1 to ℓ_2) or e_3 (from ℓ_1 to ℓ_4) in Fig. 1b.

Remark 2. Despite the non-guarantee of termination of the general EFsynth procedure, ReplayTW not only always terminates, but is also very efficient in practice: indeed, it only explores the part of the PTA corresponding to the sequence of (timed) transitions imposed by the timed word. This comes from the fact that we take the synchronized product of $\mathcal{A}$ with TW2PTA(w), the latter PTA being linear and finite.

Lemma 1. *Let pta be a PTA, and w be a timed word. Then ReplayTW(pta, w) terminates.*

3.7   Correctness

Recall that Assumption 1 assumes that there exists a valuation $v_{\mathcal{O}}$ such that $\mathcal{L}(v_{\mathcal{O}}(pta)) = \mathcal{TL}$. We show that, under Assumption 1, our resulting constraint is always non-empty and contains the valuation $v_{\mathcal{O}}$.

Theorem 1. *Let $\varphi = $ Repair($ta_{init}, \mathcal{O}$). Then $\varphi \neq \bot$ and $v_{\mathcal{O}} \models \varphi$.*

Proof. Proofs of Lemma 1 and Theorem 1 can be found in [8].

---

[3] This procedure transforms the word to a non-parametric TA; we nevertheless use the name TW2PTA for consistency with [11].

3.8 Step ⑥: Instantiation of a Repaired TA

Any assignment satisfying φ characterizes a correct TA w.r.t. the generated tests in TS; however, not all of them exactly capture the oracle behaviour. If the user wants to select one TA, (s)he can select one assignment v_{rep} of φ, and use it to instantiate the final repaired TA ta_{rep}.

In order to select one possible assignment v_{rep}, different strategies may be employed, on the base of the assumptions of the process. In this work, we assume the *competent programmer hypothesis* [22] that the developer produced an initial TA ta_{init} close to be correct; therefore, we want to generate a final TA ta_{rep} that is *not too different* from ta_{init}. In particular, we assume that the developer did small mistakes on setting the values of the clock guards.

In order to find the closest values of the clock guards that respect the constraints, we exploit the local search capability of Choco [23]:

1. we start from the observation that ta_{init} is an instantiation of pta. We therefore select the parameter evaluation v_{init} that generates ta_{init} from pta, i.e., $ta_{init} = v_{init}(pta)$;
2. we initialize Choco with v_{init}; Choco then performs a local search trying to find the assignment closest (according to a notion of distance defined later in Sect. 4) to v_{init}, and that satisfies φ.

3.9 Discussing Assumption 1

Assumption 1 assumes that the user provides a PTA pta that contains the oracle. If this is not the case, the test generation phase (Sect. 3.6) may generate a negative test (i.e., not accepted by any instance of pta) that is instead accepted by the oracle or a positive test that is not accepted by the oracle; in this case, the constraints generation phase would produce an unsatisfiable constraint φ. In this case, the user should refine the abstraction by parameterizing some other clock guards, or by relaxing the constraints on some existing parameters.

Moreover, it could be that the correct oracle has a different structure (additional states and transitions): as future work, we plan to apply other abstractions as CoPtA models [21] that allow to parametrize states and transitions.

Note that, even if the provided abstraction is wrong, our approach could still be able to refine it. In order to do this, we must avoid to use for constraint generation (step ⑤) tests that produce unsatisfiable constraints. We use a greedy incremental version of GenConstraints in which ReplayTW is called incrementally: if the constraint generated for a test w is not compatible with the other constraints generated previously, then it is discarded; otherwise it is conjuncted.

4 Experimental Evaluation

In order to evaluate our approach, we selected some benchmarks from the literature to be used as initial TA ta_{init}: the model of a coffee machine (CF) [3], of a car alarm system (CAS) [3], and the running case study (RE). For each benchmark model, Table 2 reports its number of locations and transitions.

Table 2. Benchmarks: data

Benchmark	Size of ta_{init}		# params	SD	SC (%)
	#locs.	#trans.			
RunningEx (RE)	5	4	5	2	98.33
Coffee (CF)	5	7	9	11	99.18
CarAlarmSystem (CAS)	16	25	10	12	84.24
RunningEx – different oracle (RE_{do})	5	4	5	–	98.72

The proposed approach requires that the developer, starting from ta_{init}, provides an abstraction in terms of a PTA *pta*. For the experiments, as we do not have any domain knowledge, we took the most general case and we built *pta* by adding a parameter for each guard constant; the only optimization that we did is to use the same parameter when the same constant is used on entering and/or exiting transitions of the same location (as in Fig. 1b).

In the approach, the oracle should be the real system that we can query for acceptance; in the experiments, the oracle is another TA ta_o that we obtained by slightly changing some constants on the guards. The oracle has been built in a way that it is an instance of *pta*, following Assumption 1.

In order to measure *how much* a TA (either the initial one ta_{init} or the final one ta_{rep}) is different from the oracle, we introduce a syntactic and a semantic measure, that provide different kinds of comparison with the oracle ta_o.

Given a model ta, the oracle ta_o, and a PTA *pta* having parameters $p_1, \ldots, p_n$, let v and v_o be the corresponding evaluations, i.e., $ta = v(pta)$ and $ta_o = v_o(pta)$. We define the *syntactic distance* of ta to the oracle as follows:

$$SD(ta) = \sum_{i=1}^{n} |v(p_i) - v_o(p_i)|$$

The syntactic distance roughly measures how much ta must be changed (under the constraints imposed by *pta*) in order to obtain ta_o.

The *semantic conformance*, instead, tries to assess the distance between the languages accepted by ta and the oracle ta_o. As the set of possible words is infinite, we need to select a representative set of test data TD_{SC}; to this aim, we generate, from ta_{init} and ta_o, sampled test data in the two TAs; moreover, we also add negative tests by extending the positive tests with one forbidden transition at the end. The semantic conformance is defined as follows:

$$SC(ta) = \frac{|\{t \in TD_{SC} | (t \in \mathcal{L}(ta) \wedge t \in \mathcal{L}(ta_o)) \vee (t \notin \mathcal{L}(ta) \wedge t \notin \mathcal{L}(ta_o))\}|}{|TD_{SC}|}$$

Table 2 also reports SD and SC of each benchmark ta_{init}.

Experiments have been executed on a Mac OS X 10.14, Intel Core i3, with 4 GiB of RAM. Code is implemented in Java, IMITATOR 2.11 "Butter Kouignamann" [10] is used for constraint generation, and Choco 4.10 for constraint solving. The code and the benchmarks are available at https://github.com/ERATOMMSD/repairTAsThroughAbstraction.

Table 3. Experimental results

Bench.	Policy	Time (s)					# failed tests/# tests	ta_{rep}	
		Total	Steps ②–③	Step ④	Step ⑤	Step ⑥		SD	SC (%)
RE	$P_{\pm 1}$	1.070	0.010	0.008	1.030	0.019	1/38	0	100.00
RE	$P_{minMax2}$	1.148	0.007	0.006	1.130	0.005	1/41	0	100.00
RE	$P_{minMax4}$	1.191	0.004	0.004	1.177	0.004	1/41	0	100.00
RE	P_{rnd}	0.006	0.006	0.001	0.000	0.000	0/3	2	98.33
CF	$P_{\pm 1}$	25.921	0.050	0.267	25.546	0.045	45/293	8	99.86
CF	$P_{minMax2}$	32.717	0.129	0.578	31.845	0.147	62/422	7	100.00
CF	$P_{minMax4}$	76.137	0.857	1.907	73.058	0.769	102/737	7	100.00
CF	P_{rnd}	0.134	0.098	0.035	0.000	0.000	1/11	8	99.96
CAS	$P_{\pm 1}$	59.511	0.043	0.160	59.261	0.037	174/392	2	100.00
CAS	$P_{minMax2}$	61.791	0.040	0.159	61.544	0.036	199/416	2	100.00
CAS	$P_{minMax4}$	68.341	0.716	0.467	67.037	0.584	245/464	2	100.00
CAS	P_{rnd}	0.024	0.017	0.007	0.000	0.000	0/20	12	84.24

4.1 Results

Table 3 reports the experimental results. For each benchmark and each test generation policy (see Sect. 3.4), it reports the execution time (divided between the different phases), the total number of generated tests, the number of tests that fail on ta_{init}, and SD and SC of the final TA ta_{rep}.

We now evaluate the approach answering the following research questions.

RQ1: *Is the approach able to repair faulty TAs?*

We evaluate whether the approach is actually able to (partially) repair ta_{init}. From the results, we observe that, in three cases out of four, the process can completely repair RE since SD becomes 0, meaning that we obtain exactly the oracle (therefore, also SC becomes 100%). For CF and CAS, it almost always reduces the syntactical distance SD, but it never finds the exact oracle. On the other hand, the semantic conformance SC is 100% in five cases. Note that SC can be 100% with SD different from 0 for two reasons: either the test data TD_{SC} we are using for SC are not able to show the unconformity, or ta_{rep} is indeed equivalent to the oracle, but with a different structure of the clock guards.

RQ2: *Which is the best test generation strategy?*

In Sect. 3.4, we proposed different test generation policies over $\mathcal{EPZG}$. We here assess the influence of the generation policy on the final results. $P_{\pm 1}$, $P_{minMax2}$, and $P_{minMax4}$ obtain the same best results for two benchmarks (RE and CAS), meaning that the most useful tests are those on the boundaries of the clock guards: those are indeed able to expose the failure if the fault is not too large. On the other hand, for CF, $P_{\pm 1}$ performs slightly worse than the other two, meaning that also generating tests inside the intervals (as done by $P_{minMax2}$ and $P_{minMax4}$) can be beneficial for repair. P_{rnd} is able to improve (but not totally

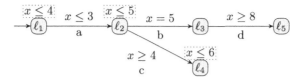

Fig. 5. Repairing TAs with different structures – another oracle TA

Table 4. Experimental results – different oracle

Bench.	Policy	Time (s)					# failed tests/# tests	ta_{rep}
		Total	Steps ②–③	Step ④	Step ⑤	Step ⑥		SC (%)
RE_{do}	$P_{\pm 1}$	2.083	0.007	0.005	2.055	0.013	10/44	98.72
RE_{do}	$P_{minMax2}$	2.718	0.005	0.004	2.693	0.013	11/47	98.72
RE_{do}	$P_{minMax4}$	2.686	0.004	0.003	2.658	0.012	11/47	98.72
RE_{do}	P_{rnd}	0.763	0.007	0.001	0.676	0.075	1/3	99.5

repair) only CF; for the other two benchmarks, it is not able to improve neither *SD* nor *SC*.

RQ3: *How long does the approach take?*

The time taken by the process depends on the size of ta_{init} and on the test generation policy. The most expensive phase is the generation of the constraints, as it requires to call IMITATOR for each test that must be accepted. As future work, we plan to optimize this phase by modifying IMITATOR to synthesize valuations guaranteeing the acceptance of multiple timed words in a single analysis. In the experiments, we use as oracle another TA that we can visit for acceptance; this visit is quite fast and so step ④ does not take too much time. However, in the real setting, the oracle is the real system whose invocation time may be not negligible; in that case, the invocation of the oracle could become a bottleneck and we would need to limit the number of generated tests.

RQ4: *Which is the process performance if pta does not include the oracle?*

Assumption 1 assumes that the user provides a PTA that contains the oracle. In Sect. 3.9, we discussed about the possible consequences when this assumption does not hold. We here evaluate whether the approach is still able to partially repair ta_{init} using an oracle having a different structure. We took the TA shown in Fig. 5 as oracle of the running example, that is structurally different from ta_{init} and *pta* shown in Fig. 1 (we name this experiment as RE_{do}); the semantic conformance SC of ta_{init} w.r.t. the new oracle is shown at the last row of Table 3[4]. We performed the experiments with the new oracle using the greedy approach described in Assumption 1, and results are reported in Table 4. We observe that policies $P_{\pm 1}$, $P_{minMax2}$, and $P_{minMax4}$, although they find some failing tests, they are not able to improve SC. This is partially due to the fact that SC is computed

---

[4] Note that it does not make sense to measure the syntactical distance, as the structure of the oracle is different.

on some timed words TD_{SC} that may be not enough to judge the improvement. On the other hand, as the three policies try to achieve a kind of coverage of *pta* (so implicitly assuming Assumption 1), it could be that they are not able to find *interesting* failing tests (i.e., they cannot be repaired); this seems to be confirmed by the fact that the random policy P_{rnd} is instead able to partially repair the initial TA using only three tests, out of which one fails. We conclude that, if the assumption does not hold, trying to randomly select tests could be more efficient.

5   Related Work

Testing timed automata. Works related to ours are approaches for test case generation for timed automata. In [1,3], a fault-based approach is proposed. The authors defined 8 mutation operators for TAs and a test generation technique based on bounded-model checking; tests are then used for model-based testing to check that System Under Test (SUT) is conformant with the specification. Our approach is different, as we aim at building a faithful representation of the SUT (i.e., the oracle). Their mutation operators could be used to repair our initial TA, as done in [14]; however, due to continuous nature of TAs, the possible mutants could be too many. For this reason, our approach symbolically represents all the possible variations of the clock guards (similar to "change guard" mutants in [3]). Other classical test generation approaches for timed automata are presented in [17,25]; while they aim at coverage of a single TA, we aim at coverage of a family of TAs described by *pta*.

Learning timed systems. The (timed) language inclusion is undecidable for timed automata [4], making learning impossible for this class. In [16,20], timed extensions of the L^* algorithm [13] were proposed for event-recording automata [5], a subclass of timed automata for which language equivalence can be decided. Learning is essentially different from our setting, as the system to be learned is usually a white-box system, in which the equivalence query can be decided. In our setting, the oracle does not necessarily know the structure of the unknown system, and simply answers membership queries. In addition, we address in our work the full class of timed automata, for which learning is not possible.

6   Conclusion and Perspectives

This paper proposes an approach for automatically repairing timed automata, notably in the case where clock guards shall be repaired. Our approach generates an abstraction of the initial TA in terms of a PTA, generates some tests, and then refines the abstraction by identifying only those TAs contained in the PTA that correctly evaluate all the tests.

As future work, we plan to adopt also other formalisms to build the abstraction where to look for the repaired timed automata; The CoPtA model [21], for example, extends timed automata with feature models and allows to specify additional/alternative states and transitions. In addition, when the oracle acts as a white-box, i.e., when the oracle is able to test language equivalence, we could also make use of learning techniques for timed automata, using the often terminating procedure for language inclusion in [26].

References

1. Aichernig, B.K., Hörmaier, K., Lorber, F.: Debugging with timed automata mutations. In: Bondavalli, A., Di Giandomenico, F.D. (eds.) SAFECOMP 2014. LNCS, vol. 8666, pp. 49–64. Springer, Cham (2014). https://doi.org/10.1007/978-3-319-10506-2_4
2. Aichernig, B.K., Jöbstl, E., Tiran, S.: Model-based mutation testing via symbolic refinement checking. Sci. Comput. Program. **97**(P4), 383–404 (2015). https://doi.org/10.1016/j.scico.2014.05.004
3. Aichernig, B.K., Lorber, F., Ničković, D.: Time for mutants—model-based mutation testing with timed automata. In: Veanes, M., Viganò, L. (eds.) TAP 2013. LNCS, vol. 7942, pp. 20–38. Springer, Heidelberg (2013). https://doi.org/10.1007/978-3-642-38916-0_2
4. Alur, R., Dill, D.L.: A theory of timed automata. Theoret. Comput. Sci. **126**(2), 183–235 (1994). https://doi.org/10.1016/0304-3975(94)90010-8
5. Alur, R., Fix, L., Henzinger, T.A.: Event-clock automata: a determinizable class of timed automata. A determinizable classof timed automata. Theoret. Comput. Sci. **211**(1–2), 253–273 (1999). https://doi.org/10.1016/S0304-3975(97)00173-4
6. Alur, R., Henzinger, T.A., Vardi, M.Y.: Parametric real-time reasoning. In: Kosaraju, S.R., Johnson, D.S., Aggarwal, A. (eds.) STOC, pp. 592–601. ACM, New York (1993). https://doi.org/10.1145/167088.167242
7. André, É.: What's decidable about parametric timed automata? Int. J. Softw. Tools Technol. Transf. **21**(2), 203–219 (2019). https://doi.org/10.1007/s10009-017-0467-0
8. André, É., Arcaini, P., Gargantini, A., Radavelli, M.: Repairing timed automata clock guards through abstraction and testing. arXiv:1907.02133 (2019)
9. André, É., Chatain, T., Encrenaz, E., Fribourg, L.: An inverse method for parametric timed automata. Int. J. Found. Comput. Sci. **20**(5), 819–836 (2009). https://doi.org/10.1142/S0129054109006905
10. André, É., Fribourg, L., Kühne, U., Soulat, R.: IMITATOR 2.5: a tool for analyzing robustness in scheduling problems. In: Giannakopoulou, D., Méry, D. (eds.) FM 2012. LNCS, vol. 7436, pp. 33–36. Springer, Heidelberg (2012). https://doi.org/10.1007/978-3-642-32759-9_6
11. André, É., Hasuo, I., Waga, M.: Offline timed pattern matching under uncertainty. In: Lin, A.W., Sun, J. (eds.) ICECCS, pp. 10–20. IEEE CPS (2018). https://doi.org/10.1109/ICECCS2018.2018.00010
12. André, É., Lin, S.-W.: Learning-based compositional parameter synthesis for event-recording automata. In: Bouajjani, A., Silva, A. (eds.) FORTE 2017. LNCS, vol. 10321, pp. 17–32. Springer, Cham (2017). https://doi.org/10.1007/978-3-319-60225-7_2
13. Angluin, D.: Learning regular sets from queries and counterexamples. Inf. Comput. **75**(2), 87–106 (1987). https://doi.org/10.1016/0890-5401(87)90052-6
14. Arcaini, P., Gargantini, A., Radavelli, M.: Achieving change requirements of feature models by an evolutionary approach. J. Syst. Softw. **150**, 64–76 (2019). https://doi.org/10.1016/j.jss.2019.01.045

15. Bengtsson, J., Yi, W.: Timed automata: semantics, algorithms and tools. In: Desel, J., Reisig, W., Rozenberg, G. (eds.) ACPN 2003. LNCS, vol. 3098, pp. 87–124. Springer, Heidelberg (2004). https://doi.org/10.1007/978-3-540-27755-2_3

16. Grinchtein, O., Jonsson, B., Leucker, M.: Learning of event-recording automata. Theoret. Comput. Sci. **411**(47), 4029–4054 (2010). https://doi.org/10.1016/j.tcs.2010.07.008

17. Hessel, A., Larsen, K.G., Mikucionis, M., Nielsen, B., Pettersson, P., Skou, A.: Testing real-time systems using UPPAAL. In: Hierons, R.M., Bowen, J.P., Harman, M. (eds.) Formal Methods and Testing. LNCS, vol. 4949, pp. 77–117. Springer, Heidelberg (2008). https://doi.org/10.1007/978-3-540-78917-8_3

18. Hune, T., Romijn, J., Stoelinga, M., Vaandrager, F.W.: Linear parametric model checking of timed automata. J. Logic Algebraic Program. **52–53**, 183–220 (2002). https://doi.org/10.1016/S1567-8326(02)00037-1

19. Jovanović, A., Lime, D., Roux, O.H.: Integer parameter synthesis for real-time systems. IEEE Trans. Softw. Eng. **41**(5), 445–461 (2015). https://doi.org/10.1109/TSE.2014.2357445

20. Lin, S.W., André, É., Liu, Y., Sun, J., Dong, J.S.: Learning assumptions for compositional verification of timed systems. Trans. Softw. Eng. **40**(2), 137–153 (2014). https://doi.org/10.1109/TSE.2013.57

21. Luthmann, L., Gerecht, T., Stephan, A., Bürdek, J., Lochau, M.: Minimum/maximum delay testing of product lines with unbounded parametric real-time constraints. J. Syst. Softw. **149**, 535–553 (2019). https://doi.org/10.1016/j.jss.2018.12.028

22. Papadakis, M., Kintis, M., Zhang, J., Jia, Y., Le Traon, Y., Harman, M.: Mutation testing advances: an analysis and survey. In: Advances in Computers. Elsevier (2018). https://doi.org/10.1016/bs.adcom.2018.03.015

23. Prud'homme, C., Fages, J.G., Lorca, X.: Choco Documentation. TASC - LS2N CNRS UMR 6241, COSLING S.A.S. (2017). http://www.choco-solver.org

24. Schrijver, A.: Theory of Linear and Integer Programming. Wiley-Interscience Series in Discrete Mathematics and Optimization. Wiley, New York (1999)

25. Springintveld, J., Vaandrager, F., D'Argenio, P.R.: Testing timed automata. Theoret. Comput. Sci. **254**(1–2), 225–257 (2001). https://doi.org/10.1016/S0304-3975(99)00134-6

26. Wang, T., Sun, J., Liu, Y., Wang, X., Li, S.: Are timed automata bad for a specification language? Language inclusion checking for timed automata. In: Ábrahám, E., Havelund, K. (eds.) TACAS 2014. LNCS, vol. 8413, pp. 310–325. Springer, Heidelberg (2014). https://doi.org/10.1007/978-3-642-54862-8_21

Proving a Non-blocking Algorithm for Process Renaming with TLA+

Aurélie Hurault and Philippe Quéinnec[✉]

IRIT, Université de Toulouse, Toulouse, France
{hurault,queinnec}@enseeiht.fr

Abstract. Shared-memory concurrent algorithms are well-known for being difficult to write, ill-adapted to test, and complex to prove. Wait-free concurrent objects are a subclass where a process is never prevented from progressing, whatever the other processes are doing (or not doing). Algorithms in this subclass are often non intuitive and among the most complex to prove. This paper presents the analysis and the proof of a wait-free concurrent algorithm that is used to rename processes. By its adaptive and non-blocking nature, the renaming algorithm resists to test, because of the cost of covering all its states and transitions even with a small input set. Thus, a proof has been conducted in TLA+ and verified with TLAPS, the TLA+ Proof System. This algorithm is itself based on the assembly of wait-free concurrent objects, the splitters, that separate processes. With just two shared variables and three assignments, a splitter seems a simple object but it is not linearizable. To avoid explicitly in-lining it and dealing with its internal state, the proof of the renaming algorithm relies on replacing the splitter with a sequential specification that is proved correct with TLAPS and verified complete by model-checking on finite instances.

Keywords: Formal verification · Non-blocking algorithm · TLA+

1 Introduction

Increase of computer performance is now obtained by multi-core multiprocessor units. Concurrent programming with locks or monitors is an old topic, and methodologies have been presented that allow developing software with few (or at least not too many) synchronization bugs. All these methodologies revolve around a *blocking* paradigm: identifying the condition for valid progress (e.g. exclusive access on a resource), and blocking while this condition is not true (e.g. waiting to acquire a lock). However, these approaches are inefficient under high load and are subject to deadlock when a process stops while holding a lock or an access. Non-blocking algorithms have been considered to alleviate these difficulties [MS98]. In a non-blocking algorithm, the delay or failure of

Supported by project PARDI ANR-16-CE25-0006.

D. Beyer and C. Keller (Eds.): TAP 2019, LNCS 11823, pp. 147–166, 2019.
https://doi.org/10.1007/978-3-030-31157-5_10

a process does not prevent the progress of other processes. Subclasses of non-blocking include lock-free, where system progress is guaranteed, and wait-free, where process progress is guaranteed [Her91]. Thus, wait-free algorithms are the most interesting to ensure individual progress in an adversary environment. Whatever the progress of the other processes, a process will be able to progress as long as the scheduler ensures that it has access to some CPU resources. Thus, wait-free algorithms are of great importance in highly concurrent environments.

Unfortunately, wait-free algorithms are hard to design and prone to bugs. They rely on low-level instructions, such as test-and-set, compare-and-swap, or shared data structures. Among these, atomic registers [Lam86,KS11] provide strong guarantees in presence of concurrency. An atomic register is a linearizable object with two operations, read and write. Progress is guaranteed even in presence of process failure. In a system where the only shared objects between processes are atomic registers, any concurrent execution (with true parallelism) is equivalent to a sequential execution on a single processor with interleaving. This nice property is instrumental in checking and verifying a wait-free algorithm as it spares us to consider true parallelism.

Nevertheless, writing a wait-free algorithm is error-prone. Correctness is often on paper only, and cannot be certified. Lastly, testing these wait-free algorithms is difficult as they generally exhibit a large reachable state space, and execution interleaving leads to a huge number of executions to consider. Bugs are often hidden in the deepest part of the algorithm and few schedulings can trigger them. Wait-free algorithms and data structures have started being used in standard libraries (for instance the `ConcurrentLinkedQueue` class in Java) but their first implementations were not always exempt of bugs [JDK08].

In this paper, we present the study of Moir and Anderson renaming algorithm [MA95]. The goal of this algorithm is to assign names (or identifiers) to processes such that the size of the namespace is small. This algorithm is wait-free, and is itself built upon wait-free objects, the splitters. This study has been conducted with the TLA$^+$ tools [Lam94] to provide a certified proof of the correctness of the renaming algorithm.

The contributions of this paper are:

- A mechanized proof of a wait-free renaming algorithm, based upon wait-free objects;
- An approach to handle the internal wait-free objects as black boxes;
- A combination of model-checking and formal proofs to verify correctness and completeness of the wait-free objects.

The *TAP Artifact Evaluation Committee* has reviewed the full artifact of our approach (available on [HQ19]). The four reviewers have found it consistent with the paper and have noted that the structure of the proofs in the artifact match their description in the paper. Regarding correctness, the four proof files have all been replayed without errors. As expected, checking the completeness is more intricate, and the reviewers have reached different upper bounds depending on their computing power.

2   TLA$^+$ Specification Language and Tools

2.1   Language

TLA$^+$ [Lam02] is a formal specification language based on untyped Zermelo-Fraenkel set theory for specifying data structures, and on the temporal logic of actions (TLA) for specifying dynamic behaviors. TLA$^+$ allows specifying symbolic transition systems with variables and *actions*. An action is a transition predicate between a state and a successor state. It is an arbitrary first-order predicate with quantifiers, set and arithmetic operators, and functions. In an action, x denotes the value of a variable x in the origin state, and x' denotes its value in the next state. Expressions rely on standard first-order logic, set operators, and several arithmetic modules. Functions are primitive objects in TLA$^+$. The application of function f to an expression e is written as $f[e]$. The set of functions whose domain is X and whose co-domain is a subset of Y is written as $[X \rightarrow Y]$. The expression DOMAIN f is the domain of the function f. The expression $[x \in X \mapsto e]$ denotes the function with domain X that maps any $x \in X$ to the expression e (which can include x). The notation $[f$ EXCEPT $![e_1] = e_2]$ is a function which is equal to the function f except at point e_1, where its value is e_2. A specification of a system is usually a disjunction of actions. Fairness, usually expressed as a conjunction of weak or strong fairness on actions, or more generally as an LTL property, ensures progression.

2.2   Tools

The TLA$^+$ toolbox contains the TLC model checker, the TLAPS proof assistant, and various tools such as a translator for the PlusCal Algorithm Language [Lam09] into a TLA$^+$ specification, and a pretty-printer that converts a textual TLA$^+$ specification into a LaTeX file.

PlusCal. Pluscal is an algorithm language that looks like a programming language (assignment, loop, conditional) augmented with constructs for describing concurrency and non-determinism. PlusCal is actually more expressive than a traditional programming language as its expressions are any TLA$^+$ expressions.

TLC. TLC, the TLA$^+$ Model Checker, is an enumerative explicit-state model-checker that can check safety and liveness properties. Its parallel implementation achieves a close to linear speedup for checking safety properties. To verify a TLA$^+$ specification, TLC requires all constants (e.g. number of processes) to be instantiated.

TLA$^+$ Proof System. TLAPS, the TLA$^+$ Proof System, is a proof assistant for writing and checking TLA$^+$ proofs [CDLM10]. TLA$^+$ proofs are written in a hierarchical and declarative style with steps and substeps. A proof manager translates these steps in proof obligations, checks the trivial ones and uses back-end provers for the other ones. These backend provers include SMT provers

(CVC3 is supplied, and Z3, CVC4, VeriT and Yices are supported), a TLA⁺ theory in Isabelle, Zenon (an automated theorem prover for first-order logic based on the tableau method), or LS4 (to prove Propositional Temporal Logic).

3   The Renaming Problem

The renaming problem consists in renaming processes so they have a unique name on a small space. Initially, every process is assumed to have a unique identifier on an arbitrary large space (for instance, the IP address of the computer it is running on and the memory address of its control block). The only property of these identifiers is that they allow distinguishing processes, that is they can be compared for equality. A renaming algorithm assigns a distinct value, called a name, to each process, so that no two processes have the same name and the range of these names is small with regard to their initial identifiers. This algorithm is useful as it allows to efficiently refer to a set of processes, for instance by using an array indexed with their names.

In a shared-memory context, a trivial algorithm can solve the renaming problem using a counter and a lock. To get a name, a process acquires the lock, gets the current value of the counter and increments it, and releases the lock. Then the range of names for renaming N processes is optimal with size N. This algorithm has two shortcomings: it is inefficient under high load because of contention on the lock, and it is not delay-tolerant or fault-tolerant. If a process is delayed or stops while holding the lock, the other processes have to wait for it to complete its invocation, potentially infinitely. This can happen for instance if a process is paused or swapped by the process scheduler, or in an adversary environment, when an evil process does a denial-of-service attack by holding the lock.

Several wait-free algorithms for the renaming problem have been proposed [MA95, AM99, GR10, CRR11, RR11]. In these wait-free algorithms, the lack of progress of one process has no impact on the progress of the others. In this paper, we focus on the first wait-free algorithm for renaming that has been proposed, by Moir and Anderson [MA95]. This algorithm renames up to N processes from an arbitrary large namespace to a namespace of size $\frac{N(N+1)}{2}$ with time complexity $\Theta(N)$. We have actually considered a more demanding variation of the original algorithm: the proven algorithm is adaptive, in the sense that the size of the resulting namespace only depends on the actual number of participants (as opposed to the maximal number of participants for non-adaptive renaming).

3.1   Informal Description

Moir and Anderson algorithm is based on a building block, the splitter (Fig. 1). A splitter is used to separate processes. When a process executes the code of a splitter, it eventually receives a value of *stop*, *right* or *down*. The main property is that at most one process ever receives *stop*, not all processes receive *right* and not all processes receive *down*. Simultaneous invocations of a splitter are

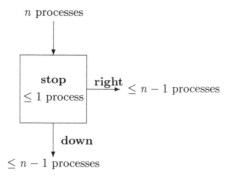

Fig. 1. Specification of a splitter

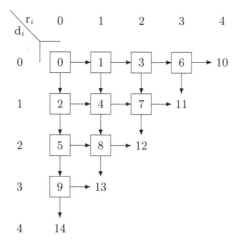

Fig. 2. Structure of Moir-Anderson algorithm for up to 5 processes

possible, and its code is concurrently executed. Equipped with this splitter, the renaming algorithm consists in a half-grid of splitters (Fig. 2).

Every process starts in the $(0,0)$ box and follows the rule of the splitter it is on. If it receives *stop*, it gets the name on this splitter and ends. If it receives *right* (resp. *down*), it moves to the right (resp. down) splitter. For N processes, a half grid of $\frac{N(N+1)}{2}$ splitters ensures that every process eventually gets a unique name (on the diagonal in the worst case, which it needs N moves to reach, thus time complexity of $\Theta(N)$, splitters being $\Theta(1)$).

3.2   Algorithm

The renaming algorithm is given Fig. 3. Each splitter at coordinate (d, r) is implemented with two atomic registers X and Y that are shared by all processes. These registers ensure that reads and writes are atomic under concurrent

```
1    initially ∀ d,r ∈ 0..N−1, d+r < N : Y[d][r] = FALSE ∧ X[d][r] = ?
2    rename(id)
3        while (d+r < N−1 ∧ ¬ stop ) do
4            X[d][r] := id;
5            if Y[d][r]
6            then r := r + 1 \* right
7            else
8                Y[d][r] := TRUE
9                if (X[d][r] = id)
10               then stop := TRUE \* stop
11               else d := d + 1        \* down
12               endif
13           endif
14       end while
15       return ½(r + d)(r + d + 1) + d
```

Fig. 3. Code of the renaming algorithm

access. More precisely, an atomic register is a linearizable object that has two operations *read* and *write*. Informally, linearizability means that each operation call appears to take effect instantaneously at some point between its invocation and its response. More rigorously, linearizability means that the object behaves as if all processes agree on a sequential history of operations that is correct with regard to the sequential definition of the object (i.e. a read returns the most recent written value), and such that this history does not reorder completed operations. From a proof point of view, it means that the algorithm behaves as an interleaving of atomic process actions, where an action can read or write at most one shared variable.

Initially, all the Y are false, and the X can hold any value. The variables d, r and stop are local to each process. An arbitrary number of processes (up to N) concurrently call **rename** with their original ids on the large namespace. Each process individually progresses at its own speed. When it gets a *stop* or reaches the diagonal, it computes a return value from its coordinates in the grid, using Cantor pairing function (a bijection from $\mathbb{N} \times \mathbb{N}$ to $\mathbb{N}$).

4   Proving the Renaming Algorithm with In-Line Splitters

4.1   A Focus on the Splitter

Let's consider one splitter in isolation (Fig. 4). A splitter is inherently concurrent, and it cannot be specified as a sequential object with a single operation. This is shown by contradiction. Assume there is a sequential object with a single operation that behaves as a splitter. As it is sequential, there exists a first process to invoke its operation. As this process may be alone, it must obtain *stop* (*right* and *down* are incorrect if it is alone). The next processes can receive either *down*

```
1   initially  Y = false ∧ X = ?
2   direction (id)
3       X := id
4       if Y then dir := right
5       else Y := true
6           if (X = id) then dir := stop
7           else dir := down
8           endif
9       endif
10      return dir
```

Fig. 4. Implementation of a splitter with two registers

or *right*, without restriction. Such a sequential object has fewer behaviors than a splitter: with a splitter, a concurrent execution allows half the processes to receive down and the other half to receive right, and none to receive stop. For instance, consider two processes that simultaneously enter the code in Fig. 4. Process 1 writes register X with its id (line 3); process 2 overwrites it with its own id; process 1 tests Y and finds it false (line 4); it checks the value of X (line 6), does not found its id, and gets *down*; then process 2 checks Y (line 4), finds it true, and gets *right*. Thus, a splitter cannot be called as a function, and its code is in-line in the code of the renaming.

Correctness Properties. The correctness properties of a splitter are:

Coherency processes are split in at least two categories, and at most one *stop*:

$$\Box \left(\begin{array}{l} \forall p, q \in Proc, dir_p = stop \wedge dir_q = stop \Rightarrow p = q \\ \wedge\ \exists p \in Proc, dir_p \neq right \\ \wedge\ \exists p \in Proc, dir_p \neq down \end{array} \right) \tag{1}$$

Termination every correct entering process eventually gets a direction:

$$\forall p \in Proc, \Box(p \text{ enters the splitter} \Rightarrow \Diamond(dir_p \in \{stop, down, right\})) \tag{2}$$

State Space. Another difficulty with the splitter (and more generally with wait-free objects) is that the reachable state space is a significant part of the possible valuations of the variables. The direction variable can hold four values (the undetermined value $\bot$, *stop*, *down*, *right*), thus the corresponding state space for N processes is 4^N. The number of valid assignments of directions that respect the property of coherency (1) is[1]:

---

[1] The percentage decrease is explained by the progressive dominance of multiple *stop* in the invalid assignments.

Number of processes	2	3	4	5	6	7	8
Possible assignments	16	64	256	1024	4096	16384	65536
Valid assignments	13	52	187	646	2185	7288	24055
Percentage	81%	81%	73%	63%	53%	44%	38%

Table 1. Model-checking of a Splitter with registers (left) and of the Renaming Algorithm with registers (right). NP is the number of processes, distinct states is the number of distinct states found by TLC, and depth (or diameter) is the length of the longest execution (ignoring stuttering loops). Times are wall-clock time. Experiments were conducted on a 32 core 2,1 GHz computer with 16 GB.

NP	distinct states	depth	time
2	98	11	
3	1389	16	
4	17164	21	
5	193115	26	2 s
6	2041458	31	15 s
7	20675305	36	1 min 50 s
8	203055896	41	12 min 24 s
9	1948989879	46	16 h 08 min

NP	distinct states	depth	time
2	142	14	
3	21260	33	1 s
4	6381732	58	56 s
5	5183748425	90	51 h 19 min

4.2 An Attempt at Proving the Renaming Algorithm

The renaming algorithm has been specified in TLA$^+$, using PlusCal [Lam09]. The steps have been chosen such that there is at most one read or write of a shared register at each step. This leads to six atomic transitions. Even if the principle and the algorithm are quite simple (13 lines, 2 matrices of shared registers, 2 conditionals and 1 loop), the proof of the uniqueness of the names is not trivial.

Correctness Properties. The renaming algorithm must verify:

Coherency processes obtain unique names:

$$\forall p, q \in Proc, p \neq q, \Box(name_p \neq \bot \wedge name_q \neq \bot \Rightarrow name_p \neq name_q) \quad (3)$$

Termination every correct entering process eventually gets a name:

$$\forall p \in Proc, \Box(p \text{ enters the renaming} \Rightarrow \Diamond(name_p \neq \bot)) \quad (4)$$

Model Checking. To get an idea of the degree of interleaving, we have model-checked both a splitter and the renaming algorithm with TLC, the TLA$^+$ model checker (Table 1). Observe that model-checking was quickly overwhelmed for the renaming algorithm. Checking with four or five processes is insufficient to get confidence in the correctness of the algorithm. Scaling from four to five processes took a lot of time (more than two days compared with less than one minute) and resources (16 GB memory and up to 110 GB disk space were required).

Proof. In the original paper, the correctness proof is given "on paper" and takes 4 pages and 12 invariants. Half of these invariants are considered trivial, and no proofs are given. Mechanically proving these *trivial* invariants was already challenging because of the intricate behavior of the splitters, and it was clear that a complete proof would require too much effort.

5 Proving the Renaming Algorithm with Linearizable Splitters

Seeing that the trivial parts of the proof were not that trivial, we decided to rethink the original algorithm:

- to reduce the interleaving, by reducing the number of step/transitions in the algorithm;
- to hide the internal parts of the splitters, as much as possible;
- to take advantage of the grid architecture (Fig. 2) by finding a way to make direct call to the splitters and being able to use theorems on splitters.

5.1 Making the Splitter Linearizable

To reduce interleaving and being able to see the splitter as a black box, the natural idea is the notion of atomic or linearizable objects [HW90]: a linearizable object behaves as if it is accessed sequentially, even in presence of concurrent invocations. Unfortunately, as shown in Sect. 4.1, a splitter is inherently concurrent, and it cannot be expressed as a linearizable object with one operation. However, the results of [CHQR19] state that the splitter can be transformed in an object with a sequential specification composed of two operations *set* and *get*.

A Set/Get Splitter. The specification of the splitter with two operations (*set* and *get*) is given in Fig. 5. Each of the operations is divided in an enabling condition (*setenabled/getenabled*) and a construction of the new state (*set/get*). The *set* operation is enabled if the process is not already in the splitter and registers that the process is entering the splitter. The *get* operation corresponds to a process receiving a direction. The pre-condition of the *get* operation ensures that the answer is valid regarding the specification in Fig. 1 and Eq. (1).

For a variable *spl* and a process $p \in Proc$, a well-formed usage of the module is a sequence of two TLA$^+$ actions: $setenabled(spl, p) \wedge spl' = set(spl, p)$, then $\exists dir \in \{Stop, Down, Right\} : getenabled(spl, p, dir) \wedge spl' = get(spl, p, dir)$.

Proofs of Correctness and Completeness. To be useful, this version of the splitter needs to be correct and complete. The correctness is the coherency property (1) and the termination property (2). The completeness means that any correct output can be delivered by the splitter with *set/get*. Indeed, the goal of this version of the splitter is to be used as a black box in the renaming algorithm. The proof of the renaming algorithm will be done with the black box version, and the implementation will use a particular implementation of the splitter, for instance the one in Fig. 4. If the black box version is not complete, the proof may omit some pathological cases.

```
┌──────────────────── MODULE Splitter ────────────────────┐
│ CONSTANT Proc   the calling processes
│ None ≜ "none"
│ Right ≜ "right"
│ Stop  ≜ "stop"
│ Down ≜ "down"
│ Direction ≜ {None, Right, Stop, Down}
│ Type ≜ [participants : SUBSET Proc,
│              stop : SUBSET Proc, down : SUBSET Proc, right : SUBSET Proc]
│
│ new ≜ [participants ↦ {}, stop ↦ {}, down ↦ {}, right ↦ {}]
│
│ setenabled(s, pid) ≜ s ∉ s.participants   set not already called
│ set(s, pid) ≜ [s EXCEPT !.participants = s.participants ∪ {pid}]
│
│ getenabled(s, pid, ans) ≜
│        ∧ pid ∈ s.participants ∧ pid ∉ (s.stop ∪ s.right ∪ s.down)   set done and get not done
│        ∧ ∨ ans = Stop   ∧ s.stop = {}                                valid answers
│          ∨ ans = Right ∧ (s.right ∪ {pid}) ≠ s.participants
│          ∨ ans = Down ∧ (s.down ∪ {pid}) ≠ s.participants
│ get(s, pid, ans) ≜ CASE
│          ans = Stop   → [s EXCEPT !.stop = {pid}]
│       □  ans = Right → [s EXCEPT !.right = s.right ∪ {pid}]
│       □  ans = Down → [s EXCEPT !.down = s.down ∪ {pid}]
└──────────────────────────────────────────────────────────┘
```

Fig. 5. The TLA$^+$ *set/get* specification of a splitter

Correctness. The correctness proof is done assuming that the splitter is well-used, i.e. that *set* is called before *get* and the enabling conditions of each operation are true. The proof of termination (2) is trivial: there is no loop and whatever were the return values to previous processes, a process can always get at least one valid value and thus cannot be blocked in the enabling condition *getenabled*. The proof of coherency (1) has been conducted with TLAPS for any number of processes (file `Splitter_correct_proof.tla` in [HQ19]).

Completeness. Completeness of this specification has also been considered. It must be shown that all correct combinations of output values are possible. The predicate *CorrectDirection(Proc, direction)* states that *direction* is a valid output array satisfying (1), and *dir* is the received values of the processes. Completeness is expressed as (where **EF**P is the CTL (computational tree logic) temporal operator stating that there exists a branch where P is eventually true):

$$Completeness \triangleq \forall direction \in [Proc \to Direction] :$$
$$CorrectDirection(Proc, direction) \Rightarrow \mathbf{EF}(dir = direction)$$

TLA$^+$ is based on LTL (linear temporal logic) and this CTL formula is not checkable. However, the negation of **EF**P is **AG**$\neg P$, and as P is a state predicate, this corresponds to the LTL invariant $\Box\neg P$. Thus, completeness can be verified in the following way. First, TLC is used to enumerate all the valid arrays of direction. Then, each of them is stated as unreachable ($\Box\neg(\ldots)$), and this property is checked with TLC. A counter-example proves that the state is actually reachable. Optimisations based on symmetry have been introduced, and the completeness of the *set/get* splitter has been verified up to 10 processes (255877 distinct states to check for reachability, reduced to 119 with permutations, 1 h 42 min on a modern quad core laptop).

5.2 The Renaming Algorithm Using Linearizable Splitters

The renaming algorithm has been rewritten using *set/get* splitters. The PlusCal version of the renaming problem using *set/get* splitters is given in Fig. 6. The translated TLA$^+$ had to be slightly tweaked because the provers have difficulties handling EXCEPT with multi-dimensional arrays, whereas the equivalent form that defines an array is fine[2].

5.3 Proof Sketch of the Coherency Property

The full proof has been conducted with TLAPS and is available online [HQ19]. The line numbers below refer to the file `Renaming.tla` that holds the algorithm and its proof.

Overall Picture. The correctness property (3) states that all the processes must have distinct names (`Uniqueness` property in the TLA$^+$ module – line 2027). This uniqueness is guaranteed if all the processes end with different coordinates (`I12` property – line 1955, whose proof (lines 1957–1979) is used to prove the `Uniqueness` property (lines 2030–2040)). A process ends either on the diagonal (condition $d + r < NP - 1$ violated, line 14 in Fig. 6) or if it gets *Stop* in a splitter that is not on the diagonal (lines 15–17 in Fig. 6). Consider two different processes that get a name (line 28):

- they both stop in a splitter that is not on the diagonal: as at most one process can stop in a splitter, they stop in different splitters and do not have the same coordinates (`StopDifferentProcessesDifferentCoordinates` property – defined line 429 and proved lines 353–434);
- one process stops in a splitter that is not on the diagonal, and the other one stops on the diagonal: they trivially do not have the same coordinates (`StopAndDoneDiffCoord` property – defined line 566 and proved lines 438–574);
- they both stop on the diagonal: this is not trivial and is explained in the following (`IDDX` property – defined line 1851 and proved lines 577–1906).

---

[2] The construct $[x \text{ EXCEPT } ![e_1] = e_2]$ is a shortcut for $[i \in \text{DOMAIN } x \mapsto \text{IF } i = e_1 \text{ THEN } e_2 \text{ ELSE } x[i]]$. For multi-dimensional arrays, provers work better with the latest.

```
 1 ┌──────────────── MODULE renaming ────────────────┐
 2  EXTENDS Naturals
 3  CONSTANT NP              – number of processes
 4  INSTANCE Splitter WITH Proc ← 1 .. NP
 5  Coord ≜ 0 .. NP − 1      – coordinate in the grid
 7  --algorithm renaming
 8  variables spl = [i ∈ Coord ↦ [j ∈ Coord ↦ new]] ;
 9  fair process proc ∈ 1 .. NP
10  variables d = 0, r = 0, name = 0 ;
11  begin
12  l0: await setenabled(spl[d][r], self) ;
13      spl[d][r] := set(spl[d][r], self) ;
14  l1: if (d + r < NP − 1) then
15  l2:     either await getenabled(spl[d][r], self, Stop) ;
16                 spl[d][r] := get(spl[d][r], self, Stop) ;
17                 goto l8 ;
18          or await getenabled(spl[d][r], self, Right) ;
19             spl[d][r] := get(spl[d][r], self, Right) ;
20             r := r + 1 ;
21             goto l0 ;
22          or await getenabled(spl[d][r], self, Down) ;
23             spl[d][r] := get(spl[d][r], self, Down) ;
24             d := d + 1 ;
25             goto l0 ;
26          end either
27      end if ;
28  l8: name := ((r + d) ∗ (r + d + 1) ÷ 2) + d ;
29  end process
30  end algorithm
31 └──────────────────────────────────────────────────┘
```

Fig. 6. Renaming algorithm in PlusCal using set/get splitters.

Number of Participants in a Splitter. To prove this last case, the key inductive invariant is that (NbParticipants property – line 588):

$$\forall i, j \in Coord : Cardinality(splitters[j][i].participants) = 0$$
$$\lor Cardinality(splitters[j][i].participants) \leq NP - (i + j)$$

The first disjunction handles the case where the coordinates are outside the half-grid $(i+j \geq NP)$, and the second one handles the case where the coordinates are inside the half-grid $(i + j < NP)$.

A simple induction using that processes enter a splitter (i, j) either from the splitter on top $(i − 1, j)$ or from the splitter on left $(i, j − 1)$, and that not all processes can go down or right, gives that there is at most $NP - (i - 1 + j) - 1 + NP - (i + j - 1) - 1$, i.e. $2 * (NP - (i + j))$ processes in the splitter (i, j). This basic induction fails. As an example, consider the splitter $(1, 1)$. To receive $NP - 2$ processes from the splitter $(0, 1)$, there must be at least $NP - 1$ processes in the splitter $(0, 1)$. It means that there is at most 1 process in the splitter $(1, 0)$. This process, alone, stops in this splitter and no process comes from the splitter $(1, 0)$ to the splitter $(1, 1)$.

Since a simple induction fails, another invariant is needed (NbParticipantsBis property – line 795):

$$\forall i, j \in Coord : Cardinality(\{p \in ProcSet : d[p] \geq j \wedge r[p] \geq i\}) = 0$$
$$\vee Cardinality(\{p \in ProcSet : d[p] \geq j \wedge r[p] \geq i\}) \leq NP - (i + j)$$

This invariant considers the triangle below and to the right of (i, j), i.e. the triangle with coordinates (i, j), $(NP - 1 - i, j)$ and $(i, NP - 1 - j)$. In the following, we refer to this triangle as *the (i, j) triangle*.

The proof is done by proving that the property is preserved by all the transitions. For the (i, j) triangle, the two non-trivial cases are when a process in a splitter in column $i - 1$ moves right, or a process in a splitter in line $j - 1$ moves down. In both cases, the number of processes in the (i, j) triangle increases. These two cases are symmetric, and only the first one is discussed.

The intuition behind the proof is shown in Fig. 7.

- The induction hypothesis gives that in the $(i - 1, j)$ triangle (green in Fig. 7), there are less than $NP - i - j + 1$ processes.
- The fact that *self* can move right ensures that there is at least another process in the splitters including or below the one of *self* (orange in Fig. 7). This property (2InColumnWhenRight property – line 1380) is proved thanks to another invariant that states that if at one point there is a participant in a splitter, there will always be (at least) a process in the column of the splitter (AlwaysOneInColumn property – line 1248). This last one is proved thanks to the correctness of the splitter: not all processes can go right (EnableRightExistsOtherNotRight – line 199 in the Splitter.tla file).

This means that before *self* moves, there is at most $NP - i - j + 1 - 2$ processes in the (i, j) triangle (blue in the Fig. 7). So after the transition, there are at most $NP - i - j + 1 - 2 + 1 = NP - i - j$ processes in the (i, j) triangle. QED.

Metrics of the Proof. The first version was 3000 lines, and after cleaning (factorization into lemma and removing steps not needed by TLAPS), it consists in 2000 lines of TLAPS for the renaming, and 200 lines for the splitter, with a total of 70 lemmas and theorems, and 963 proof steps.

The splitter proofs are composed of 93 proof obligations. Among them, 43 are obvious and discharged by tlapm (the TLA$^+$ proof manager). The other 50 are proved by SMT (we use CVC3, VeriT and Z3).

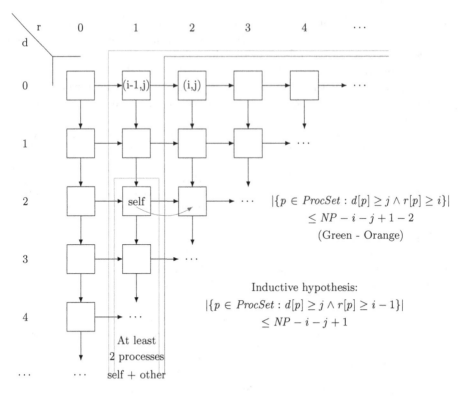

Fig. 7. Intuition behind the proof of Moir-Anderson algorithm (Color figure online)

The renaming proof is composed of 1541 proof obligations. Among them, 914 are trivial and proved by tlapm. Among the 627 left, 108 are proved by Zenon (an automated theorem prover), 35 are proved by LS4 (temporal logic), 475 are proved by SMT and 9 are proved by Isabelle (properties on sets).

To check the proof, TLAPS takes 10 min on a quad core modern laptop.

5.4 Proof Sketch of the Termination Property

The second correctness property is the termination (4): every correct process eventually gets a name. To do this, we show by induction that, for each process, (d, r) lexicographically increases until either the sum reaches NP, or the process receives a *Stop* and terminates. Assume a process is at $l0$ (Fig. 6, lines 12–13), that its current value of (d, r) is (i, j) and that (d, r) has lexicographically increased until that point, meaning that it is the first time it reaches (i, j). At $l0$, *setenabled* is true as the process has not previously called *set* on the splitter (i, j). The process reaches $l1$ (line 14). At $l1$, the process can go to $l8$ and terminate (QED), or continue to $l2$. At $l2$ (lines 15–27), *getenabled* is true as the process has previously called *setenabled* on this splitter, the process has not previously called *get* on this splitter (first occurrence of (i, j)), and at least

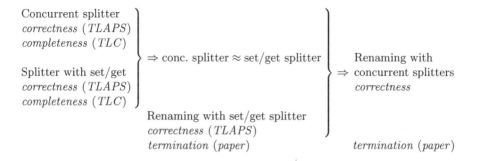

Fig. 8. Summary of the approach. For each property, the verification method is given (proof with TLAPS, model-checking with TLC, proof on paper).

one of the choices $\{Stop, Right, Down\}$ is enabled (the specification of a splitter (Fig. 5) guarantees that the three sets *stop*, *down* and *right* are disjoint, thus at least one choice is enabled). If the process gets *Stop*, it goes to $l8$ and terminates (QED); if it gets *Down* or *Right*, d or r increases, thus (d, r) becomes $(i + 1, j)$ or $(i, j + 1)$, and so lexicographically increases. The condition in $l1$ eventually becomes false, and the process reaches $l8$ (QED).

TLAPS does not support checking liveness properties, and this proof has not been mechanically verified.

5.5   Back to the Original Algorithm

The last step to prove the original Moir-Anderson algorithm of Fig. 3 consists in putting back the concurrent splitters implemented with registers in place of the linearizable splitters with *set/get*. Both versions of the splitter have been proved equivalent by proving that they satisfy the same correctness properties (properties (1) and (2)) and are both complete[3]. For the concurrent splitter, the proof of coherency (1) has been done in TLAPS (file `Splitter_register.tla` in [HQ19]). It consists in 8 lemmas and theorems that prove 17 elementary properties with 30 proof steps. The proof of termination (2) is trivial as it is straight-line code. The proof of completeness has been done by model-checking just like for the linearizable splitter (Sect. 5.1).

Regarding termination of the renaming algorithm with concurrent splitters (4), a similar argument to 5.4 shows that, for each process, (d, r) lexicographically increases until either the sum reaches NP, or the process receives a *Stop* and terminates.

---

[3] Another approach would have been to show a bisimulation between their transition systems. Note that it requires to exhibit a *parameterized* bisimulation, as we have to consider any number of concurrent invocations. We had already proved the properties on the concurrent splitter during our initial attempt at proving the renaming algorithm (Sect. 4.2) and it seemed simpler to continue onward.

A summary of the approach we have used to prove the original Moir-Anderson algorithm is shown in Fig. 8.

6   Related Work

Wait-free data structures were introduced by Herlihy [Her91], and then automatically derived from a sequential implementation using universal simulations [Her93]. However, the state of the art universal construction [CER10] is still far too slow compared to the hand-crafted lock-free or lock-based versions. In [TP14], the authors observe that wait-free implementations are notoriously hard to design and often inefficient. One approach consists in designing a lock-free data structure, and then in manually transforming it into a wait-free data structure. [TP14] presents a mechanical transformation of lock-free data structures to wait-free ones. The limits of this work is first, the existence of the lock-free implementation, which has to be written and proven, and secondly, that this implementation must have a normalized form to be convertible.

[GGH05] is a rare example of the certified proof of a lock-free algorithm. The proof of safety has been conducted in PVS, while the proof of progress is on paper. Building on this experience, [GH04] presents a reduction theorem that allows reasoning about a lock-free program to be designed on a higher level than the elementary synchronization primitives. Lamport's refinement mappings are used to prove that the lower-level specification correctly implements the higher-level one. The reduction theorem has been verified with PVS.

Wait-free implementation of tasks have been mechanically proven (e.g. [ORV+10, TSR14, DGH13]). However, to the best of our knowledge, no non-trivial wait-free algorithm built upon wait-free tasks has been mechanically proved. Our intuition for this situation is that proofs cannot be made modular and compositional when using bricks which are inherently concurrent if their internal structure must be visible to take into account this concurrency. Several complex and original algorithms can be found in the literature such as Moir and Anderson renaming algorithm [MA95] that we have considered in this paper, stacks implemented with elimination trees [ST97], lock-free queues with elimination [MNSS05]. In these papers, the correctness proofs are intricate as they must consider the algorithm as a whole, including the tricky part involving wait-free objects, and they have not been mechanically checked. Our approach which exposes a more simple and sequential specification (instead of a complex concurrent implementation) seeks to alleviate this limitation.

Other works have studied the replacement of the complex implementation of part of a system with a simpler one to ease the proof. For example in [GKR+15], the authors use the notion of deep specification to verify a layer-based architecture. By taking into account the context, a given deep specification may have several implementations which all yield equivalent behaviors. Then, a proof of a whole program can be done using the deep specification of a subprogram (which is simpler than the implementations) and it will stay valid when replacing this subprogram with its implementation. Our approach is similar with a non-layered algorithm, and the set/get specification can be seen as a deep specification, adhering to the coherency property and compatible with the non-linearizable nature of the splitter.

7   Conclusion

Mechanically proving and certifying a wait-free algorithm built upon wait-free objects is a challenging task. An important step is the replacement of the internal wait-free objects with objects having a sequential specification. This allows a compositional approach to the proof, where theorems are proved on the internal objects and reused in the proof of the algorithm. Moreover, this black box view greatly reduces the number of control points in the algorithm, and thus the number of interleavings.

TLA$^+$ has been found well adapted for this task. It natively contains advanced data structures (sets, arrays and maps) with the usual mathematical foundations and notations. Concurrency is intrinsic, both in algorithm description and in reasoning. Tool support is adequate, allowing tests (possibly exhaustively on small models) and proofs. The hierarchical structure advocated by Lamport [Lam12] helps in incrementally building the proofs, by focusing on the important cases of a theorem and delaying the proofs of the obvious or marginal cases. Proving a realistic algorithm such as Moir-Anderson algorithm requires various theories: numbers (coordinates in the grid), sets (cardinality and partitioning), functions (arrays), temporal logic (invariants). The hierarchical structure allows decomposing the proof of a theorem that requires several theories in steps where only one is needed. This in turn allows using the most adequate prover for this theory and simplifies automation of the proof.

A   Description of the Artifact

This artifact [HQ19] allows to replicate all the results that we claim in the paper:

- the proof of correctness of the splitter with registers,
- the proof of correctness of the splitter with set/get,
- the way to check the completeness of the splitter with set/get,
- the way to check the completeness of the splitter with registers,
- the proof of correctness of the renaming algorithm using the set/get splitter.

Combining these results implies that the renaming algorithm is correct when used with the original splitter with registers.

A.1   Requirements

Running the artifact relies on the TLA+ Toolbox and the TLA+ Proof System. Both are included in the distributed files, and a script is supplied to install them. The verification of the correctness proofs is achievable on a standard laptop, checking the completeness requires much more resources (at least a quad core with 8 GB of memory, and a 32 core computer with 16 GB was used for the largest numbers of processes).

A.2   Proofs of Correctness

The proof of correctness of Moir-Anderson renaming algorithm is built upon the four following files:

- `Splitter.tla`: the set/get splitter with some lemma needed for the correctness proof of the renaming;
- `Splitter_correct_proof.tla`: the proof of correctness of the set/get splitter;
- `Renaming.tla`: the Renaming algorithm and its proof of correctness;
- `Splitter_register.tla`: the splitter based on register and its proof of correctness.

One just has to load them in the toolbox and launch the verification, as explained in the artifact distribution.

A.3   Proofs of Completeness

The goal is to verify the completeness of an implementation w.r.t a property P, i.e. that all the valid (w.r.t to P) assignments of the variables are reachable in the implementation.

Our approach consists in two steps: first generate all the valid assignments; then, for each of these assignments, verify that it is reachable. As we rely on TLC, the TLA$^+$ model checker, this approach works for a given number of processes.

1. Choose a number of processes;
2. `generate-states nbproc Splitter_config.tla`
   The module Splitter_config.tla is used to generate all the return values that satisfy the correctness property of the splitter, for **nbproc** processes.
3. `check-reachability vars XXX.tla`
   For each valuation (read from stdin), a module is built with an invariant

$$\text{INVARIANT } Unreachable \triangleq vars \neq valuation$$

   and it is model-checked with the specification in **XXX**. It should end with a violation, which proves that this state is reachable.
4. Once all states have been checked, this proves the completeness of **XXX** for this number of processes.

A script **runall** enumerates the verification of both splitter specifications for 1, 2, 3 etc. processes. One can also check a specific size.

References

[AM99]   Afek, Y., Merritt, M.: Fast, wait-free (2k)-renaming. In: 18th Annual ACM Symposium on Principles of Distributed Computing, pp. 105–112 (1999)

[CDLM10] Chaudhuri, K., Doligez, D., Lamport, L., Merz, S.: Verifying safety properties with the TLA$^+$ proof system. In: Giesl, J., Hähnle, R. (eds.) IJCAR 2010. LNCS (LNAI), vol. 6173, pp. 142–148. Springer, Heidelberg (2010). https://doi.org/10.1007/978-3-642-14203-1_12

[CER10] Chuong, P., Ellen, F., Ramachandran, V.: A universal construction for wait-free transaction friendly data structures. In: 22nd ACM Symposium on Parallelism in Algorithms and Architectures, pp. 335–344 (2010)

[CHQR19] Castaneda, A., Hurault, A., Queinnec, P., Roy, M.: Modular machine-checked proofs of concurrent algorithms built from tasks. In: Submitted to DISC 2019 (2019)

[CRR11] Castañeda, A., Rajsbaum, S., Raynal, M.: The renaming problem in shared memory systems: an introduction. Comput. Sci. Rev. **5**(3), 229–251 (2011)

[DGH13] Drăgoi, C., Gupta, A., Henzinger, T.A.: Automatic linearizability proofs of concurrent objects with cooperating updates. In: Sharygina, N., Veith, H. (eds.) CAV 2013. LNCS, vol. 8044, pp. 174–190. Springer, Heidelberg (2013). https://doi.org/10.1007/978-3-642-39799-8_11

[GGH05] Gao, H., Groote, J.F., Hesselink, W.H.: Lock-free dynamic hash tables with open addressing. Distrib. Comput. **18**(1), 21–42 (2005)

[GH04] Gao, H., Hesselink, W.H.: A formal reduction for lock-free parallel algorithms. In: Alur, R., Peled, D.A. (eds.) CAV 2004. LNCS, vol. 3114, pp. 44–56. Springer, Heidelberg (2004). https://doi.org/10.1007/978-3-540-27813-9_4

[GKR+15] Gu, R., et al.: Deep specifications and certified abstraction layers. In: 42nd ACM Symposium on Principles of Programming Languages, pp. 595–608 (2015)

[GR10] Gafni, E., Rajsbaum, S.: Recursion in distributed computing. In: Dolev, S., Cobb, J., Fischer, M., Yung, M. (eds.) SSS 2010. LNCS, vol. 6366, pp. 362–376. Springer, Heidelberg (2010). https://doi.org/10.1007/978-3-642-16023-3_30

[Her91] Herlihy, M.: Wait-free synchronization. ACM Trans. Program. Lang. Syst. **13**(1), 124–149 (1991)

[Her93] Herlihy, M.: A methodology for implementing highly concurrent objects. ACM Trans. Program. Lang. Syst. **15**(5), 745–770 (1993)

[HQ19] Hurault, A., Quéinnec, P.: TLA$^+$ proof of Moir-Anderson renaming algorithm (2019). http://hurault.perso.enseeiht.fr/RenamingProof

[HW90] Herlihy, M., Wing, J.M.: Linearizability: a correctness condition for concurrent objects. ACM Trans. Program. Lang. Syst. **12**(3), 463–492 (1990)

[JDK08] Bug JDK-6785442: ConcurrentLinkedQueue.remove() and poll() can both remove the same element (2008)

[KS11] Kshemkalyani, A.D., Singhal, M.: Distributed Computing: Principles, Algorithms, and Systems. Cambridge University Press, Cambridge (2011)

[Lam86] Lamport, L.: On interprocess communication. Distrib. Comput. **1**(2), 77–101 (1986)

[Lam94] Lamport, L.: The temporal logic of actions. ACM Trans. Program. Lang. Syst. **16**(3), 872–923 (1994)

[Lam02] Lamport, L.: Specifying Systems. Addison Wesley, Boston (2002)

[Lam09] Lamport, L.: The PlusCal algorithm language. In: Leucker, M., Morgan, C. (eds.) ICTAC 2009. LNCS, vol. 5684, pp. 36–60. Springer, Heidelberg (2009). https://doi.org/10.1007/978-3-642-03466-4_2

[Lam12] Lamport, L.: How to write a 21st century proof. J. Fixed Point Theory Appl. **11**(1), 43–63 (2012)

[MA95] Moir, M., Anderson, J.H.: Wait-free algorithms for fast, long-lived renaming. Sci. Comput. Program. **25**(1), 1–39 (1995)

[MNSS05] Moir, M., Nussbaum, D., Shalev, O., Shavit, N.: Using elimination to implement scalable and lock-free FIFO queues. In: 17th ACM Symposium on Parallelism in Algorithms and Architectures, pp. 253–262 (2005)

[MS98] Michael, M.M., Scott, M.L.: Nonblocking algorithms and preemption-safe locking on multiprogrammed shared memory multiprocessors. J. Parallel Distrib. Comput. **51**(1), 1–26 (1998)

[ORV+10] O'Hearn, P.W., Rinetzky, N., Vechev, M.T., Yahav, E., Yorsh, G.: Verifying linearizability with hindsight. In: 29th ACM Symposium on Principles of Distributed Computing, pp. 85–94 (2010)

[RR11] Rajsbaum, S., Raynal, M.: A theory-oriented introduction to wait-free synchronization based on the adaptive renaming problem. In: 25th IEEE International Conference on Advanced Information Networking and Applications, pp. 356–363 (2011)

[ST97] Shavit, N., Touitou, D.: Elimination trees and the construction of pools and stacks. Theory Comput. Syst. **30**(6), 645–670 (1997)

[TP14] Timnat, S., Petrank, E.: A practical wait-free simulation for lock-free data structures. In: ACM Symposium on Principles and Practice of Parallel Programming, PPoPP 2014, pp. 357–368 (2014)

[TSR14] Tofan, B., Schellhorn, G., Reif, W.: A compositional proof method for linearizability applied to a wait-free multiset. In: Albert, E., Sekerinski, E. (eds.) IFM 2014. LNCS, vol. 8739, pp. 357–372. Springer, Cham (2014). https://doi.org/10.1007/978-3-319-10181-1_22

Tame Your Annotations with MetAcsl: Specifying, Testing and Proving High-Level Properties

Virgile Robles[1]([⊠])(iD), Nikolai Kosmatov[1,2](iD), Virgile Prevosto[1](iD),
Louis Rilling[3](iD), and Pascale Le Gall[4](iD)

[1] Institut LIST, CEA, Université Paris-Saclay, Palaiseau, France
{virgile.robles,nikolai.kosmatov,virgile.prevosto}@cea.fr
[2] Thales Research and Technology, Palaiseau, France
[3] DGA, Rennes, France
louis.rilling@irisa.fr
[4] Laboratoire de Mathématiques et Informatique pour la Complexité et les Systèmes,
CentraleSupélec, Université Paris-Saclay, Gif-Sur-Yvette, France
pascale.legall@centralesupelec.fr

Abstract. A common way to specify software properties is to associate a contract to each function, allowing the use of various techniques to assess (e.g. to prove or to test) that the implementation is valid with respect to these contracts. However, in practice, high-level properties are not always easily expressible through function contracts. Furthermore, such properties may span across multiple functions, making the specification task tedious, and its assessment difficult and error-prone, especially on large code bases. To address these issues, we propose a new specification mechanism called meta-properties. Meta-properties are enhanced global invariants specified for a set of functions, capable of expressing predicates on values of variables as well as memory related conditions (such as separation) and read or write access constraints. This paper gives a detailed presentation of meta-properties and their support in a dedicated Frama-C plugin MetAcsl, and shows that they are automatically amenable to both deductive verification and testing. This is demonstrated by applying these techniques on two illustrative case studies.

1 Introduction

Function contracts are a common way of specifying the functional behavior of a program in a modular manner. In this setting, each function of the program is annotated with both preconditions (properties expected to be ensured by the caller of the function) and postconditions (properties that must be ensured after the function returns). Various assessment techniques exist to check the validity of a function implementation with respect to its contract.

This is the case in the Frama-C [1] framework, built for the analysis of C programs. Frama-C allows the user to specify function contracts in its companion

© Springer Nature Switzerland AG 2019
D. Beyer and C. Keller (Eds.): TAP 2019, LNCS 11823, pp. 167–185, 2019.
https://doi.org/10.1007/978-3-030-31157-5_11

specification language ACSL [2] and to express first-order properties on program variables. A variety of *plugins* can be used to assess the validity of the C program with respect to these contracts, for example via static (deductive) verification or dynamic verification (runtime assertion checking).

Motivation. However, some categories of properties over a C program are not easily expressible via function contracts. In particular, some properties, which we may call *global* properties, are spanning across multiple functions. For instance, we might want to ensure that all accesses to some data are guarded by a proper authentification mechanism. Writing contracts for each function encompassed by a global property is tedious and error-prone, especially on large code bases. In the end, there is no guarantee other than manual verification that the set of provided contracts correctly and completely expresses the global property: in the example above, checking that all accesses are indeed guarded by an appropriate annotation would quickly become very difficult. In this situation, even when all contracts are verified, it cannot be directly deduced with a high level of confidence that the global property is indeed true.

This can become even harder when the contract clauses related to the global property are mixed with other, usual clauses: when updating the contract of a function, it becomes very easy to invalidate the global property since there is no explicit link between this property and the associated contract clauses. This need for global properties arises in two different case studies we tackled, each one involving both safety and security properties over a whole library of functions.

To address these issues, we propose a new specification mechanism within FRAMA-C called *meta-properties* (whose main ideas were briefly presented in [3]), which provides the verification engineer with a means to easily specify global properties on a C program. An automated translation of meta-properties into ACSL annotations allows using existing analysis plugins for the assessment.

This paper provides a rigorous description of the notion of meta-property and its instantiation mechanism, along with multiple extensions that were implemented in the METACSL plugin, and an evaluation of assessment techniques for meta-properties using static and dynamic verification.

Contributions. More precisely, the contributions of this paper include :

- a proper formalization of the notion of meta-property and its translation into ACSL (Sects. 2 and 3),
- several extensions to basic meta-properties allowing the user to write more expressive properties on a larger class of programs (Sect. 4),
- a detailed description of a previous case study regarding confidentiality (introduced in [3]), and a new case study about smart houses, that are both specified using meta-properties (Sect. 5),
- a demonstration that meta-properties are amenable to a new assessment method, runtime verification (Sect. 6), and
- an evaluation of two assessment techniques—deductive verification and runtime assertion checking—on the two case studies (Sect. 6).

With respect to the previous tool demo paper [3] (which gave an informal presentation of meta-properties and briefly illustrated their usage for deductive verification only), the present paper gives a complete formal description of meta-properties, illustrated by several examples, provides more detail on several recent extensions, the proposed transformation-based approach and the considered case studies, and demonstrates the capacity of the proposed approach to be combined with both deductive verification and runtime assertion checking.

2 Specification of Meta-Properties

Meta-properties are a way of expressing a category of *high-level, global* program properties. It basically consists of a local property, a notion of scope (a set of target functions) indicating which parts of the program have to respect the property, and a notion of context determining what kinds of situations (e.g. which instructions) in the target functions must be constrained by the property. This section formalizes and illustrates this notion.

2.1 Definition of a Meta-Property

We assume that we are working on a *complete* C program, where all functions are defined in one of the source files composing the program. Moreover, statements have been normalized such that each instruction modifies at most one single memory location. In Frama-C, this normalization phase is enforced by the kernel.

In this setting, let $\mathcal{F}$ denote the set of all functions defined in the program under analysis. We define as usual the control-flow graph (CFG) of each function as a directed graph (V, E) where each vertex $v \in V$ is a *single* C instruction and an edge $e \in E$ from v_1 to v_2 indicates that after executing v_1 the program may execute v_2 (conditional statements may have two successors, while normal instructions, such as assignments, have exactly one).

A *meta-property* is then defined as a triple $(F, \mathcal{C}, P)$ where :

- $F \subseteq \mathcal{F}$ is the *target set*, delimiting the scope of the meta-property.
- $\mathcal{C}$ is a called a *context*. It is defined as a pair $(\mathcal{M}, \theta)$ where $\mathcal{M}$ is a (potentially empty) set of names that we call *meta-variables* and θ is a *contextualization mapping*. Given a C function f having a CFG (V, E), θ associates f with a set whose elements are pairs (e, m) where $e \in E$ and m is an *environment mapping* which maps each name of $\mathcal{M}$ to an ACSL term. Informally, the contextualization mapping defines a criterion for selecting a set of locations in a C function and may associate additional information to these locations, by setting values (ACSL terms) for some special variables, that we call *meta-variables*. Sect. 2.3 presents examples of contexts with their corresponding meta-variables, and Fig. 2 gives a full example of one of them.
- P is an ACSL predicate over a subset of $\mathcal{G} \cup \mathcal{M}$, where $\mathcal{G}$ is the set of variables defined in the global scope of the program. Given a location-environment pair (e, m) returned by θ, we can construct an ACSL property, denoted P_m, where every meta-variable v is replaced by $m(v)$.

```
1  int A, B, C;
2  int level, secret_size; // level is the current confidentiality level
3  int* secret; // a secret array with secret_size elements
4
5  void main(); // main entry point
6  void def_level(int val); // set confidentiality level
7  void backdoor_root(); // backdoor that can always access secret
8  int read_secret(unsigned n); // return secret only if level is sufficient
9  /*@
10    //A always remains equal to B in function main
11    meta \prop, \name(AB_same), \targets({main}), \context(\strong_invariant),
12       A == B;
13    //The level can only be modified in def_level or backdoor_root
14    meta \prop, \name(modif_level),
15       \targets(\diff(\ALL, {def_level, backdoor_root})),
16       \context(\writing), \separated(\written, &level);
17    //The secret can only be read if level is at least ROOT_LEVEL
18    meta \prop, \name(can_read_secret), \targets(\ALL), \context(\reading),
19       \separated(\read, &secret[0 .. secret_size - 1]) \/ level >= ROOT_LEVEL;
20    //Function backdoor_root is never called
21    meta \prop, \name(no_backdoor), \targets(\ALL), \context(\calling),
22       \separated(\called, backdoor_door); */
```

Fig. 1. Examples of meta-properties and contexts

Given the target set F, the context $\mathcal{C} = (\mathcal{M}, \theta)$ and the property P, the meta-property $(F, \mathcal{C}, P)$ is interpreted as:

$$\forall f \in F, \ \forall (e, m) \in \theta(f), \ P_m \text{ holds on } e.$$

In other words, for every function of F and for every point in this function selected by θ, P must hold at this point when its meta-variables have been instantiated according to the environment mapping.

One simple example of meta-property, with no meta-variable, is the specification of a predicate P as a *strong invariant*: $M_{si}(P) = (\mathcal{F}, (\emptyset, \theta_{si}), P)$ where θ_{si} returns every edge of the CFG with a trivial environment mapping.

2.2 ACSL Syntax and First Examples

To specify meta-properties in Frama-C, we propose an extension of ACSL for explicitly providing each element of the triple $(F, \mathcal{C}, P)$. It is mandatory to *name* the property. This allows traceability between the meta-property and the generated ACSL assertions. Figure 1 gives a few examples of meta-properties that are detailed below. Concretely, a meta-property is defined as follows:

```
1 /*@ meta \prop, \name(...), \targets(...), \context(...), P; */
```

The target set is provided using the usual set syntax of ACSL. It can be explicit ({f1,...,fn}), or use set operators such as \union or \inter. We also added the \diff operator for set difference, which does not exist in ACSL.

Since the goal for meta-properties is to be able to easily and automatically specify properties on large code bases, giving the explicit set of targets is rarely a practical solution. Instead we provide a special variable \ALL which refers to $\mathcal{F}$ (the set of all functions in the program), and is very convenient, along with the \diff operation, to specify target sets of the form "all functions except...".

As an additional way to ease the delimitation of the targets, we provide two constructs \callees and \callers. \callees(f) is the set containing f and all functions (transitively) called by f. \callers(f) is the dual set containing f and all functions that (transitively) call f. It is especially useful when dealing with programs with clearly defined entry points.[1]

The combination of these simple constructs allows for a convenient way to specify the scope of a meta-property without having to rewrite the target set when new functions are added to the implementation.

2.3   Available Contexts

We define several contexts that the user can use when writing a meta-property, by indicating the context name in the \context(...) field. It turns out that these few and simple contexts, combined with the expressiveness of ACSL itself, are enough to write quite interesting properties.

Weak Invariant, Pre/Post-condition. The \precond context returns only the starting edge of the CFG with no meta-variable, while \postcond does the same with the ending edges, and \weak_invariant combines both.

Strong Invariant. As mentioned earlier, the \strong_invariant context simply provides a contextualization mapping returning every edge of the CFG of a given function without defining any meta-variables. However, it is sometimes necessary even for a strong invariant to be temporarily broken. Equality between two variables (e.g. AB_same in Fig. 1) is an example of that, as there is no way to change the value of the two variables in a single instruction. To overcome this issue, we add a lenient modifier that can be applied on a block of code to exclude the edges inside it from the scope of strong invariants.

Upon Writing the \writing context is the pair $(\{\backslash\texttt{written}\}, \theta_w)$, where θ_w returns all edges of the CFG of a given function leading to an instruction that writes into the memory (through e.g. the assignment of a variable) with an environment that maps \written to the address modified by that instruction. The action of mapping θ_w is illustrated in Fig. 2.

Since \written is a meta-variable of this context, it can then be used by the predicate P to form a useful meta-property. A simple example would be to forbid any local modification of some global variable, as shown by meta-property modif_level on Line 14 of Fig. 1. It states that for any function that is not def_level or backdoor_root, whenever some memory location is modified locally, it must be unrelated to the global variable level. In ACSL, the \separated(p1,p2) predicate states that the memory locations referred to by given (sets of) pointers p1,p2 are physically disjoint (or *separated*). Since we consider only local modification, a call to def_level inside another function

---

[1] This feature relies on the FRAMA-C plugin CALLGRAPH, which makes gross over-approximations of these sets in the presence of indirect calls (i.e. function pointers).

```
1  int* G;
2
3  /*@ assigns
4     T[0 .. 40];
5  */
6  void bar(int* T);
7  //bar is declared
8  //but not defined
9
10 void foo(int* p) {
11    int i = *p;
12    while(--i) {
13       *p = i;
14       bar(G);
15    }
16 }
```

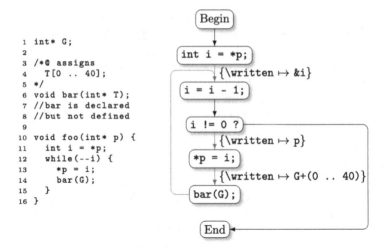

Fig. 2. Illustration of the contextualization mapping θ_w (for \writing context) for function foo. Red arrows indicate the edges returned by θ_w (leading to writing operations), and the corresponding environment mapping is shown by a label on such an edge (indicating that meta-variable \written is mapped to the (potentially) modified variable(s)). (Color figure online)

not allowed to modify level does not violate modif_level, even if def_level itself modifies level. Thus, modif_level can be seen as enforcing the proper encapsulation of level.

Upon Reading. The \reading context is identical to the \writing context except that it selects all edges leading to an instruction that *reads from* the memory and associates a meta-variable \read with the addresses being read by the instruction. It is illustrated by property can_read_secret in Fig. 1.

Upon Calling. In a similar fashion, the \calling context selects all edges preceding a function call and maps a meta-variables \called with the function (or function pointer) that is being called. It is used in the no_backdoor property.

3   Instantiation of Meta-Properties

Several existing FRAMA-C plugins provide useful and efficient analysis of ACSL-annotated C code, such as deductive verification [4] or runtime assertion checking [5]. Following the usual FRAMA-C approach of *tool collaboration*, we wish to take benefit of existing analyzers without re-implementing them for meta-properties. To do that, we designed a way to transform meta-properties into plain ACSL annotations while keeping links between the original meta-properties and their ACSL translation. Hence, the existing tools can understand and analyze the translation and their results for the translated ACSL annotations can then be interpreted in terms of meta-properties.

```
1  meta \prop,
2    \name(G_is_constant),
3    \targets({foo}),
4    \context(\writing),
5    \separated(\written, G);
```

```
1   void foo(int* p) {
2     int i = *p;
3     while(1) {
4       /*@assert \sep(&i, G);*/
5       i = i - 1;
6       if(i ≠ 0) break;
7       /*@assert \sep(p, G);*/
8       *p = i;
9       //Invalid assertion
10      /*@assert \sep(G+(0..40), G);*/
11      bar(p);
12    }
13  }
```

Fig. 3. A meta-property and its instantiation for function foo of Fig. 2

Since meta-properties have more expressive power than ACSL, it is often impossible to transform a meta-property into a single ACSL annotation. In some cases, a meta-property is translated into function contract clauses (e.g. for weak invariants) but in most cases it has to be captured by assertions inserted directly into the body of a function. More precisely, we use the ACSL annotation /*@ assert P; */, which means that P must hold at the particular point where the assertion is inserted. This allows a verification process that sticks closely to the definition of a meta-property $(F, \mathcal{C}, P)$: for each function f in F, once the set of edges of f defined by $\mathcal{C}$ is determined, it suffices to assert that for each edge/environment pair (e, m), P_m (P with meta-variables substituted with their values in m) must be valid in the context of e. The transformation process materializes this assertion by inserting a concrete ACSL annotation /*@ assert P_m; */ at the point between two instructions corresponding to the edge e. Note however that P_m must be correctly typed at this point, as discussed in Sect. 4.1. This **assert** is called an *instantiation* of the meta-property. Translation of a meta-property then consists in instantiating it for each edge/environment pair, as illustrated by Fig. 3, showing a simple *Upon Writing* meta-property and its translation for function foo of Fig. 2. Note that, as most Frama-C plugins, we rely on the presence of an **assigns** clause specifying the side effects of a function whose body is unknown (as function bar in Fig. 2).

This translation technique can be performed automatically and is correct by definition *with respect to the semantics given to meta-properties*: there is a one-to-one mapping between CFG edges and assertions in the instrumentation. We implemented it in the METACSL plugin of Frama-C.

Performance Considerations. While the proposed technique is simple, it entails that a meta-property is instantiated for each selected edge in each target function. Thus, the number of instantiations can quickly become high enough (for example when using the *Strong Invariant* context) to become a problem for the FRAMA-C plugins that are expected to analyse the translated program, resulting in potentially long analysis times or loss of precision in the results.

However, we have observed that when a meta-property has been instantiated, there are a lot of cases where the resulting assertion is trivial to prove or disprove. For example if P is \separated(\written, &A) and P_m is \separated(&B, &A) where A and B are different variables (thus separated by definition), this instantiation is trivially valid and its actual insertion can be skipped.

Thus, METACSL performs a *simplification phase* for assertions where simple patterns such as the one mentioned above are recognized and replaced by their truth value, which is then propagated through the property. Hence, the instantiations left in the code are those that could not be simplified, and for which other plugins should attempt a more thorough verification. The quantitative evaluation of this simplification is discussed in Sect. 5.

4   Extensions of Meta-Properties

The basic definition of meta-properties presented in Sect. 2 enables the specification of many useful properties, as seen in the examples. However, the case studies (described in Sect. 5) showed that it had several limitations, in both expressiveness and adaptability to the structure of programs. To address these limitations, we introduce some extensions to meta-properties.

4.1   Typing Issues

A context is defined as a pair $(\mathcal{M}, \theta)$ where $\mathcal{M}$ is the set of meta-variables, i.e. names that are mapped to different ACSL terms at each point defined by θ. Each meta-variable can then be used in the property P to refer to those terms.

However, notice that while each mapped ACSL term has a well-defined type, the meta-variable itself does not. Or rather, its type is the union of types of the mapped terms. Yet, this set of types is not known in advance when writing a meta-property. Thus, nothing can be assumed for example about the type of \written when specifying a meta-property in the *Upon Writing* context, except that it is always a pointer type (since it refers to the set of addresses that are modified). Any other assumption would create a risk of typing error. For example, assuming there exists a C structure struct S with an x field, the presence of \written->x == 0 in P would make any instance of the meta-property related to an assignment to a location of another type ill-defined, while \separated(\written, &global_variable) would not, since the \separated predicate only requires its parameters to be of pointer types.

While this suffices to express interesting properties such as separation, it does not allow reasoning about the value of the meta-variable. To address this issue, we introduce a construct to make assumptions about the type of a meta-variable while having a safeguard in case these assumptions were wrong. More precisely, we add two functions \tguard and \fguard that take an unsafe predicate (where a typing error might happen), behave as the identity if there is no error, and return respectively \true and \false otherwise. This allows the user to specify the previous example as \tguard(\written->x == 0). If a particular instance of \written is of the expected type struct S then its field is checked, else the property defaults to \true (i.e. we are only interested in modifications on locations of that type). Had \fguard been chosen instead of \tguard, any instantiation of that meta-property on a type that is not struct S would have defaulted to \false, effectively forbidding write operations to those types.

Intuitively, these functions should be used to guard any predicate that may be invalid for some instantiation of the meta-property. The default value to choose should reflect if these failures are expected in some cases or not: in our example, \tguard allowed and ignored failures while \fguard did not.

4.2 Labels in Meta-Properties

While meta-properties allow specifying a property when some event defined by the context happens (e.g. a memory operation) and the safeguarding constructs enable that property to talk about the values of the meta-variables, sometimes we need to talk about the *effect* of the memory operation on these values.

For example, one may want to globally guarantee that some initially null global variable G is initialized only once to a strictly positive value. However it is not possible to specify this without a mean to refer to G *before* and *after* each modification, which would be needed to characterize our notion of initialization.

In ACSL, one can use the \at(expression, label) construct to refer to the value of an expression *at a specific point of the program* identified by a *label*. An expression used without \at refers to its value at the point where it appears (which can be used explicitly with the Here label). There also exists two built-in labels Pre and Post referring respectively to the state before and after the current function.[2] Furthermore, any previously defined C label can be used as a label in \at. The \at construct can naturally be used in P, with labels Pre, Post and Here keeping their meanings.

To tackle the aforementioned problem, we define two additional labels that are specific to meta-properties and their context: Before and After that are used to refer to the states before and after the statements considered by the context, if any. These special labels may be mapped to actual ACSL labels by the contextualization mapping of a context when it makes sense to do so.

For example, the \precond does not define them. The \writing context maps Before to Here (since by definition the edge returned by the context *precedes* a statement modifying the memory) and After to a C label inserted after the statement modifying the memory.

With these labels, we can now write our previously problematic initialization meta-property:

```
1 meta \prop, \name(G_unique_initialization),
2     \targets(\ALL), \context(\writing),
3     \separated(\written, &G) \/ (\at(G, Before) == 0 /\ \at(G, After) > 0);
```

---

[2] Technically, Post can only be used in assigns statements or contract post-conditions.

which means that each instruction either does not modify G or modifies it such that its value is 0 before the modification and strictly positive after it.

4.3 Referring to Non-global Values

As meta-properties are *global* properties that are not declared in the scope of any particular function, they can only refer to global variables and meta-variables. This is a strong limitation to the kind of properties that can be written, as some programs have few interesting objects declared in the global scope and typically pass them as arguments. To tackle this issue, we came up with two different mechanisms: the \formal construct and the notion of *local binding*.

Referring to Function Parameters. If there is an object present in every target function of a meta-property, but as a consistently named function parameter (which is called a *formal*) instead of a global variable, we introduce the \formal keyword to refer to such a parameter in the property P of a meta-property. When \formal(some_param) appears in a meta-property, each instantiation of the meta-property triggers the check that some_param is indeed a formal of the current target function. If it is, the \formal call is safely replaced by some_param. Otherwise, a typing error is triggered at the point where it is used.

Thus, \formal is best used when combined with the safeguarding constructs \tguard and \fguard (Sect. 4.1), since it allows the specification engineer to *assume* that a formal is consistently defined in every target function and use it in a property, but to safely default to a conservative property if this assump-

```
1 meta \prop, \name(),
2      \targets(\ALL),
       \context(\calling),
3      \tguard(
4          \separated(\called,
               \formal(pre_process))
5          \/ \separated(do_not_call,
               \formal(pre_process))
6      );
```

tion is wrong. For example, the above property specifies that if a function in the programs takes a function pointer pre_process as a parameter, then it can only be called if it is distinct from a do_not_call function. If this parameter does not exist in a function, then the property defaults to \true since there is nothing to verify.

Referring to Bound Names. If it is not possible to rely on a consistent naming of formals across functions, we introduce a notion of *binding* to overcome this difficulty with some help from the user.

We introduce two special functions, \bind and \bound. The first one is to be used outside of a meta-property, in the body of a C function, to *bind* a name to the value of a C expression at that point. This name can then be used in a meta-property to formulate an interesting property about the value it refers to. A name can actually be bound multiple times to different value at different points of a program, meaning that the name inside a meta-property refers to the whole set of associated values. The whole process is illustrated in Fig. 4. Notice that the bound values are constant but may be pointers referring to changing memory. We are then specifying a property across all the memory states of the different instantiations, which makes \bound a meta-variable.

```
1  int lock;
2  int* create_cell() {
3    char* c = malloc(1);
4    //@ meta \bind(c, cells);
5    return c;
6  }
7  int safe_modify_cell
8  (int* cell, int val) {
9    if(!lock) {
10     lock = 1;
11     *cell = val;
12     lock = 0;
13     return 0;
14   }
15   else return -1;
16 }
17 void unsafe_modify_cell
18 (int* cl, int val) {
19   *cll = val;
20 }
21
22 /*@ //Pointers returned by create_cell
23     //are not modified if the lock is on
24     meta \prop,
25     \name(cell_modif_is_critical),
26     \targets(\ALL), \context(\writing),
27     \separated(\written, \bound(cells))
                    V lock;
28 */
```

Fig. 4. *Bindings* usage example

To actually instantiate (as described in Sect. 3) a meta-property with bindings, the program must be further instrumented using *ghost code.*

Ghost variables are declared for specification purposes only and cannot be used by the original C code, while ghost statements may only modify ghost variables. Thus, ghost code altogether cannot modify the original behavior of the code but may facilitate verification.

For each bound name, we allocate an associated ghost global array whose role is to store the set of associated values. Consequently, each instance of \bind(v, n) is replaced by a ghost instruction adding v to the array n_set associated to n and every instance of a predicate $P(n)$ involving a bound name is replaced by a quantified predicate $\forall v \in$ n_set, $P(v)$. This is illustrated in Fig. 5, which is the translation of Fig. 4. Notice that the type of the array is inferred from the \bind calls. As such, it is the responsibility of the user to ensure that every bound value is of the same type and to use the bound name appropriately.

5   Case Studies and Their Specification

We applied our technique to two different case studies for the purpose of evaluating its relevance on actual code and properties. First, we describe the content of these case studies and how useful properties about them are specified using meta-properties.[3] Then in Sect. 6, various assessment techniques are used to check the validity of the implementation with respect to these meta-properties.

5.1   Confidentiality

The first case study, which was submitted by an industrial partner, deals with a confidentiality-oriented page management system. We assume a system where a confidentiality level is associated to each memory page. Two different pages may have the same level but the set of confidentiality levels must be totally ordered.[4]

---

[3] The case studies and their specifications are available at https://huit.re/metatap.

[4] We assume a total order for simplicity, but it would also work with a partial one.

```
1  int lock;
2  //@ ghost char* cells_set = NULL;
3  //@ ghost size_t cells_set_size = 0;
4  int* create_cell() {
5      char* c = malloc(1);
6      //@ ghost add_to_array(cells_set, c);
7      return c;
8  }
9  int safe_modify_cell(int* cell, int val) {
10     if(!lock) {
11         /*@ assert ∀ size_t i; i < cells_set_size ⇒
12                     \separated(&lock, cells_set[i]) ∨ !lock; */
13         *cell = val;
14         lock = 1;
15         //@ assert ∀ i; ... \separated(cell, cells_set[i]) ∨ !lock;
16         *cell = val;
17         //@ assert ∀ i; ... \separated(&lock, cells_set[i]) ∨ !lock;
18         lock = 0;
19         return 0;
20     }
21     else return -1;
22 }
23 void unsafe_modify_cell(int* cl, int val) {
24     //@ assert ∀ i; ... \separated(cl, cells_set[i]) ∨ !lock;
25     *cl = val;
26 }
```

Fig. 5. Translation of Fig. 4

We call *agent* any entity (a process, for example) which may happen to read or write from such pages, and give to each agent a confidentiality level as well.

The two basic guarantees that such a system should offer are:

C_1: An agent can never **read** from a page with a confidentiality level **higher** than its own (to preserve the confidentiality of the data written on the page),

C_2: An agent can never **write** to a page with a level **lower** than its own (to prevent the agent's data from being read by lower agents in the future).

Notice that these properties ensure *confidentiality* but not *integrity*, which is not considered here but could be similarly specified.

We wrote a simple implementation of this case study, where the system is modelled by a stateful API of functions to allocate, free, write to or read from pages. The confidentiality level of the calling agent is represented by a global variable, which is assumed to be securely modified when the context changes.

There are several other properties needed for C_1 and C_2 to be useful in ensuring confidentiality:

C_3: The confidentiality level of an allocated page remains constant,

C_4: The allocation status of a page can only be modified by the allocation and de-allocation functions,

C_5: Non allocated pages are neither accessed nor modified,

C_6: Non allocated pages do not retain old data.

We also consider an extension of this system introducing *encryption* as a means to decrease the confidentiality level of a page. Two functions to encrypt

```
1  //Never read from a higher confidentiality page
2  meta \prop, \name(C_1), \targets(\ALL),
3    \context(\reading),
4      forall_page(p,
5        page_allocated(p) ∧ user_level < page_level(p) ⇒
6        \separated(page_data(p), \read)
7      );
8  //The confidentiality of an allocated page is constant outside of encryption
9  meta \prop, \name(C_3'), \targets(\diff(\ALL, {page_encrypt, page_decrypt})),
10   \context(\writing),
11     forall_page(p,
12       page_allocated(p) ⇒ \separated(&p->confidentiality_level, \written)
13     );
14
15 //The content of a free page is always null
16 meta \prop, \name(C_6), \targets(\ALL),
17   \context(\strong_invariant),
18     forall_page(p, !page_allocated(p) ⇒ clean_page(p));
```

Fig. 6. Specification of some confidentiality properties using meta-properties

and decrypt a page are added to the API with a key based on the confidentiality level of the caller, and we weaken C_3 into:

C_3': The confidentiality level of an allocated page remains constant, except in encryption/decryption functions.

All of these properties can be expressed using meta-properties, as illustrated in Fig. 6 where properties C_1, C_3' and C_6 are specified. The `forall_page` predicate is a formula-shortening macro which quantifies over the globally-stored array of pages (both free and allocated).

5.2 Smart House

The second case study models a smart house command system on which we tried to specify and verify interesting safety and security properties.

The house is modelled as a set of rooms, each containing a door that can be locked or unlocked by authorized users, a window that can be opened or closed and an AC system that can be enabled or disabled. There is also an alarm that can be triggered by anyone in case of emergency.

We assume each room contains a terminal authenticating users and relaying their instructions to a central command system. The system is again modelled as a stateful API, this time with a single entry point where instructions from terminals are received and processed. We also add some administration functions that should not be called by terminals.

Some desirable properties that we specified for this system are:

S_1: Every door is unlocked when the alarm is ringing,
S_2: The AC system cannot be enabled when the window in the room is open,
S_3: A door can only be unlocked by authorized users,
S_4: The alarm cannot be silenced by users,

```
1  #define USER_SET (\callees(receive_command))
2  /*@
3  meta \prop, \name(S_2), \targets(\ALL),
4    \context(\strong_invariant),
5    forall_room(r,
6      r->window_state == 0
7      ⇒ r->ac_state == AC_DISABLED
8  );
9
10 meta \prop, \name(S_3),
11     \targets(USER_SET),
12     \context(\writing),
13     forall_room(r,
14         \at(r->door_lock_state, Before) ≠ 0
15         ∧ \at(r->door_lock_state, After) == 0
16         ∧ \fguard(user_permissions[\formal(uid)] < r->clearance_needed)
17         ⇒ \separated(\written, &r->door_lock_state)
18     );
19
20 meta \prop, \name(S_4), \targets(USER_SET),
21     \context(\writing),
22     \at(alarm_status, Before) == ALARM_NONE
23     ∨ \at(alarm_status, After) ≠ ALARM_NONE
24     ∨ \separated(\written, &alarm_status);
25 */
```

Fig. 7. Specification of some smarthouse-related properties using meta-properties

Their formalization into meta-properties is represented in Fig. 7. Notice the use of both the \formal construct (Sect. 4.3) to refer to the parameters of the different functions (combined with \fguard to default to a false predicate if there is no such parameter), as well as the \at construct with labels Before and After (Sect. 4.2) in S_3 to express the fact that a door is locked before an instruction and unlocked after it, needed to express the notion of unlocking. Finally, notice the use of the \callees function in USER_SET to refer to the set of every function called by the single entry point (receive_command), in order to exclude the administration functions (if they are indeed not called) from the scope of the meta-properties.

6   Assessment of the Case Studies

Having two case studies specified with meta-properties, we want to evaluate the ability to assess them with the usual FRAMA-C tools, after translating meta-properties into native ACSL with METACSL. To that end, we wrote a correct C implementation of the different functions for both the confidentiality and smart house case studies. Then, to increase the number of benchmarks, we used a FRAMA-C plugin[5] to generate mutations of this correct implementation, providing a set of modified implementations, potentially invalid with respect to the meta-properties. In this way, we obtain respectively 126 and 69 mutants for the confidentiality and the smarthouse case study. The mutations consist in the replacement of binary operators, the negation of conditions and the modification

---

[5] See https://github.com/gpetiot/Frama-C-Mutation.

Number of:	functions	meta-properties	generated asserts	gen. asserts with simplif.	invalid mutants/ total mutants
Confidentiality	11	11	408	273	42/126
Smarthouse	14	7	156	87	19/69

Fig. 8. Statistics about the METACSL instrumentation on case studies

Case study	Confidentiality		Smarthouse	
Assessment type	WP	E-ACSL	WP	E-ACSL
False Positives	0	29	0	6
False Negatives	0	0	0	0
Interrupted (RTE)	N/A	19	N/A	11

Fig. 9. Assessment of automatic approaches, relative to a manual verification

of numerical values. They simulate frequent programming errors in the code. The specification for the mutants remains the same as for the initial implementation.

For each mutant, we manually check if the introduced mutation violates one of the meta-properties of the case study. If so, the mutant is considered invalid. The proportion of invalid mutants is reported in Fig. 8 along with some quantitative information about the case studies and their instrumentation by METACSL. Here we can observe that the simplification phase described in Sect. 3 significantly reduces the number of generated assertions, thus easing the job of the tools that are subsequently run on the resulting translated programs.[6]

For each benchmark (initial version or one of the mutants, including all valid and invalid mutants), we first apply METACSL to generate an instrumented C program. We wish then to investigate whether, thanks to the instrumentation with METACSL, different FRAMA-C tools are able to assess the validity of the benchmarks with respect to the meta-properties.

We test two existing assessment techniques, namely deductive verification with the WP plugin and runtime verification with the E-ACSL plugin. For both plugins, Fig. 9 indicates the number of false positives (cases where the mutant is invalid but no violation was detected) and false negatives (cases where the mutant is valid, but flagged as violating a meta-property; this can happen in case of proof failure or faulty translation). We detail both techniques in the rest of the section.

6.1 Deductive Verification

Deductive verification allows users to formally prove that the implementation of a function is correct with respect to its specification. If a function is specified by annotations (a contract, invariants and/or assertions), then logical formulas encoding the semantics of these annotations and known as *proof obligations*

---

[6] For example, simplification saves 8 s on the deductive verification of the correct confidentiality implementation (for a total of 24 s).

(POs) can be generated and given to automated theorem provers. If all POs are validated, the body of the function fulfills its specification. This technique is implemented by FRAMA-C plugin WP.

We attempt to run WP on each benchmark. While a proof success is definitive, a proof failure may have different causes: the property to be proved may be false, there could be insufficient assumptions available to the prover or it could simply exceed the capacity of the prover in its allocated time. Thus if every proof failure is classified as a judgement of invalidity, false negatives are to be expected. To mitigate this phenomenon, we first manually annotated the case studies with partial function contracts for the correct implementations to be successfully proved.

The results are encouraging. Every valid mutant was successfully proved as valid, and the proof failed for each invalid mutant (see Fig. 9)[7], thus confirming the correctness of the transformation. These results demonstrate that the spec-to-spec translation with METACSL creates a convenient, fully automatic toolchain for deductive verification of global properties in Frama-C. As usual for deductive verification, some additional annotations were necessary to prove the different functions (respectively 40 and 5 lines of specification were needed, loops being the main point of effort) but their number was much smaller than the number of relevant assertions automatically generated from the meta-properties.

6.2   Runtime Verification on Test Cases

We now wish to study if it is also possible to verify meta-properties at runtime—without any additional annotations—thanks to the E-ACSL [5] plugin for runtime assertion checking. It automatically translates an ACSL-annotated C program into another program that fails at runtime if an annotation is violated.

Since our two case studies are APIs without any `main` function, we wrote small test suites of complete programs that can be actually compiled and executed. In both cases, they contain simple functional tests and do not aim at covering every possible usage case. They feature sequences of respectively 40 and 20 calls to the APIs.

We then applied runtime assertion checking to the execution of every instrumented benchmark on all tests of both test suite. The results (Fig. 9) are also promising and allowed us to identify several issues and future work directions.

The additional row refers to cases where the generated binary detected a violation of a safety property[8], thus stopping the execution and preventing us to know if a meta-property violation would have been detected or not. In the future, it would be desirable to filter out safety-violating mutants, and only keep mutations simply modifying the semantics of the code.

There are no false negatives, confirming that the instrumentation of both METACSL and E-ACSL does not introduce any bug. There is a significant

---

[7] The last row is not relevant for deductive verification, see Sect. 6.2.

[8] E-ACSL add checks to ensure that no runtime error (segfaults, overflow, ...) will occur and stops the program upon violation.

number of false positives (incorrect mutants for which no test failed). There are several reasons for this. First, our initial test suites are not complete and some mutants are not killed by these tests. In the future, we plan to address this by using the STADY [6] plugin, which combines static and dynamic verification and allows the automatic generation of test cases that can exhibit counter-examples for invalid properties. The second reason is that E-ACSL only supports a subset of ACSL: some properties involving complex constructions such as the \at keyword are simply ignored by E-ACSL, thus they cannot possibly be violated at runtime. This support should be improved in the future.

This study demonstrates that it is easy to check meta-properties at runtime without extra annotation effort thanks to the combination of METACSL and E-ACSL, as long as the specified properties are supported by the tools. This is especially useful for properties that are not easily tractable with deductive verification: for example, a property using bindings (Sect. 4.3) might be very difficult to verify using WP without writing extensive function contracts, while it can be immediately tested with E-ACSL.

7 Related Work

ACSL is a specification language inspired by previous efforts such as JML [7], a behavioural interface specification language for Java. JML has similar limitations regarding the expression of global properties on a software module, and we believe that our approach could be useful in this context as well. However a subset of meta-properties is already expressible in JML, such as weak invariants (using JML class invariants). Another high-level specification feature of JML is the notion of *constraint*, which allows the specification of a property relating the states before and after every method of a class, or a given set of methods (similar to our notion of target set).

The idea of extending a contract-based specification language to support high-level properties has been explored before. For example, Cheon and Perumandla [8] extended JML, allowing the specification of *protocols*, i.e. properties related to the order of call sequences. Protocols could be specified using the \calling context of meta-properties and ghost code to model an automaton, but may not be as usable as the simple syntax provided by this work. Another such example is the work of Trentelman and Huisman [9], which extends JML to enable the expression of temporal properties. Meta-properties can express a subset of temporal properties with the extension detailed in Sect. 4.2, but this is not the aim of the tool (the Frama-C plugins AORAÏ [10] and CAFE [11] are already devoted to this task).

Within Frama-C, extending ACSL by writing a plugin that translates the extension back into normal ACSL has been used previously for the support of relational properties with RPP [12] or temporal logic with AORAI [10].

The proposed transformation technique is related to the work of Pavlova et al. [13] as they generate annotations whose verification implies the validity of a high-level property as well. However, their specified properties are in the form of pre-/post-conditions on a well-defined set of *core* functions that are then propagated throughout the code, while we define properties that are not always pertaining to some core functions and use a simpler propagation method.

The general idea of defining a high-level concept in the global scope and then *weaving it* into the implementation is analogous to the Aspect-Oriented Programming (AOP) [14] paradigm, as meta-properties can be seen as cross-cutting concerns on the specification side rather than the implementation side. Contexts can then be related to *pointcuts*, which in AOP are a set of control flow points where the code needed by the concern should be added.

8   Conclusion and Future Work

We proposed in this paper a complete description of a new specification mechanism for high-level properties in FRAMA-C. Meta-properties provide a useful extension to function contracts, offering the possibility to express a variety of high-level safety- and security-related properties, and reducing the risk of errors inherent to the manual specification of such properties, especially when updating the program specification or code. Today, meta-properties are capable to express the different types of high-level properties that motivated this work (e.g. isolation properties for verification of a hypervisor, confidentiality-oriented security properties, various global invariants, etc.).

The extensions to meta-properties we presented are helpful for expressing richer properties (e.g. referring to different states) on a larger class of C programs (by allowing the properties to refer to objects that are not necessarily in the global scope), as demonstrated for the specification of the two case studies.

We provided an automatic transformation-based method to enable the assessment of the meta-properties and showed that the result can successfully be assessed by existing deductive verification and runtime assertion checking techniques. This enables both users ready to put some effort into the specification of their program and users with a complete test suite, to assess the validity of their program with strong levels of confidence.

Finally, we emphasize that our goal is to propose a *pragmatic class of properties amenable to a high level of automation*; we do not claim they offer more expressiveness than other classes of properties on the logical level.

Future Work. We plan to perform a formalization and a formal soundness proof for our transformation technique, thereby allowing METACSL to be reliably used for critical code verification. There is a plan to tackle existing industrial case studies to demonstrate the ability of meta-properties to specify programs that are not necessarily verification-friendly. Finally, we wish to refine the transformation technique in order to allow the proof of the generated specification to scale better when the number of meta-properties or the size of the code increases.

Acknowledgment. This work was partially supported by the project VESSEDIA, which has received funding from the EU Horizon 2020 research and innovation programme under grant agreement No 731453. This work was also partially supported by

ANR (grant ANR-18-CE25-0015-01). The work of the first author was partially funded by a Ph.D. grant of the French Ministry of Defense. Many thanks to the anonymous referees for their helpful comments.

References

1. Kirchner, F., Kosmatov, N., Prevosto, V., Signoles, J., Yakobowski, B.: Frama-C: a software analysis perspective. Formal Aspects Comput. **27**, 573–609 (2015)
2. Baudin, P.: ACSL: ANSI/ISO C Specification Language (2018). https://framac.com/acsl.html
3. Robles, V., Kosmatov, N., Prevosto, V., Rilling, L., Le Gall, P.: METACSL: specification and verification of high-level properties. In: Vojnar, T., Zhang, L. (eds.) TACAS 2019. LNCS, vol. 11427, pp. 358–364. Springer, Cham (2019). https://doi.org/10.1007/978-3-030-17462-0_22
4. Baudin, P., Bobot, F., Correnson, L., Dargaye, Z.: WP plugin manual (2010). http://frama-c.com/wp.html
5. Signoles, J., Kosmatov, N., Vorobyov, K.: E-ACSL, a runtime verification tool for safety and security of C programs (tool paper). In: International Workshop on Competitions, Usability, Benchmarks, Evaluation, and Standardisation for Runtime Verification Tools, pp. 164–173 (2017)
6. Petiot, G., Kosmatov, N., Botella, B., Giorgetti, A., Julliand, J.: How testing helps to diagnose proof failures. Formal Aspects Comput. **30**, 629–657 (2018)
7. Leavens, G.T., Baker, A.L., Ruby, C.: JML: a notation for detailed design. In: Kilov, H., Rumpe, B., Simmonds, I. (eds.) Behavioral Specifications of Businesses and Systems. SECS, vol. 523, pp. 175–188. Springer, Boston (1999). https://doi.org/10.1007/978-1-4615-5229-1_12
8. Cheon, Y., Perumandla, A.: Specifying and checking method call sequences in JML. In: International Conference on Software Engineering Research and Practice, pp. 511–516 (2005)
9. Trentelman, K., Huisman, M.: Extending JML specifications with temporal logic. In: Kirchner, H., Ringeissen, C. (eds.) AMAST 2002. LNCS, vol. 2422, pp. 334–348. Springer, Heidelberg (2002). https://doi.org/10.1007/3-540-45719-4_23
10. Stouls, N., Groslambert, J.: Vérification de propriéts LTL sur des programmes C par génération d'annotations. Research Report (French) (2011)
11. de Oliveira, S., Prevosto, V., Bensalem, S.: CaFE: a model-checker collaboratif. In: Approches Formelles dans l'Assistance au Developpement Logiciel (2017)
12. Blatter, L., Kosmatov, N., Le Gall, P., Prevosto, V., Petiot, G.: Static and dynamic verification of relational properties on self-composed C code. In: Dubois, C., Wolff, B. (eds.) TAP 2018. LNCS, vol. 10889, pp. 44–62. Springer, Cham (2018). https://doi.org/10.1007/978-3-319-92994-1_3
13. Pavlova, M., Barthe, G., Burdy, L., Huisman, M., Lanet, J.L.: Enforcing high-level security properties for applets. In: Quisquater, J.J., Paradinas, P., Deswarte, Y., El Kalam, A.A. (eds.) Smart Card Research and Advanced Applications VI. IFIP International Federation for Information Processing, vol. 153, pp. 1–16. Springer, Boston (2004). https://doi.org/10.1007/1-4020-8147-2_1
14. Kiczales, G., et al.: Aspect-oriented programming. In: Akşit, M., Matsuoka, S. (eds.) ECOOP 1997. LNCS, vol. 1241, pp. 220–242. Springer, Heidelberg (1997). https://doi.org/10.1007/BFb0053381

Property-Based Test Case Generators
for Free

Emanuele De Angelis[1(✉)], Fabio Fioravanti[1(✉)], Adrián Palacios[2(✉)],
Alberto Pettorossi[3(✉)], and Maurizio Proietti[4(✉)]

[1] DEC, University "G. d'Annunzio" of Chieti-Pescara, Pescara, Italy
{emanuele.deangelis,fabio.fioravanti}@unich.it
[2] MiST, DSIC, Polytechnic University of Valencia, Valencia, Spain
apalacios@dsic.upv.es
[3] University of Rome Tor Vergata, Rome, Italy
pettorossi@info.uniroma2.it
[4] CNR-IASI, Rome, Italy
maurizio.proietti@iasi.cnr.it

Abstract. Property-Based Testing requires the programmer to write
suitable *generators*, i.e., programs that generate (possibly in a random
way) input values for which the program under test should be run. However, the process of writing generators is quite a costly, error-prone activity. In the context of Property-Based Testing of Erlang programs, we
propose an approach to relieve the programmer from the task of writing
generators. Our approach allows the automatic, efficient generation of
input test values that satisfy a given specification. In particular, we have
considered the case when the input values are data structures satisfying complex constraints. That generation is performed via the symbolic
execution of the specification using constraint logic programming.

1 Introduction

Over the years, Property-Based Testing (PBT), as proposed by Claessen and
Hughes [8], has been established as one of the favorite methods for testing software. The idea behind PBT is as follows: instead of supplying specific inputs,
i.e., test cases, to a program under test, the developer defines properties to be
satisfied by the program inputs and outputs. Then, random inputs are generated
and the program is run with those input values, thereby producing output values
and checking whether or not the input-output pairs satisfy the desired property.
If the output associated with a particular input does not satisfy the property,
the counterexample to the property reveals an undesirable behavior. Then, the
developer can modify the program under test so that the counterexample is no
longer generated. The fact that input values are generated in a random way plays

This work has been partially supported by the EU (FEDER) and the *Spanish Mini-
sterio de Ciencia, Innovación y Universidades*/AEI, grant TIN2016-76843-C4-1-R and
by the *Generalitat Valenciana*, grant PROMETEO-II/2015/013 (SmartLogic).

D. Beyer and C. Keller (Eds.): TAP 2019, LNCS 11823, pp. 186–206, 2019.
https://doi.org/10.1007/978-3-030-31157-5_12

a key role in the PBT techniques, because randomicity enables the generation of valid inputs which originally could have escaped the attention of the developer.

QuickCheck [8] is the first tool that implemented Property-Based Testing and it works for the functional language Haskell. Then, a similar approach has been followed for various programming languages, and among many others, let us mention: (i) Erlang [2,27], (ii) Java [22,39], (iii) Scala [33], and (iv) Prolog [1].

In this paper we will focus on the dynamically typed functional programming language Erlang and, in particular, we will refer to the PropEr framework [27,30]. Typically, in PropEr the set of valid input data is defined through: (i) a type specification, and (ii) a filter specification (that is, a constraint), which should be satisfied by the valid inputs. When working with user-defined types and filters, the developer must provide a *generator*, that is, a program that constructs input data of the given type satisfying the given filter. PropEr supports writing generators by providing a mechanism for turning type specifications into data generators, and also providing primitives for constraining data size and assigning frequencies to guide data generation. However, the task of writing a generator that satisfies all constraints defined by a filter is left to the developer. Unfortunately, writing and maintaining generators is a time-consuming and error-prone activity. In particular, hand-written generators may result in the generation of sets of non-valid inputs or, even worse, sets of inputs which are too restricted.

In this paper we explore an approach that relieves the developer from the task of writing data generators of valid inputs. We assume that the data generation task is specified by providing: (i) a *data type specification*, using the Erlang language for that purpose, and (ii) a *filter specification* provided by any boolean-valued Erlang function. We have constructed a symbolic interpreter, written in the *Constraint Logic Programming* (CLP) language [20], which takes the data type and the filter specification, and automatically generates data of the given type satisfying the given filter. Our interpreter is *symbolic*, in the sense that it is able to run Erlang programs (in particular, the filter functions) on symbolic values, represented as CLP terms with possibly variable occurrences.

The symbolic interpreter works by exploiting various computational mechanisms which are specific to CLP, such as: (i) *unification*, instead of matching, which enables the use of predicate definitions for generating terms satisfying those predicates, (ii) *constraint solving*, which allows the symbolic computation of sets of data satisfying given constraints, and (iii) *coroutining* between the process of generating the data structures and the process of applying the filter. By using the above mechanisms we realize an efficient, automated data generation process following a *constrain-and-generate* computation pattern, which first generates data structure skeletons with constraints on its elements, and then generates random concrete values satisfying those constraints. Finally, these concrete data are translated back into inputs for the Erlang program under test.

The paper is structured as follows. In Sect. 2, we recall some basic notions on the Erlang and CLP programming languages. In Sect. 3, we present the framework for Property-Based Testing based on PropEr [27]. In Sect. 4, we show how from any given data type definition, written in the type language of Erlang, we derive a CLP generator for such data type. In Sect. 5, we describe our CLP interpreter for a sequential fragment of Erlang. In Sect. 6, we show the use of coroutining and, in Sect. 7, we present some experimental results obtained by the ProSyT tool, which implements our PBT technique. Finally, in Sect. 8, we compare our approach with related work in constraint-based testing.

2   Preliminaries

In this section we present the basic notions of the Erlang and CLP languages.

The Erlang language. Erlang is a concurrent, higher-order, functional programming language with dynamic, strong typing [36]. Its concurrency is based on the Actor model [19] and it allows asynchronous communications among processes. These features make the Erlang language suitable for distributed, fault-tolerant, and soft real-time applications. An Erlang program is a sequence of function definitions of the form: $f(X_1, \ldots, X_n)$ -> e, where f is the function name, $X_1, \ldots, X_n$ are variables, and e is an Erlang expression, whose syntax is shown in the box below, together with that of values and patterns. For reasons of simplicity, we have considered a subset of Core Erlang, that is, the intermediate language to which Erlang programs are translated by the Erlang/OTP compiler language [12]. This subset, in particular, does not include letrec expressions, nor commands for raising or catching exceptions, nor primitives for supporting concurrent computations.

Values $\ni$ v $::=$ l | $c(v_1, \ldots, v_n)$ | fun $(X_1, \ldots, X_n)$ -> e

Patterns $\ni$ p $::=$ p' when g

p' $::=$ l | X | $c(X_1, \ldots, X_n)$

Expressions $\ni$ e $::=$ l | X | f | $c(e_1, \ldots, e_n)$ | $e_0(e_1, \ldots, e_n)$ | let $X = e_1$ in e

| case e of $(p_1$ -> $e_1)$; $\ldots$; $(p_n$ -> $e_n)$ end | fun $(X_1, \ldots, X_n)$ -> e

---

In these syntactic definitions: (i) by 'Values $\ni$ v' we mean that v (possibly with subscripts) is a meta-variable ranging over Values, and analogously for Patterns and Expressions, (ii) l ranges over literals (such as integers, floats, atoms, and the empty list []), (iii) c is either the list constructor [_|_] or the tuple constructor $\{\_, \ldots, \_\}$, (iv) X (possibly with subscripts) ranges over variables, (v) fun $(X_1, \ldots, X_n)$ -> e denotes an anonymous function (we stipulate that the free variables in the expression e belong to $\{X_1, \ldots, X_n\}$), (vi) g ranges over *guards*, that is, boolean expressions (such as comparisons of terms using =<, ==, etc.) (vii) f ranges over function names.

The evaluation of an expression is performed in the *call-by-value* regime and returns a value. Variables are bound to values via the usual *pattern matching* mechanism. In Erlang each variable is bound to a value only once (this feature is known as *single assignment*). During the evaluation of a function call, the patterns of the case-of expression are considered, one after the other, in left-to-right order. The first pattern for which the pattern matching succeeds with a true guard, determines the corresponding expression to be evaluated. If there is no matching pattern with a true guard, a `match_fail` run-time error occurs.

The running example: a faulty insertion program. Below we show an Erlang function which is intended to insert an integer I in a list L of integers sorted in ascending order, thereby producing a new, extended sorted list. That function has an error as we have indicated in the line `ERR`. In what follows we will show how to automatically generate input values for detecting that error.

```
insert(I,L) -> case L of
  [] -> [I];
  [X|Xs] when I=<X -> [X,I|Xs];   % ERR: [X,I|Xs] should be [I,X|Xs]
  [X|Xs] -> [X] ++ insert(I,Xs)   % '++' denotes list concatenation
end.
```

Constraint Logic Programming. By CLP(X) we denote the CLP language based on constraints in the domain X, where X is: either (i) FD (the domain of integer numbers belonging to a finite interval), or (ii) R (the domain of floating point numbers), or (iii) B (the domain of boolean values) [20].

A *constraint* is a quantifier free, first-order formula whose variables range over the domain X. A *user-defined predicate* is a predicate symbol not present in the constraint language. An *atom* is an atomic formula $p(t_1, ..., t_k)$, where p is a user-defined predicate and $t_1, ..., t_k$ are first-order terms constructed out of constants, variables, and function symbols. A CLP(X) program is a set of *clauses* of the form either A. or A :- c, A1, ..., An., where A, A1, ..., An are atoms and c is a constraint on the domain X. A *query* is written as ?- c, A1, ..., An. A term, or an atom, is said to be *ground* if it contains no variables. As an example, below we list a CLP(FD) program for computing the `factorial` function ('#>' and '#=' denote the greater-than and equality relations, respectively):

```
factorial(0,1).
factorial(N,FN) :- N #> 0, M #= N-1, FN #= N*FM, factorial(M,FM).
```

For the operational semantics of CLP(X), we assume that, in the normal execution mode, constraints and atoms in a query are selected from left to right. In Sect. 6 we will see how the selection order is altered by using *coroutining* constructs (in particular, by using `when` declarations). When a constraint is selected, it is added to the *constraint store*, which is the conjunction of all constraints derived so far, thereby deriving a new constraint store. Then, the satisfiability of the new store is checked. The search for a clause whose head is unifiable with a given atom is done by following the textual top-down order of the program and, as usual for Prolog systems, the search tree is visited in a depth-first manner.

3 A Framework for PBT of Erlang Programs

In this section we introduce the fragment of the PropEr framework developed by Papadakis and Sagonas [27], which we use to specify PBT tasks. PropEr relies on a set of predefined functions for specifying the properties of interest for the Erlang programs. We consider the following PropEr functions.

- ?FORALL(Xs, XsGen, Prop), which is the main function used for property specification. Xs is either a variable, or a list of variables, or a tuple of variables. XsGen is a *generator* that produces a value for Xs. Prop is a boolean expression specifying a property that we want to check for the program under test. We assume that Xs includes all the free variables occurring in Prop. For instance, ?FORALL(X, integer(), mult1(X) >= X) (i) uses the predefined generator integer(), which generates an integer, and (ii) specifies the property mult1(X) >= X for the function mult1(X) -> X*(X+1).

- ?LET(Xs, XsGen, InExpr), which allows the definition of a *dependent generator*. Xs and XsGen are like in the ?FORALL function, and InExpr is an expression whose free variables occur in Xs. ?LET(Xs, XsGen, InExpr) generates a value obtained by evaluating InExpr using the value of Xs produced by XsGen. For instance, ?LET(X, integer(), 2*X) generates an even integer.

- ?SUCHTHAT(Xs, XsGen, Filter), which allows the definition of a generator of values satisfying a given *filter* expression. Xs and XsGen are like in the ?FORALL function, and Filter is a boolean expression whose free variables occur in Xs. ?SUCHTHAT(Xs, XsGen, Filter) generates a value, which is a value of Xs produced by XsGen, for which the Filter expression holds true. For instance, ?SUCHTHAT(L, list(integer()), L=/=[]) generates non-empty lists of integers.

In PropEr a generator is specified by using: (i) type expressions, (ii) ?LET functions, and (iii) ?SUCHTHAT functions. We consider generators of first-order values only. However, higher-order functions may occur in Prop, InExpr, and Filter.

A *type expression* (whose semantics is a set of first-order values) is defined by using either the following PropEr *predefined types*:

- any(): all first-order Erlang values;
- integer(L,H): the integers between L and H (these bounds can be omitted);
- float(L,H): the floats between L and H (these bounds can be omitted);
- atom(): all Erlang atoms;
- boolean(): the boolean values true and false;

or PropEr *user-defined types*, which are defined by using type parameters and recursion, as usual. For instance, the type of binary trees with elements of a parameter type T can be defined as follows:

```
-type tree(T) :: 'leaf' | {'node',tree(T),T,tree(T)}.
```

Compound type expressions can be defined by the following *type constructors*:

- {T_1,...,T_N}: the tuples of N elements of types T_1,...,T_N, respectively;
- list(T): the lists with elements of type T;
- [T_1,...,T_N]: the lists of N elements of types T_1,...,T_N, respectively;
- union([T_1,...,T_N]): all elements x such that x is of type either T_1 or ... or T_N;
- exactly(lt): the singleton consisting of the literal lt.

Types can be used for specifying a *contract* [1] for an Erlang function `Func` by writing a declaration of the form:

```
-spec Func(ArgType1, ..., ArgTypeN) -> RetType.
```

A property is specified by declaring a nullary function (whose name, by convention, starts with `prop_`) of the form:

```
prop_name() -> ?FORALL(Xs, XsGen, Prop)
```

Here is an example of a *property specification*, which we will use for testing the `insert` function presented in Sect. 2.

```
prop_ordered_insert() ->                              % property_spec
  ?FORALL({E,L}, {integer(),ne_ordered_list()}, ordered(insert(E,L))).
ne_ordered_list() ->                                  % generator_1
  ?SUCHTHAT(L, non_empty(list(integer())), ordered(L)).
non_empty(T) -> ?SUCHTHAT(L, T, L=/=[]).              % generator_2
ordered(L) -> case L of                               % filter
  [A,B|T] -> A =< B andalso ordered([B|T]);
  _ -> true
end.
```

In order to run the `prop_ordered_insert()` function, PropEr needs an *ad-hoc* implementation of the function `ne_ordered_list()` that generates a *non-empty ordered* list. If such a function is not provided by the user, PropEr executes the `ne_ordered_list()` generator in a very inefficient way by randomly generating non-empty lists of integers until it produces a list which is ordered [27, Sect. 4.2].

The main contribution of this paper is a technique that relieves the programmer from implementing generator functions and, instead, it derives efficient generators directly from their specifications. By doing so, we mitigate the problem of ensuring that the implementation of the generator is indeed correct, and we also avoid, in most cases, the inefficiency of a generate-and-test behavior by a suitable interleaving (via coroutining) of the process of data structure generation with the process of checking the constraint satisfaction (that is, filter evaluation). The implementation of our technique consists of the following six components.

1. A *translator from PropEr to CLP*, which translates the property specification, together with the definitions of Erlang/PropEr types and functions that are used, to a CLP representation.
2. A *type-based generator*, which implements a CLP predicate `typeof(X,T)` that generates datum `X` of any given (predefined or user-defined) type `T`. `typeof` queries can be run in a symbolic way, thereby computing for `X` a term containing variables, possibly subject to constraints.
3. A *CLP interpreter* for filter functions, that is, functions occurring in filter expressions. The interpreter handles the subset of the Core Erlang language presented in Sect. 2. In particular, it defines a predicate `eval(In,Env,Out)` such that, for an Erlang expression `In` whose variables are bound to values in an environment `Env`, `eval` computes, according to the semantics of Erlang,

---

[1] More detailed information about types and contract specifications can be found at http://erlang.org/doc/reference_manual/typespec.html

an output expression Out. The evaluation of eval is performed in a *symbolic* way, as the values in the bindings in Env may contain CLP variables, possibly subject to constraints. Thus, by running a query consisting of the conjunction of a typeof atom and an eval atom, we get as answer a term whose ground instances are values of the desired type, satisfying a given filter.

4. A *value generator*, which takes as input a term produced by running the type-based generator (Component 2) and then the interpreter (Component 3). The value generator can also be run immediately after the type-based generator, if no filter is present. Term variables, if any, may be subject to constraints. Concrete instances of the term (i.e., ground terms) satisfying these constraints are generated by choosing values (in a deterministic or random way) from the domains of the variables.

5. A *translator from CLP to Erlang*, which translates the values produced by the value generator (Component 4) to Erlang values.

6. A *property evaluator*, which evaluates, using the Erlang system, the boolean Erlang expression Prop whose inputs are the values produced by the translator (Component 5). Then the property evaluator checks whether or not one of the following three cases occurs: (i) Prop holds, (ii) Prop does not hold, or (iii) the evaluation of Prop crashes, that is, produces a runtime error.

The above six components have been implemented in a fully automatic tool, called ProSyT[2] (Property-Based Symbolic Testing).

4   Type-Based Value Generation

Type-based generation (Component 2 of our ProSyT tool) is achieved through the implementation of the typeof predicate. Given a type T, the predicate typeof(X,T) holds iff X is a CLP term encoding an Erlang value of type T. If T is a predefined type, typeof invokes a T-specific predicate for generating the term X. For example, for the type list(A), that is, the type of the lists whose elements are of type A, typeof is implemented by the following clause:

```
typeof(X,list(A)) :- list(X,A).
```

where the binary predicate list is defined by the following two clauses:

```
list(nil,T).
list(cons(X,Xs),T) :- typeof(X,T), list(Xs,T).
```

where nil and cons are the CLP representations of the Erlang empty list and list constructor, respectively. If T is a user-defined type, typeof invokes the clause:

```
typeof(X,T) :- typedef(T,D), typeof(X,D).
```

where typedef(T,D) holds iff D is the (CLP representation of the Erlang) definition of type T. The clauses for typedef are generated during the translation from Erlang to CLP. For example, for the definition of the type tree(T) of binary trees, introduced in Sect. 3, we have the following clause:

---

[2] https://fmlab.unich.it/testing/

```
typedef(tree(T), union([
      exactly(lit(atom,leaf)),
      tuple([exactly(lit(atom,node)),tree(T),T,tree(T)]) ])).
```

where: (i) `union([T1,T2])` denotes the union of the two types T1 and T2, (ii) `exactly(E)` denotes a type consisting of the term E only, and (iii) `tuple(L)` denotes the type of the tuples $\{t_1, \ldots, t_n\}$ of terms such that t_i has the type specified by the i-th element of the list L of types.

Apart from the case when the type T is `exactly(lit(...))`, the query `?- typeof(X,T)` returns answers of the form X=t, where t is a non-ground term, whose variables may be subject to constraints. Here follow some examples of use of the `typeof` predicate. If we run the query `?- typeof(X,integer)` we get a single answer of the form X=lit(int,_1320), _1320 in inf..sup, where _1320 is a variable that can take any integer value in the interval inf..sup, where `inf` and `sup` denote the minimum and the maximum integer, respectively. We can explicitly specify a range for integers. For instance, the answer to the query `?- typeof(X,integer(10,20))` is X=lit(int,_1402), _1402 in 10..20.

The query `?- typeof(X,list(integer))` produces a first answer of the form X=nil. If we compute an additional answer for that query, then we get X=cons(lit(int,_1618), nil), _1618 in inf..sup denoting the nil terminated list containing a single integer value. If we continue asking for additional answers, then by the standard Prolog execution mechanism, based on backtracking and depth-first search, we get answers with lists of increasing length.

When dealing with recursively defined data types, we have to care about the size of the generated terms, with the objective of avoiding the possible non-termination of the evaluation of the `typeof` predicate. The size of a term is defined to be the number of list or tuple constructors occurring in it. Thus, for instance, the term `lit(X,integer)` encoding an integer, has size 0, and the size of a list of integers is equal to its length. The size of any term generated by `typeof` is constrained to be in the interval `min_size..max_size`, where `min_size` and `max_size` are configurable non-negative integers.

As an alternative to the built-in mechanisms for size management, we also provide the predicate `typeof(X,T,S)` which holds if X is a term of type T and size S. By using specific values of S or providing constraints on S, the user can specify the term size he desires and can control the answer generation process.

The user can also generate terms of *random* size, instead of terms of increasing size, as obtained by standard Prolog execution. For this purpose, we provide configuration options allowing `typeof` to generate data structures whose size is randomly chosen within the interval `min_size..max_size`.

It is also possible to use randomness during the generation of tuples and unions. For instance, every run of the query `?- typeof(X,tree(integer),2)` using standard Prolog execution, produces the same *first* answer, which is a tree consisting of the root and its right child. In order to modify such a behavior, we have introduced the `random_tuple` option that makes `typeof` generate tuples by randomly choosing one of its elements. (Recall that non-empty trees are indeed defined as tuples.) By doing so, the first answer to the above query is the tree consisting of the root and either its right child or its left child.

Similarly, for union types, we can introduce randomness through the use of the random_union option. For example, suppose that the type color has the two values black and white only. Thus, its translation into CLP is as follows:

```
typedef(color,union([exactly('black'),exactly('white')])).
```

Then, if we run the query ?- typeof(X,color) using the standard Prolog execution mechanism, we will always obtain black as the first answer. However, if we use the random_union option we may get either black or white with equal frequency. More in general, we provide a weighted_union type, which allows the association of frequencies with types using non-negative integers, so that elements of types with higher frequencies are generated more often.

Random generation of *ground* terms (Component 4 of ProSyT) is achieved through the use of the rand_elem(X) predicate. For example, the clauses used for the generation of (possibly, non-flat) lists of integers are the following ones:

```
rand_elem(nil).
rand_elem(cons(X,L)) :- rand_elem(X), rand_elem(L).
rand_elem(lit(int,V)) :- rand_int(V).
rand_int(V) :- int_inf(V,Inf), int_sup(V,Sup), random_between(Inf,Sup,V).
```

where rand_int(V) holds iff V is a random integer value in the range Inf..Sup, Inf and Sup being the minimum and maximum values that V can take, subject to the constraints that are present in the constraint store. For instance, the query:

```
?- typeof(X,list(integer(1,10)),3), rand_elem(X). may return the answer:
X = cons(lit(int,6), cons(lit(int,4), cons(lit(int,9), nil))).
```

A similar mechanism is used for generating ground terms containing floats.

Finally, ground CLP terms are translated to Erlang values (Component 5 of ProSyT) by using the write_elem predicate. For instance, if we append write_elem(X) to the above query, we get the Erlang list [6,4,9].

5   The Interpreter of Filter Functions

The CLP interpreter, which is Component 3 of ProSyT, provides the predicate eval(In,Env,Out) that computes the output value Out of the input expression In in the environment Env. The environment Env, which maps variables to values, is represented by a list of pairs of the form ('X',V), where 'X' is the CLP constant representing the Erlang variable X and V is the CLP term representing its value. By means of a symbolic representation of Erlang expressions and values occurring in the environment (by using possibly non-ground CLP terms subject to suitable constraints), the evaluation of any input expression via the interpreter allows the exhaustive exploration of all program computations without explicitly enumerating all the concrete input values.

In the interpreter, a function definition is represented by a CLP term of the form fun(Pars,Body), where Pars and Body are the formal parameters and the function body, respectively. As an example of how the interpreter is defined, Fig. 1 lists the CLP implementation of the semantic rule for function application, represented by a term of the form apply(Func,IExps), where Func is the name of the function to be applied to the actual parameters IExps.

The behavior is as follows. First, the interpreter retrieves (at line 1) the definition of the function Func. Then, it evaluates (at line 2) the actual parameters IExps in the environment Env, thereby deriving the list of expressions AExps. Then, the interpreter binds (at line 3) the formal parameters

```
eval(apply(Func,IExps),Env,Out) :-
    fundef(Func,fun(Pars,Body)),        % 1
    eval_args(IExps,Env,AExps),         % 2
    zip_binds(Pars,AExps,Binds),        % 3
    constrain_output_exp(Func,Out),     % 4
    eval(Body,Binds,Out).               % 5
```

Fig. 1. CLP interpreter for applying the function Func to the actual parameters IExps.

Pars to the actual parameters AExps, thereby deriving the new environment Binds. If a contract for Func has been provided (see Sect. 3) and the --force-spec option of ProSyT has been used, then (at line 4) a constraint is added on the CLP variables occurring in the output expression Out. For instance, let us suppose that the programmer specifies the following contract for the listlength function that computes the length of a list:

```
-spec listlength(list(any())) -> non_neg_integer().
```

where the non_neg_integer() type requires the output of listlength on lists of any type to be a non-negative integer. Thus, the constraint M#>=0 is imposed on the CLP variable M occurring in the output expression lit(int,M) computed by listlength. Finally, the interpreter evaluates (at line 5), the Body of the function Func in the new environment Binds, thereby deriving the output expression Out.

Now, let us consider the filter function ordered_list of Sect. 3. In order to generate symbolic ordered lists, which will be used for producing the test cases for insert, we run the following query:

```
?- typeof(I,non_empty(list(integer))),
   eval(apply(var('ordered',1),[var('L')]),[('L',I)],lit(atom,true)).
```

In the above query eval calls ordered in an environment where the 'L' parameter is bound to I, and outputs an expression denoting the atom true. As a result of query evaluation, typeof binds the CLP variable I to a nonempty list of integers and eval adds constraints on the elements of the list enforcing them to be in ascending order. Among the first answers to the query we obtain:

```
I = cons(lit(int,_54),cons(lit(int,_55),nil)), _55#>=_54 ;
I = cons(lit(int,_51),cons(lit(int,_52),cons(lit(int,_53),nil))),
    _52#>=_51, _53#>=_52
```

Then, by running the predicates rand_elem and write_elem, for each non-ground list whose elements are in ascending order, we can (randomly) generate one or more ordered Erlang lists, without backtracking on the generation of lists whose elements are not ordered. The following command runs ProSyT on the file ord_insert_bug.erl that includes the bugged insert function and the prop_ordered_insert() property specification.

```
$ ./prosyt.sh ord_insert_bug.erl prop_ordered_insert
```

By default, ProSyT runs 100 tests by generating non-ground ordered lists of increasing length, which are then instantiated by choosing integers from the interval -1000..1000. The 100 tests produce as output a string of 100 characters such as (we show an initial part of that string only):

```
x.x.xxxxxxx...xxxx.xxxxxxx.xxxxx.xxxx..
```

Each character represents the result of performing a test case: (i) the character '.' means that the desired property prop_ordered_insert holds, and (ii) the character 'x' means that it does not hold, hence revealing a bug.

The generation of the ordered lists for the 100 test cases takes 42ms (user time) on an Intel® Core™ i7-8550U CPU with 16GB running Ubuntu 18.04.2.

6   Coroutining the Type-Based Generator and the Filter Interpreter

The process of symbolic test case generation described in the previous section has a good performance when the filter does not specify constraints on the *skeleton* of the data structure, but only on its *elements*. For instance, in the case of ordered lists, the filter ordered(L) does not enforce any constraint on the length of the symbolic list L generated by the type-based generator, but only on its elements.

Now, let us consider the following filter function avl, which checks whether or not a given binary tree is an AVL tree, that is, a *binary search tree* that satisfies the constraint of being *height-balanced* [10].

```
avl(T) -> case T of
   leaf -> true;
   {node,L,V,R} ->
     B = height(L)-height(R) andalso B >= -1 andalso B =< 1 andalso   % 1
     ltt(L,V)   andalso   gtt(R,V)   andalso                          % 2
     avl(L)   andalso   avl(R);
   _ -> false
 end.
```

The recursive clause of the **case-of** checks whether or not any tree {node,L,V,R} rooted in V (the value of the node) is height-balanced (line 1), all the values in the left subtree L are smaller than V, and all the values in the right subtree R are larger than V (line 2). avl uses the following utility functions: (i) height(T), which returns the height of the tree T, (ii) ltt(T,V), and (iii) gtt(T,V), which return true if the value of each node n in the tree T is less than, or greater than V, respectively. In order to generate AVL trees, we run the following query:

```
?- typeof(X,tree(integer)),
   eval(apply(var('avl',1),[var('T')]),[('T',X)],lit(atom,true)),
   rand_elem(X).
```

However, unlike the case of ordered lists, among the answers to the query typeof(X,tree(integer)) just a few instances of X turn out to be AVL trees. Hence, eval repeatedly fails until typeof generates a binary tree satisfying the constraints specified by the filter. As an example, for trees of size 10, eval finds 10 AVL trees out of 9000 trees generated by typeof.

In order to make the generation process more efficient, we use the *coroutining* mechanism to implement a data-driven cooperation [23], thereby interleaving the execution of the type-based generator `typeof` and that of the interpreter `eval`. Coroutining is obtained by interchanging the order of the `typeof` and `eval` atoms in the query, so that the `eval` call is selected before the `typeof` call. However, the execution of `eval` is *suspended* on inputs of the filter function that are not instantiated enough to decide which clauses of a `case-of` expression can be used to proceed in the function evaluation. The execution of `eval` is then *resumed* whenever the input to the filter function gets further instantiated by the `typeof` execution. By doing so, during the generation of complex data structures, `typeof` must comply with the constraints enforced by `eval`. This mechanism can dramatically improve efficiency, because the unsatisfiability of the given constraints may be detected before the entire data structure is generated.

Coroutining is implemented by using the `when(Cond,Goal)` primitive provided by SWI-Prolog [35], which suspends the execution of `Goal` until `Cond` becomes true. In particular, `when` declarations are used in the rule of the interpreter shown below, which defines the operational semantics of `case-of` expressions.

```
eval(case(CExps,Cls),Env,Exp) :-
   eval(CExps,Env,EExps),
   suspend_on(Env,EExps,Cls,Cond),
   when(Cond,( match(Env,EExps,Cls,MEnv,Cl), eval(Cl,MEnv,Exp) )).
```

The evaluation of expressions of the form 'case CExps of Cls end.', encoded as `case(CExps,Cls)`, in the environment `Env` behaves as follows. The expressions `CExps` are evaluated in the environment `Env`, thereby getting the expressions `EExps` to be matched against one of the patterns of the clauses `Cls`. Then, `suspend_on(Env,EExps,Cls,Cond)` generates a condition `Cond` of the form $(\text{nonvar}(V_1), \ldots, \text{nonvar}(V_n))$, where $V_1,\ldots,V_n$ are the CLP variables occurring in `EExps` that would get bound to either a list or a tuple while matching the expressions `EExps` against the patterns of the clauses `Cls`. Such a condition forces the suspension of the evaluation of the goal occurring as a second argument of the `when` primitive until all of these variables get bound to a non-variable term. If the evaluation of the `case-of` binds all the variables to terms which are neither lists nor tuples, then `suspend_on` produces a `Cond` that holds `true`. Thus, when the goal of the `when` primitive is executed: (i) `match(Env,EExps,Cls,MEnv,Cl)` selects a clause `Cl` from `Cls` whose pattern matches `EExps`, hence producing the environment `MEnv` that extends `Env` with the new bindings derived by matching, and (ii) `eval(Cl,MEnv,Exp)` evaluates `Cl` in `MEnv` and produces the output expression `Exp`. Now, if we run the following query:

```
?- eval(apply(var('avl',1),[var('T')]),[('T',X)],lit(atom,true)),
   typeof(X,tree(integer)),
   rand_elem(X).
```

the CLP variable `X`, shared between `typeof` and `eval`, forces the type-based generator and the filter to cooperate in the generation of AVL trees. Indeed, as soon as the `typeof` (partially) instantiates `X` to a binary tree, the evaluation of the filter function adds constraints on the skeleton of X (corresponding to the properties at lines 1 and 2 of the definition of the avl function). The advantage of this approach is that the constraints on X restrict the possible ways in which its left and right subtrees can be further expanded by recursive calls of typeof. As an example, suppose we want to test the following function avl_insert that inserts the integer element E into the AVL tree T:

```
avl_insert(E,T) -> case T of
  {node,L,V,R} when E < V -> re_balance(E,{node,avl_insert(E,L),V,R});
  {node,L,V,R} when E > V -> re_balance(E,{node,L,V,avl_insert(E,R)});
  {node,L,V,R} when E == V -> {node,L,V,R};
  leaf -> {node,leaf,E,leaf}
end.
```

This function uses the following utility functions shown below: (i) re_balance, which given an integer element E and a binary search tree T, performs suitable rotations on T so as to make it height-balanced, and (ii) right_rotation, and (iii) left_rotation, which perform a right rotation, and a left rotation on T, respectively. The definition of re_balance has two errors: (1) at line ERR_1, where '<' should be '>', and (2) at line ERR_2, where '>' should be '<'.

```
re_balance(E,T) ->
  {node,L,V,R} = T,
  case height(L) - height(R) of
    2 -> {node,_,LV,_} = L,               % Left unbalanced tree
    if E < LV -> right_rotation(T);
       E > LV -> right_rotation({node,left_rotation(L),V,R})
    end;
    -2 -> {node,_,RV,_} = R,              % Right unbalanced tree
    if E < RV -> left_rotation(T);                            % ERR_1
       E > RV -> left_rotation({node,L,V,right_rotation(R)})  % ERR_2
    end;
    _ -> T
  end.

right_rotation({node,{node,LL,LV,LR},V,R}) ->
  {node,LL,LV,{node,LR,V,R}}.

left_rotation({node,L,V,{node,RL,RV,RR}}) ->
  {node,{node,L,V,RL},RV,RR}.
```

The following test case specification states that after inserting an integer element E in an AVL tree, we get again an AVL tree:

```
avl() -> ?SUCHTHAT(T, tree(integer()), avl(T)).
prop_insert() ->
  ?FORALL({E,T}, {integer(),avl()}, avl(avl_insert(E,T))).
```

The following command runs ProSyT on the file avl_insert_bug.erl that includes the above bugged avl_insert function and the test case specification.

```
$ ./prosyt.sh avl_insert_bug.erl prop_insert --force-spec\
  --min-size 3 --max-size 20 --inf -10000 --sup 10000 --tests 200
```

In this command we have used the following options:
(i) `--min-size` and `--max-size` specify the values of `min_size` and `max_size`, respectively, determining the size of the data structure (see Sect. 3), (ii) `--inf` and `--sup` specify the bounds of the interval where integer elements are taken from (see Sect. 3), and (iii) `--tests N` specifies the number of tests to be run.

Here is an initial part of the string of characters we get:

`..x...x...cx..x.xxc....x..c.x..x..x.c..`

The generation of the 200 test cases takes 550ms (user time). Several 'x' characters are generated, corresponding to runs of `avl_insert` that do not return an AVL tree, and hence reveal bugs. Moreover, the 'c' characters in the output string correspond to crashes of the execution, due to the fact that the `right_rotation` or `left_rotation` functions threw a `match_fail` exception when applied to a tree on which those rotations cannot be performed.

7   Experimental Evaluation

In this section we present the experimental evaluation we have performed for assessing the effectiveness and the efficiency of the test case generation process we have presented in this paper and we have implemented in ProSyT.

Benchmark suite. The suite consists of 10 Erlang programs: (1) `ord_insert`, whose input is an integer and an ordered list of integers (see Sect. 2); (2) `up_down_seq`, whose input is a list of integers of the form: $[w_1, \ldots, w_m, z_1, \ldots, z_m]$, with $w_1 \leq \ldots \leq w_m$ and $z_1 \geq \ldots \geq z_m$; (3) `n_up_seqs`, whose input is a list of ordered lists of integers of increasing length; (4) `delete`, whose input is a triple $\langle w, u, v \rangle$ of lists of integers such that w is the ordered permutation of the list obtained by concatenating the ordered lists u and v; (5) `stack`, whose input is a pair $\langle s, n \rangle$, where s is a stack encoded as a list of integers, and n is the length of that list; (6) `matrix_mult`, whose input is a pair of matrices encoded as a pair of lists of lists, (7) `det_tri_matrix`, whose input is a lower triangular matrix encoded as a list of lists of increasing length of the form: $[[v_{11}], [v_{21}, v_{22}], \ldots, [v_{n1}, \ldots, v_{nn}]]$, (8) `balanced_tree`, whose input is a height-balanced binary tree [10]; (9) `binomial_tree_heap`, whose input is a binomial tree satisfying the minimum-heap property [10]; (10) `avl_insert`, whose input is an AVL tree (see Sect. 6). The benchmark suite is available online as part of the ProSyT tool (the suffixes `_bug.erl` and `_ok.erl` denotes the buggy and correct versions of the programs, respectively).

Experimental processes. We have implemented the following two experimental processes. (*i*) *Generate-and-Test*, which runs PropEr for randomly generating a value of the given data type, and then tests whether or not that value satisfies the given filter; this process uses the predefined generator for lists and a simple user-defined generator for trees. (*ii*) *Constrain-and-Generate*, which runs ProSyT by coroutining the generation of the skeleton of a data structure and the evaluation of the filter expression (see Sect. 6), and then randomly instantiating that skeleton.

Table 1. Column *Time* reports the seconds needed to generate N ($\leq$ 100,000) test cases of size in the interval [10, 100] within the time limit of 300 s.

Program	PropEr		ProSyT	
	Time	N	*Time*	N
1. ord_insert	300.00	0	300.00	67,083
2. up_down_seq	300.00	0	300.00	22,500
3. n_up_seqs	300.00	0	300.00	24,000
4. delete	300.00	0	9.21	100,000
5. stack	143.71	100,000	19.57	100,000
6. matrix_mult	300.00	0	300.00	76,810
7. det_tri_matrix	300.00	304	32.28	13,500
8. balanced_tree	300.00	121	21.54	100,000
9. binomial_tree_heap	300.00	0	43.45	4,500
10. avl_insert	300.00	0	300.00	23,034

Technical resources. The experimental evaluation has been performed on a machine equipped with an Intel® Core™ i7-8550U CPU @ 1.80GHz × 8 processor and 16GB of memory running Ubuntu 18.04.2 LTS. The timeout limit for each run of the test cases generation process has been set to 300 s.

Results. We have run PropEr and ProSyT for generating up to 100,000 test cases whose size is in the interval [10, 100], and we made the random generator for integer and real values to take values in the interval [−10000, 10000]. ProSyT has been configured so that the random instantiation phase can produce at most 1500 concrete test cases for every data structure skeleton found. The results of the experimental evaluation are summarized in Table 1.

The experiments show that the *Constrain-and-Generate* process used by ProSyT performs much better than the *Generate-and-Test* process used by PropEr. Indeed, *Generate-and-Test* is able to find valid test cases only when the filter is very simple. Actually, in some examples, PropEr generates test cases with very small size only (less than the minimum specified size limit of 10). In particular, for the ord_insert program, PropEr generates ordered lists of length at most 8, while ProSyT is able to generate lists of length up to 53. Also for the programs det_tri_matrix and balanced_tree, the size of the largest data structure generated by PropEr (a 5×5 matrix and a 15 node balanced tree) is much smaller than the largest data structure generated by ProSyT (a 12×12 matrix and a 22 node balanced tree). Finally, note that for the programs det_tri_matrix and binomial_tree_heap, ProSyT halted before the time limit of 300 s because no more skeletons exist within the given size interval.

8   Related Work

Automated test generation has been suggested by many authors as a means of reducing the cost of testing and improving its quality [32]. Property-Based Testing, and in particular the QuickCheck approach [8], is one of the most well-established methods for automating test case generation (see also the references cited in the Introduction).

PropEr [27,30] is a popular Property-Based Testing tool for Erlang programs that follows the QuickCheck approach. PropEr was proposed as an open-source alternative to Quviq QuickCheck [2], a proprietary, closed-source tool for Property-Based Testing of Erlang programs. In addition, PropEr was designed to be integrated with the Erlang type specification language.

However, a critical point of PropEr (and of other PBT frameworks) is that the user bears most of the burden of writing correct, efficient generators of test data. Essentially, PropEr only provides an automated way for converting type specifications into generators of *free* data structures, but very limited support is given to automatically generate data structures subject to *constraints*, such as the sorted lists and AVL-trees we have considered in this paper. In this respect, the main contribution of our work is a technique for the automated generation of test data from PropEr specifications. Indeed, our approach, based on a CLP interpreter for (a subset of) Erlang, allows the automated generation of test data in an efficient way. Test data are generated by interleaving, via corouting, the data structure generation, the filtering of those data structures based on constraint solving, and the random instantiation of variables. This mechanism, implemented in the ProSyT tool, has demonstrated good efficiency on some non-trivial examples.

The work closest to ours is the one implemented by the FocalTest tool [6]. FocalTest is a PBT tool designed to generate test data for programs and properties written in the functional language Focalize. Its main feature is a translation of Focalize programs into CLP(FD) programs extended with the *constraint combinators* `apply` and `match`, which encode function application and pattern matching, respectively. `apply` and `match` are implemented by using *freeze* and *wake-up* mechanisms based on the instantiation of logical variables, and in particular, the evaluation of `apply` and `match` is waken up when their arguments are bound to non-variable terms.

A difference between FocalTest and ProSyT comes from the fact that, Focalize is a statically typed language and Erlang is a dynamically typed language. Static type information is used by FocalTest for instantiating variables, while in ProSyT type-based instantiation is performed through the `typeof` data structure generator. Static typing is also exploited in the proof of correctness of FocalTest, whose operational semantics has been formalized in Coq [5]. In contrast, we handle Erlang's dynamic typing discipline by writing an interpreter of (a subset of) the language, which also models failure due to runtime typing errors.

The development of the CLP interpreter for Erlang and, more in general, for the PropEr framework, is indeed the most significant and distinctive feature of our approach. From a methodological point of view, a direct implementation of the operational semantics in a rule-based language like CLP, requires a limited effort for the proof of correctness with respect to a formal semantics (we did not deal with this issue in the present paper, but we tested our interpreter on several examples). From a practical point of view, the use of the interpreter avoids the need of extending CLP with special purpose constraint operators like `apply` and `match`. Moreover, our interpreter-based approach lends itself to possible optimizations for improving the efficiency of test case generation, such as *partial evaluation* [21], for automatically deriving specialized test case generators.

The freeze and wake-up mechanisms used by FocalTest are quite related to the coroutining mechanism implemented by ProSyT, which, however, is realized by the interpreter, rather than by the constraint solving strategy.

Other differences between FocalTest and ProSyT concern numerical variables and random instantiation. FocalTest handles integer numerical variables using the CLP(FD) constraint solver and randomly instantiates those variables using a strategy called *random iterative domain splitting*. ProSyT handles integer and float numerical variables using CLP(FD) and CLP(R), respectively, for solving constraints on those variables, and their random instantiation is done by using CLP(FD) and CLP(R) built-ins. ProSyT is also able to perform random generation of data structures, by using a randomized version of the predicate `typeof` (see Sect. 4), possibly specifying a distribution for the values of a given type.

The idea of interleaving, via coroutining, the generation of a data structure with the test of consistency of the constraints that the data structure should satisfy, is related to the lazy evaluation strategy used by *Lazy SmallCheck* [31], a PBT tool for Haskell. Lazy SmallCheck checks properties for partially defined values and lazily evaluates parallel conjunction to enable early pruning of the set of candidate test data. Lazy SmallCheck does not use symbolic constraint solving, and exhaustively generates all values up to a given bound.

Besides functional programming languages, PBT has also been applied to Prolog [1]. Similarly to ProSyT, the PrologCheck tool [1] implements randomized test data generation for Prolog. However, when the test data specification contains constraints, PrologCheck follows a *generate-and-test* approach, and no mechanism is provided by the tool for coroutining data generation and constraint solving (unless this is coded directly by the programmer).

The use of constraint-based reasoning techniques for test case generation is a well-established approach [11,16,18,25], which has been followed for the implementation of several tools in various contexts. Among them, we would like to mention: GATeL [26], a test sequence generator for the synchronous dataflow language LUSTRE, AUTOFOCUS [29], a model-based test sequence generator for reactive systems, JML-TT [3], a tool for model-based test case generation from specifications written in the Java Modeling Language (JML), Euclide [17], a tool for testing safety-critical C programs, and finally, tools for *concolic testing*, such as PathCrawler [37], CUTE [34], and DART [15], which combine concrete execution with constraint-based path representations of C programs.

Our work is also related to approaches and tools proposed in the context of languages for specifying and testing meta-logic properties of formal systems. In particular, αCheck [7] follows an approach very much inspired by PBT for performing bounded model-checking of formal systems specified in αProlog, which is a Horn clause language based on nominal logic. Related concepts are at the basis of QuickChick, a PBT tool for the Coq proof assistant [28]. Lampropoulos et al. [24] also address the problem of deriving correct generators for data satisfying suitable inductive invariants on top of QuickChick. In that work, the mechanism for data generation makes use of the narrowing technique, which similarly to our resolution-based approach, builds upon the unification algorithm.

Declarative approaches for test data generation have been proposed in the context of *bounded-exhaustive testing* (BET) [9], whose goal is to test a program on all input data satisfying a given invariant, up to a fixed bound on their size. One of the most well-known declarative frameworks for BET is Korat [4], which is a tool for testing Java programs. Given a Java predicate specifying a data structure, subject to a given invariant and a size bound on its input, Korat uses backtracking to systematically explore the bounded input space of the predicate by applying a generate-and-test strategy. JMLAutoTest [38] implements a technique, based on statistical methods, for avoiding the generation of many useless test cases by exploiting JML specifications.

A different domain-specific language for BET of Java programs is UDITA [14]. It provides non-deterministic choice operators and an interface for generating linked structures. UDITA improves efficiency with respect to the generate-and-test approach by applying the *delayed choice* principle, that is, postponing the instantiation of a variable until it is first accessed.

It has been shown that CLP-based approaches, which exploit built-in unification and special purpose constraint solving algorithms, can be very competitive with respect to domain-specific tools for BET [13].

9 Conclusions

We have presented a technique for automated test case generation from *test case specifications*. We have considered the Erlang functional programming language and a test case specification language based on the PropEr framework [27,30].

In this paper we have shown how we can relieve the programmer from writing generators of test data by using constraint logic programming (CLP). However, even if our approach to automated PBT is based on CLP, the programmer is not required to deal with any concept related to logic programming, and Prolog code is fully transparent to the programmer. Indeed, we provide both (i) a translator from PropEr and Erlang specifications and programs to CLP, and (ii) a translator of the generated test data from CLP syntax to Erlang syntax.

At present, the ProSyT tool, which implements our PBT technique, does not provide any *shrinking* mechanism to try to generate an input of *minimal* size in case the program under test does not satisfy the property of interest. However, we think that this mechanism can efficiently be realized by using the primitives for controlling term size provided by our tool, together with Prolog default search strategy based on backtracking.

Finally, we would like to notice that, even if we developed our technique in the context of PBT of Erlang programs, the approach we followed is to a large extent independent of the specific programming language, as it is based on writing a CLP interpreter of the programming language under consideration. Thus, as future work, we plan to apply a similar scheme to other programming languages by providing suitable CLP interpreters.

Acknowledgements. We would like to thank the anonymous reviewers for their very helpful and constructive comments.

E. De Angelis, F. Fioravanti, A. Pettorossi, and M. Proietti are members of the INdAM Research group GNCS. E. De Angelis, F. Fioravanti, and A. Pettorossi are research associates at CNR-IASI, Rome, Italy.

A. Palacios was partially supported by the EU (FEDER) and the Spanish *Ayudas para contratos predoctorales para la formación de doctores* and *Ayudas a la movilidad predoctoral para la realización de estancias breves en centros de I+D* (MICINN) under FPI grants BES-2014-069749 and EEBB-I-17-12101.

References

1. Amaral, C., Florido, M., Santos Costa, V.: PrologCheck – property-based testing in Prolog. In: Codish, M., Sumii, E. (eds.) FLOPS 2014. LNCS, vol. 8475, pp. 1–17. Springer, Cham (2014). https://doi.org/10.1007/978-3-319-07151-0_1
2. Arts, Th., Hughes, J., Johansson, J., Wiger, U.T.: Testing telecoms software with Quviq QuickCheck. In: Feeley, M., Trinder, Ph.W., (eds.) Proceedings of the 2006 ACM SIGPLAN Workshop on Erlang, Portland, Oregon, USA, 16 September 2006, pp. 2–10. ACM (2006)
3. Bouquet, F., Dadeau, F., Legeard, B.: Automated boundary test generation from JML specifications. In: Misra, J., Nipkow, T., Sekerinski, E. (eds.) FM 2006. LNCS, vol. 4085, pp. 428–443. Springer, Heidelberg (2006). https://doi.org/10.1007/11813040_29
4. Boyapati, C., Khurshid, S., Marinov, D.: Korat: automated testing based on Java predicates. In: Proceedings of the 2002 ACM SIGSOFT International Symposium on Software Testing and Analysis, pp. 123–133. ACM, New York (2002)
5. Carlier, M., Dubois, C., Gotlieb, A.: A first step in the design of a formally verified constraint-based testing tool: FocalTest. In: Brucker, A.D., Julliand, J. (eds.) TAP 2012. LNCS, vol. 7305, pp. 35–50. Springer, Heidelberg (2012). https://doi.org/10.1007/978-3-642-30473-6_5
6. Carlier, M., Dubois, C., Gotlieb, A.: FocalTest: a constraint programming approach for property-based testing. In: Cordeiro, J., Virvou, M., Shishkov, B. (eds.) ICSOFT 2010. CCIS, vol. 170, pp. 140–155. Springer, Heidelberg (2013). https://doi.org/10.1007/978-3-642-29578-2_9
7. Cheney, J., Momigliano, A.: αCheck: a mechanized metatheory model checker. Theory Pract. Log. Program. **17**(3), 311–352 (2017)
8. Claessen, K., Hughes, J.: QuickCheck: a lightweight tool for random testing of Haskell programs. In: Odersky, M., Wadler, Ph. (eds.) Proceedings of the 5th ACM SIGPLAN International Conference on Functional Programming (ICFP 2000), Montreal, Canada, 18–21 September 2000, pp. 268–279. ACM (2000)
9. Coppit, D., Le, W., Sullivan, K.J., Khurshid, S., Yang, J.: Software assurance by bounded exhaustive testing. IEEE Trans. Softw. Eng. **31**(4), 328–339 (2005)

10. Cormen, T.H., Leiserson, C.E., Rivest, R.L., Stein, C.: Introduction to Algorithms, 3rd edn. MIT Press, Cambridge (2009)
11. Dick, J., Faivre, A.: Automating the generation and sequencing of test cases from model-based specifications. In: Woodcock, J.C.P., Larsen, P.G. (eds.) FME 1993. LNCS, vol. 670, pp. 268–284. Springer, Heidelberg (1993). https://doi.org/10.1007/BFb0024651
12. Carlsson, R., et al.: Core Erlang 1.0.3. language specification. Technical Report, Department of Information Technology, Uppsala University, Uppsala, Sweden (2004). https://www.it.uu.se/research/group/hipe/cerl/doc/core_erlang-1.0.3.pdf
13. Fioravanti, F., Proietti, M., Senni, V.: Efficient generation of test data structures using constraint logic programming and program transformation. J. Log. Comput. **25**(6), 1263–1283 (2015)
14. Gligoric, M., Gvero, T., Jagannath, V., Khurshid, S., Kuncak, V., Marinov, D.: Test generation through programming in UDITA. In: Kramer, J., Bishop, J., Devanbu, P.T., Uchitel, S. (eds.) Proceedings of the 32nd ACM/IEEE International Conference on Software Engineering, Cape Town, South Africa, 2–8 May 2010, pp. 225–234. ACM (2010)
15. Godefroid, P., Klarlund, N., Sen, K.: DART: directed automated random testing. In: Sarkar, V., Hall, M.W. (eds.) Proceedings of the ACM SIGPLAN 2005 Conference on Programming Language Design and Implementation, Chicago, IL, USA, 12–15 June 2005, pp. 213–223. ACM (2005)
16. Gómez-Zamalloa, M., Albert, E., Puebla, G.: Test case generation for object-oriented imperative languages in CLP. Theory Pract. Log. Program. **10**(4–6), 659–674 (2010)
17. Gotlieb, A.: Euclide: a constraint-based testing framework for critical C programs. In: 2nd International Conference on Software Testing, Verification and Validation, ICST 2009, Denver, Colorado, USA, 1–4 April 2009, pp. 151–160. IEEE Computer Society (2009)
18. Gotlieb, A., Botella, B., Rueher, M.: A CLP framework for computing structural test data. In: Lloyd, J. (ed.) CL 2000. LNCS (LNAI), vol. 1861, pp. 399–413. Springer, Heidelberg (2000). https://doi.org/10.1007/3-540-44957-4_27
19. Hewitt, C., Bishop, P., Steiger, R.: A universal modular ACTOR formalism for artificial intelligence. In: Proceedings of the 3rd International Joint Conference on Artificial Intelligence, IJCAI 1973, San Francisco, CA, USA, pp. 235–245. Morgan Kaufmann Publishers Inc. (1973)
20. Jaffar, J., Maher, M.: Constraint logic programming: a survey. J. Log. Program. **19**(20), 503–581 (1994)
21. Jones, N.D., Gomard, C.K., Sestoft, P.: Partial Evaluation and Automatic Program Generation. Prentice Hall, Upper Saddle River (1993)
22. junit-quickcheck: Property-based testing, JUnit-style. https://github.com/pholser/junit-quickcheck
23. Kowalski, R.A.: Logic for Problem Solving. North Holland, Amsterdam (1979)
24. Lampropoulos, L., Paraskevopoulou, Z., Pierce, B.C.: Generating good generators for inductive relations. In: Proceedings of the ACM on Programming Languages, vol. 2, pp. 45:1–45:30 (2017)
25. Marre, B.: Toward automatic test data set selection using algebraic specifications and logic programming. In: Furukawa, K. (eds.) Logic Programming, Proceedings of the 8th International Conference, Paris, France, 24–28 June 1991, pp. 202–219. MIT Press (1991)

26. Marre, B., Arnould, A.: Test sequences generation from LUSTRE descriptions: GATeL. In: Proceedings of the 15th IEEE International Conference on Automated Software Engineering, ASE 2000, Grenoble, France, 11–15 September 2000, p. 229. IEEE Computer Society (2000)
27. Papadakis, M., Sagonas, K.: A PropEr integration of types and function specifications with property-based testing. In: Rikitake, K., Stenman, E. (eds.) Proceedings of the 10th ACM SIGPLAN Workshop on Erlang, Tokyo, Japan, 23 September 2011, pp. 39–50. ACM (2011)
28. Paraskevopoulou, Z., Hriţcu, C., Dénès, M., Lampropoulos, L., Pierce, B.C.: Foundational property-based testing. In: Urban, C., Zhang, X. (eds.) ITP 2015. LNCS, vol. 9236, pp. 325–343. Springer, Cham (2015). https://doi.org/10.1007/978-3-319-22102-1_22
29. Pretschner, A., Lötzbeyer, H.: Model based testing with constraint logic programming: first results and challenges. In: Proceedings of the 2nd ICSE Workshop on Automated Program Analysis, Testing and Verification (WAPATV), pp. 1–9 (2001)
30. PropEr: Property-Based Testing for Erlang. http://proper.softlab.ntua.gr/
31. Runciman, C., Naylor, M., Lindblad, F.: SmallCheck and lazy SmallCheck: automatic exhaustive testing for small values. In: Gill, A. (ed.) Proceedings of the 1st ACM SIGPLAN Symposium on Haskell, Haskell 2008, Victoria, BC, Canada, 25 September 2008, pp. 37–48. ACM (2008)
32. Rushby, J.: Automated test generation and verified software. In: Meyer, B., Woodcock, J. (eds.) VSTTE 2005. LNCS, vol. 4171, pp. 161–172. Springer, Heidelberg (2008). https://doi.org/10.1007/978-3-540-69149-5_18
33. ScalaCheck: Property-Based Testing for Scala. http://www.scalacheck.org/
34. Sen, K., Marinov, D., Agha, G.: CUTE: a concolic unit testing engine for C. In: Wermelinger, M., Gall, H.C. (eds.) Proceedings of the 10th European Software Engineering Conference held jointly with 13th ACM SIGSOFT International Symposium on Foundations of Software Engineering, 2005, Lisbon, Portugal, 5–9 September 2005, pp. 263–272. ACM (2005)
35. The SWI Prolog Logic Programming System. http://www.swi-prolog.org/
36. Virding, R., Wikström, C., Williams, M.: Concurrent programming in Erlang, 2nd edn. In: Armstrong, J. (ed.) Prentice Hall International Ltd, Hertfordshire (1996)
37. Williams, N., Marre, B., Mouy, P., Roger, M.: PathCrawler: automatic generation of path tests by combining static and dynamic analysis. In: Dal Cin, M., Kaâniche, M., Pataricza, A. (eds.) EDCC 2005. LNCS, vol. 3463, pp. 281–292. Springer, Heidelberg (2005). https://doi.org/10.1007/11408901_21
38. Xu, G., Yang, Z.: JMLAutoTest: a novel automated testing framework based on JML and JUnit. In: Petrenko, A., Ulrich, A. (eds.) FATES 2003. LNCS, vol. 2931, pp. 70–85. Springer, Heidelberg (2004). https://doi.org/10.1007/978-3-540-24617-6_6
39. Yatoh, K., Sakamoto, K., Ishikawa, F., Honiden, S.: ArbitCheck: a highly automated property-based testing tool for Java. In: Proceedings of the 7th IEEE International Conference on Software Testing, Verification, and Validation Workshops, ICSTW 2014, Cleveland, Ohio, USA, 31 March–April 4 2014, pp. 405–412. IEEE Computer Society (2014)

Author Index

Printed in the United States
By Bookmasters